PALM SPRINGS
TRUE CRIME

Connect with the Author
Twitter.com/EricGMeeks
Facebook.com/EricGMeeks
www.EricGMeeks.com

Complete Works

Fiction
The Author Murders
Witch of Tahquitz
Six Stories

Non-Fiction
Intuitive Reflections: The Art of Ron Klotchman
The Best Guide Ever to Palm Springs Celebrity Homes
P. S. I Love Lucy: Lucille Ball's Palm Springs
Roberta Linn: Lawrence Welk's First Television Champagne Lady
Not Now Lord, I've Got Too Much to Do
Reversing Discrimination

Downloads
Currently about 25 titles available

Edited by Eric G. Meeks
1853 Cavalry Quest for a Southwest Railroad Route

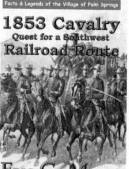

Facts & Legends of the Village of Palm Springs
1853 Cavalry
Quest for a Southwest
Railroad Route
Eric G. Meeks
Author of WITCH OF TAHQUITZ

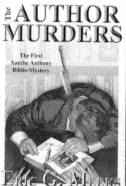

The
AUTHOR
MURDERS
The First
Xanthe Anthony
Biblio-Mystery
Eric G. Meeks
Author of WITCH OF TAHQUITZ

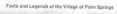

Facts and Legends of the Village of Palm Springs
The Best Guide Ever to
PALM SPRINGS
CELEBRITY HOMES

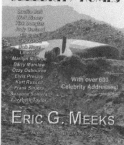

Lucille Ball
Walt Disney
Kirk Douglas
Judy Garland
Cary Grant
Bob Hope
Liberace
Marilyn Monroe
Barry Manilow
Ozzy Osbourne
Elvis Presley
Kurt Russell
Frank Sinatra
Suzanne Somers
Elizabeth Taylor

With over 800
Celebrity Addresses!

Eric G. Meeks

Champagne Lady

Roberta Linn

E. G. Meeks

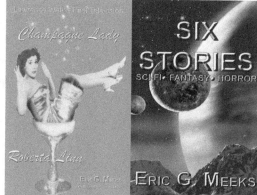

SIX
STORIES
SCI-FI · FANTASY · HORROR

Eric G. Meeks

Facts and Legends of the Village of Palm Springs
WITCH
of
TAHQUITZ

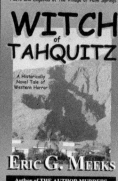

A Historically
Novel Tale of
Western Horror

Eric G. Meeks
Author of THE AUTHOR MURDERS

A Corporate Wars Story
APOLLO THORN
The Moons of Jupiter

Eric G. Meeks

Lucille Ball's
Palm Springs

Eric G. Meeks
Author of
The Best Guide Ever to Palm Springs Celebrity Homes

PALM SPRINGS TRUE CRIME

ERIC G. MEEKS

Horatio Limburger Oglethorpe, Publisher

Palm Springs True Crime
© 2015 by Horatio Limburger Oglethorpe, Publisher

ISBN-13: 978-0-9862189-9-6
ISBN-10: 0-9862189-9-6

Third Printing
Hardback Edition
Updated 1-29-2017

The chapter Tribal Casino Origins, The Octopus,and Indian
Head Nichols has also been printed as its own book.

The chapter Palm Springs Madam has been removed.

The story on Jeremy Crocker has been re-edited.

Printed in the United States of America

Dedication

To the police, fire and other public safety officers of the Palm Springs area. Without their dedication and service, the city I love wouldn't be nearly as great a place to live.

Special Thanks

To my editors, Don Reece and Kathy Baskerville, who have stuck by me through every mispelling and grammatical error.

To Dawn Martinez and Sherrie Leuder for their contributing photographs to the story: Cliff Lambert and The Boiz.

And,
To my first generation of Beta-Readers:
John Nichols, Loraine Slook, and Marlene Talley.
You all really helped make this a better book.

Thank you,
EGM

Table of Contents

PREFACE

A Quick Word

Thank you for taking this stroll with me down some of the darker paths of Palm Springs.

In this book you'll find some of the crime stories to be historic in nature, others will be fairly current. All are stories I've heard about or read about throughout my life. I've lived in Palm Springs since 1976 and you can't be a resident here without picking up on some local headlines.

Most of these stories are written in third person. I did a ton of research to collect the data contained herein. Occasionally, you'll find a story with first-hand knowledge peppered in when the information came from personal experience. In those stories, I use the word "I" a lot. A few stories are written entirely in the first person.

From 1996 to 2002, I served as a member of the Palm Springs Police Advisory committee; originally on a formative committee and then for nearly 3 years as its Chairman. The insight gained from this experience gave me a great deal of respect for our valley's officers.

Crime is, unfortunately, inevitable everywhere. I've been a victim of it several times in my life. Thankfully, it's always been at the level of bicycle thefts. Not everyone can claim such innocuous victimhood. Crime is a shame and blight on society in any form.

I try to not glamorize the criminals. They don't deserve it. Well, excepting maybe for my Dad and his "T" runs. That was pretty fun. It wasn't really a crime though. You'll understand when you read the story. Chalk it up to living in interesting times.

PALM SPRINGS TRUE CRIME

ERIC G. MEEKS

HOMICIDE

Producer, Director Al Adamson

ERIC G. MEEKS

Horror, Sexploitation and Murder

Al Adamson, born July 25, 1929, was the son of a filmmaker. In 1961, at the age of 42, he worked with his dad, Victor Adamson, on the movie *Halfway to Hell,* and decided he wanted to make movies himself. Al formed a partnership with Sam Sherman and created Independent-International Pictures and made his wife, Regina Carrol, a busty blonde who liked big sunglasses and loose fitting tops, the star of many of his films.

Independent-International became known for B-grade horror and Sci-Fi films with lots of sexual exploitation. Aging actors and actresses were cast against a desert backdrop fighting aliens or biker gangs for their very survival or for the chastity of their women. Adamson owned the Casablanca Motor Lodge at 1342 East Palm Canyon Drive, in the Deepwell neighborhood of Palm Springs and he could house the cast and crew during production. It was a great way to keep costs down.

His early films include: *Psycho a Go-Go* (1965), *Blood of Dracula's Castle* (1969), *Satan's Sadists* (1969), *Five Bloody Graves* (1969) and *Horror of the Blood Monsters* (1970). Several of his earliest films starred John Carradine, an actor with a long list of credits and the father of David Carradine, who would play Grasshopper on the TV show *Kung Fu.* In 1971, he made his most famous horror film: *Dracula vs. Frankenstein* starring Lon Chaney, Jr. and J. Carrol Naish. (Naish also owned a hotel in Palm Springs).

In 1969, Al Adamson had a close brush with one of America's most notorious killers, though at the time Adamson, his wife, Regina, and his film crew was unaware of the murderous spree that was to

15

erupt only two months later. They were filming scenes for the film *Satan's Sadists*, about a motorcycle gang led by a bushy bearded, crazy-eyed, tough guy named Satan. His gang called themselves "The Sadists." Together they wreaked havoc on the lives of unsuspecting citizens with barbaric acts of violence. The film was shot at Spahn Ranch in the San Fernando Valley while the ranch was being simultaneously rented by Charles Manson and his band of followers, including Sharon Tate and Charles "Tex" Watson.

During the filming, it was noted that Manson had a slew of young girls living there. He called them his Family. All of them were very unkempt; dirty bare feet, unwashed bodies and straggly hair, rumpled and dirty clothing. They were underfed and would come creeping out of the barns and from behind bushes, slowly gravitating to the on-set food area usually reserved for the cast and crew. They were so thin no one complained about the groups partaking of some of the donuts and sandwiches.

What were noticed though was how they all had these far-away eyes that didn't seem to be able to focus and how they explained their living at the ranch in wispy voices with little definition as to what they were doing with their lives.

Charles Manson however was another story. He had clear definition. He sang to his followers often. They girls would sit around his feet on the scrubby ground in a hypnotic trance as he sang the words "I've got to be me," a song he wrote himself.

The similarities that Manson had and further developed to match the lead character in *Satan's Sadists* were disturbing. When the press released arrest photographs of Charles Manson, after his orchestrating the Sharon Tate-La Bianca murders in August 1969, Manson was a dead ringer for the motorcycle gang leader Satan, with his wild long black hair and that death defying cultish stare. Adamson and Carrol both wondered if their movie had had an effect on Manson due to the similarities of their lead character's background history, brought out in the theme song to the movie, Satan's being an orphaned child by a mother who was too busy as a prostitute to take care of her natural born son, since Manson's mother had done the same thing to him as a child.

On the set however, Manson seemed to hang around the fringes of the shooting, looking for some way to be involved. At one point, when a dune buggy broke down, it was Charles Manson who jumped in to help fix the vehicle. He displayed excellent skills at understanding engines and mechanical things and had the car fixed enough to keep the production moving along.

Overall, Adamson and Carrol considered themselves fortunate that the worst the Spahn Ranch-*Satan's Sadists*-Charles Manson event was a weird experience and extreme coincidence.

As Adamson's filmmaking continued in the 1970s, he purchased a large estate in the Movie Colony in Palm Springs at 899 North Avenida De Las Palmas, which was formally owned by Harold Lloyd. To his film making, he added more sexualized productions, beginning with *The Female Bunch* (1971), to his repertoire and attracted other falling stars like Robert Livingstone and Yvonne De-Carlo. It was DeCarlo who shared her aging beauty with filmgoers in Adamson's almost pornographic film *Blazing Stewardesses* (1975). Sexploitation films proved profitable and he made a dozen more, including *Angel's Wild Women* (1972), *Girls for Rent* (1974), *Cinderella 2000* (1977) and *Nurse Sherri* (1978).

In the late 1970s, Adamson crossed racially divisive lines by making several black action films, a subgenre classified these days as Blacksploitation, including *Black Heat* (1976), *Uncle Tom's Cabin* (1976), and *Black Samurai* (1977).

In all he made 30 films in just less than 20 years, barely scratching headlines and never once was nominated for an Oscar. After releasing his last film *Lost* (1983), starring Sandra Dee and Jack Elam and still not receiving any recognition for his contribution to the dramatic arts, Adamson hung up his camera and retired from the industry. He wouldn't make serious headlines until his murder,

12 years later.

Regina died of cancer in 1992. Al sold the Palm Springs hotel and moved to Indio, stretching out his retirement money and buying a nice home with a Jacuzzi. He loved that Jacuzzi. In the summer of 1995, Al made friends with a handyman/contractor named Fred Fulford, 46, who was allowed to live at Al's 2-story home with the promise of completing some renovations. Al only lived at the Indio home on Avenue 49 part-time, having residences in Texas and Las Vegas, and enjoyed a travelling lifestyle.

On July 26, 1995, Al's brother, Kenneth Adamson, contacted Indio police claiming that Al had been missing for about a month and sought their help in locating him. He feared something criminal might have happened to Al. Working from several anonymous tips; the police searched the Indio home. Fulford was nowhere to be found. There was a recently completed new tile floor where the Jacuzzi once sat. The police dug up the renovated room and found Al Adamson's body, stuffed in a large blanket and buried under four tons of cement.

A homicide arrest warrant was issued for Fred Fulford. He was not easily found. Using credit card receipts, he was discovered to have been residing for about a week in a St. Petersburg, Florida hotel. East coast authorities were called. Fulford was arrested and extradited back to California for prosecution.

Fulford had Indio attorney Robert DeAztlan representing him early on. However, then Fulford decided to represent himself. Delays and extensions from a legally inexperienced Fulford haunted the proceedings. Eventually the judge convinced Fulford to accept another attorney, Robert Hurley, or suffer a doomed defense. It took four years to go to trial.

In October, 1999, during his opening statements, Deputy District Attorney Paul Vinegrad said he would show the jury evidence that Fred Fulford had bashed in Al Adamson's skull with a heavy object and then dumped his body into a hole where a Jacuzzi once stood. He did this so he could steal the victim's money and use his check book and credit cards, often forging Al Adamson's name. Furthermore, Vinegrad said, he would show that Fulford had sold several of Adamson's cars, shipping them to Florida to hide the tracings of his transactions. Fulford's motive for the killing was to prevent Adamson from collecting on Fulford's debts and to keep him from alerting authorities. In short, Fulford wanted to be able to continue stealing from Adamson.

Robert Hurley, Fulford's attorney, said the evidence was "Circumstantial" and would not meet the standard of "Beyond a reasonable doubt." He even indicated Fulford would eventually take the stand in his own defense and went on to say that Fulford could profit more from Adamson being alive than dead. In essence, Fred Fulford was being framed.

At the trial, Kenneth Adamson testified that in their past phone conversation his brother, Al, had complained to him that Fulford had ran up $4,000 in bills while living in Al's home. Al claimed Fulford was stealing from him, wanted restitution and wanted Fulford out of his house. Adamson had threatened Fulford with getting the police involved if he didn't pay the money back. Al called Fulford's conduct criminal. The day after the phone conversation, Kenneth went to go see his brother at the Indio home. Fulford answered the door and said Al wasn't home. Kenneth hung around a while. Al didn't return and Kenneth eventually left.

A movie stunt man and friend of Al Adamson's, Gary Kent, testified that he'd had a similar conversation where Al complained about a man living with him had been stealing from him and running up his credit cards.

On October 27, 1999, prosecutors called forth more witnesses. Ernesto Perez, a laborer, testified that he and his brother had been hired by Fulford to remove the Jacuzzi on June 21, 1995. At the end of the day Fulford had told them to come back the next day and help him fill the hole. Upon their return, they noticed a big hump of dirt in the middle of the hole and Fulford was watering it down, creating a sort of circular moat, around the mound. Perez and his brother filled the hole with cement blocks and a load of cement delivered by a truck.

Detective, Jack Anderson, described the crime scene that police found upon searching the home and how after removing the tile floor and breaking through the cement, a job that took several hours; they'd discovered Adamson's body rotting in the hole. As the police dug through the cement and dirt below, they could smell the body decomposing.

Fred Fulford was the first witness called to his defense by his attorney. He took the stand on November 9, 1999. He confirmed that he had met Al Adamson in 1994 in Las Vegas and had agreed to come live at his home in Indio while remodeling not one, but two homes at the Avenue 49 address and then went on to admit to forgery, perjury and taking Al Adamson's money but, he denied repeatedly having killed the man and burying his body under cement. He was in the witness box testifying all day. Fulford, 50, plainly stated, "I did not kill that man." He claimed that if Adamson had lived he would make more money and fully reimburses his employer because their agreement was to sell the homes and then split the profits, which would exceed the $4,000 in debt he owed to Adamson. Fulford testified that his name had been added to the credit card by Adamson as a way to purchase supplies for the remodel since Adamson was so frequently out of town and that the cars Fulford were trying to sell in Florida had been given to him although Adamson had yet to transfer the titles. Fulford defended his actions and claimed no knowledge that Adamson was buried under the Jacuzzi even though he admitted that he did remove the Jacuzzi as part of the remodel and then have the hole filled with cement. The only explanation he could give was that somebody else, somebody unknown, had come in and dumped Al Adamson's body in the empty hole during the night.

The second witness for the defense was a structural engineer who testified that there was nothing unusual about a contractor filling a hole left by the Jacuzzi with cement.

On November 17, 1999, Defense and Prosecuting Attorney's made their closing arguments. Robert Hurley, for the defense, claimed there was no direct evidence linking his client to the actual murder and summarized his alternate theory that Fred Fulford was simply a man doing a remodel who may have overstepped his financial authority and then was framed for the murder. Deputy District Attorney Paul Vinegrad was relentless in his final closing accusations that Fred Fulford was the man who committed the murder and showed the jury several gruesome photographs of Al Adamson's decomposing body, found by detectives as it lay in the hole left from the removal of four tons of cement.

The jury went out to deliberate and less than two hours later came back with a decision of "Guilty." Fred Fulford was convicted of First Degree murder.

Fred Fulford, as he had for most of the six-week trial, showed little emotion as the jury made their decision public. His attorney told reporters that they would appeal based on several trial issues that he would not presently discuss. Prosecutors said they were not surprised by the decision or the defense's claim to appeal but that the jury had made the right decision based on the evidence. A sentencing hearing was scheduled for December 17.

The sentencing hearing went through several delays and finally happened on Friday, March 3rd, 2000. Judge Graham Cribbs denied a defense request to reduce the First Degree murder charge and cited the crime as "Cold hearted and calculated" and "It's right out of a script of a horror movie" then he sentenced Fred Fulford to 25 years to life in prison. His current place of residence is San Quentin State Prison.

Sources:

John M. Glionna, HORROR FILM DIRECTOR FOUND SLAIN, BURIED UNDER FLOOR, Los Angeles Times (.com), August 8, 1995.

John Horn, MOVIE DIRECTOR AL ADAMSON SLAIN, BURIED UNDER OWN HOUSE, Associated Press, San Francisco Examiner.

Jeanne King, MOVIE-LOT SATAN PORTENT OF DEATH, http://www.cielodrive.com/archive/movie-lot-satan-portent-of-death/, December 28, 1969.

Greg Krieger, ARTICLES ON AL ADAMSON, http://gregkrieger.tripod.com/aladamson/adamsontrial.html.
Christine Mahr, 4-YEAR-OLD MURDER CASE TO GO TO TRIAL NEXT WEEK: HANDYMAN CHARGED IN DEATH OF FILMMAKER BURIED IN CEMENT, The Desert Sun, October 2, 1999.

Christine Mahr, TESTIMONY BEGINS IN TRIAL OVER FILMMAKER'S SLAYING, The Desert Sun, October 26, 1999.
Christine Mahr, DETECTIVE DETAILS TO JURY HOW OFFICIALS FOUND BURIED BODY, The Desert Sun, October 27, 1999.

Christine Mahr, TRIAL IN MURDER OF AL ADAMSON COULD BE FASTER THAN EXPECTED, The Desert Sun, November 1, 1999.

Christine Mahr, DEFENDANT DENIES KILLING DIRECOR, The Desert Sun, November 10, 1999.

Christine Mahr, MOVIE-DIRECOR MURDER CASE MAY BE SENT TO JURY TODAY, The Desert Sun, November 16, 1999.

Christine Mahr, FULFORD CASE GOES TO JURY AFTER CLOSING STATEMENTS, The Desert Sun, November 17, 1999.

Christine Mahr, MAN GUILTY OF FIRST DEGREE MURDER, The Desert Sun, November 18, 1999.

Christine Mahr, ADAMSON'S DEATH WAS LIKE SCENE FROM FILM, FRIEND SAYS, The Desert Sun, November 18, 1999.

Christine Mahr, MURDERER GETS SENTENCED, The Desert Sun, March 4, 2000.

Unknown author, FAMED B-GRADE HORROR DIRECTOR AL ADAMSON MURDER 6/21/1995 INDIO, CA *FRIEND FRED FULFORD CONVICTED OF HIS MURDER, SENTENCED TO 25 YEARS TO LIFE IN PRISON*, https://mylife-ofcrime.wordpress.com/2012/12/05/famed-b-grade-horror-dire ctor-al-adamson-murder-6211995-indio-ca-friend-fred-fulford-convicted-of-his-murder-sentenced-to-25-years-to-life-in-prison/

Various contributors, AL ADAMSON, IMDB database, http://www.imdb.com/name/nm0011467/.

Various contributors, AL ADAMSON, https://en.wikipedia.org/wiki/Al_Adamson , Wikipedia.org.

The Friendly Murders

The pool man showed up to do his bi-weekly chore of skimming and vacuuming, maintaining the crystal waters in the backyard of 893 West Camino Sur, a 1961 modernist styled home in the swanky Las Palmas neighborhood. Normally there would have been a momentary greeting of the pretty housewife as she went about her daily duties, a slight nod of the head and a quick, "Good morning mam." The home was unusually quiet. The summer temperatures had already dipped from the 100+ degrees of September. On October 13th, 1978, it might only reach ninety.

Still seeking polite pleasantries, the pool man took a quick look in the kitchen window. He doesn't want to be seen peering into his employers privacy. He wondered if they were home. When he looked inside, he saw something out of place. The kitchen was somewhat messy. In the dining room beyond, the table was set, awaiting dinner. A few wine glasses were knocked over as if an earthquake had come and gone; though no quake had happened last night. Unusual. He knew they had staff here to keep things straight and they wouldn't usually leave the place in disarray. He looked further and noticed the maid; a pleasant elderly woman who was often around the house was on the ground, half sticking out from behind the kitchen island. She was not moving and her hair was unkempt. A dark pool of something spilled on the floor had surrounded her head. The pool man grew concerned and drove to a nearby telephone and dialed 911.

The first responders were patrolmen. They go to the home and gain entry. Inside they found the maid had been shot with a single bullet to the head. They called for back-up; a detective, and crime scene technicians.

Within an hour the home was filled with officers taking pictures and collecting evidence.

The oven was on, indicating the killings happened just before dinner.

A second victim was found. Sophia friendly, the beautiful trophy wife, was discovered sprawled in the hallway. Her reading glasses were still held in her hand. It would appear she had been attempting to flee when the killer – or killers – shot her in the head from behind. The bullet left an exit wound near the bridge of her nose.

A third victim was found in the study, slumped awkwardly in his favorite chair: Edward Friendly. The television was on. Loud. Edward was known to be hard of hearing. The noise most likely helped mask the intruders trespass. Edward had been shot twice; once in the chest and one to the top of his head. It split his head open like a rip piece of fruit.

Police cordoned off the home and street with tape and squad cars. Neighbors were questioned. No one saw or heard anything. No vehicles coming or going. No loud noises. No gunshots. No unusual suspects in the neighborhood. It was not difficult to imagine. The home, while open to the street, had high back yard fences and lots of mature landscaping. The lot was impressively large, about twice the size of most people's, some 17,000sf. The home itself was just over 3,000sf. Neighbors would have been watching the evening news or eating their own meals. Many ate out. They could afford to.

The Las Palmas neighborhood did not attract working class homeowners. It was and still is filled with the city's elite: the wealthy, many celebrities, generally older residents who could afford to pay for nice things. Pay extra for privacy. Tall trees lined the perimeter of each home, most had gates and fences to prevent the public's prying eyes. Only the best architects were hired to design the stylish houses. No one could easily tell if their neighbor was home.

By talking to the neighbors, the pool man and the maid's family, the police pieced together a profile of the victims.

The maid, Frances Williams, 67, had worked for the Friendly's for the better part of a year as both maid and cook. She worked about five days of the week and was on call whenever they were expected to arrive in town.

The wife, Sophia Friendly, 71, was matriarch of the family. Her lineage came from a wealthy line of San Francisco socialites, the Brownells. She brought more than good looks to the marriage. She'd brought money and prestige.

Initially, it was the husband, Edward Friendly, 74, who police thought was the primary source of motive for the killings. Edward had purchased their Palm Springs home just a year earlier, in 1977, for just over $200,000. It was to be his retirement home, a place to relax and enjoy life after decades of hard work. His working years had been filled with selling real estate in San Francisco and Salt Lake City. His largest sale was in the 1950s when he sold Tanforan Race Track, a horse racing track where some of Edward's privately owned thoroughbreds had raced. His commission had been in the millions. The killers may have simply wanted to rob the Friendly's. Jewelry was missing. Cash was gone. Some miscellaneous items: silver and other valuables had disappeared. The crime scene smelled like an organized crime, maybe mafia, smash and grab gone very very wrong.

Ballistics would determine the murder weapon was a .45 caliber Star Model PD pistol. It appeared that the killings had been done by a professional hit man. The home showed no signs of breaking and entering. Beyond the facts so far disclosed, there were no solid clues to make a determination with absolute certainty as to the killer's identity.

After first considering the husband's ties, the police focused on the Sophia Friendly and found that shortly after her murder Sophia would have come into a large sum of money via a trust fund inheritance. As a younger woman, she'd been married to Curtis Wood Hutton, a nephew of E. F. Hutton, the stock broker champion of the early 1900s. C. W. Hutton was first cousin to Barbara Woolworth Hutton, heiress to the Woolworth's department store fortune who Donnell knew as a former wife of Cary Grant's from the local history of the two honeymooning in Palm Springs in the 1940s. It was Barbara's connection to C. W. Hutton that raised Donnell's eyebrows. Follow the money. He'd discovered that in the 1930s Barbara had given C. W. $1 million to help sustain him. When C. W. had gone into the U. S. Navy that same decade, the money had been placed in a trust in case he should suffer a fatality and thereby allowing the money to pass, relatively untaxed to his wife Sophia, his beneficiary.

Decades passed. C. W. lived through the war and he and Sophia eventually divorced. The trust did not change its inheritance instructions. In 1978, when now Sophia Friendly and her husband Edward were killed, C. W. was still alive, though battling a deadly strain of Cancer. Two weeks after the Friendly's murders, C. W. died also, of natural causes. Instead of his now multi-million dollar trust fund passing on to Sophia Friendly, it would instead pass on to their now adult children, Sophia Hutton and Edward Hutton.

In late October of 1978, just two weeks after the murders, PSPD detectives found and questioned Edward Hutton and two of his employees, Anthony Garrido and David St. John, about the murder of his mother and step-dad in Palm Springs and about the inheritance. Edward now ran a restaurant in Houston called La Seule Etoile, or The Lone Star, an expensive French restaurant in an area known as The Richmond Strip. Through the interviews detectives discovered Edward had a criminal friend, Andreas Christensen, from Scandinavia, who had both been in Houston with Edward in 1978, shortly before the murders, and that he also knew the Friendly's. He might have made his entry into the home, and should he have wanted, easily, with no need of forcing entry. One of the employees, Anthony Garrido, also admitted to purchasing the .45 caliber Star pistol for

Christensen at a local pawn shop. The police didn't find the gun and so there was nothing real, nothing physical to link Christensen to the crime. Still, he fled before police could question him, escaping to Rhodesia (which would become Zimbabwe) on his European passport. Zimbabwe was a country involved in a deadly Civil War, where vicious squads and thugs marched the streets with machetes, killing anyone who opposed them. The chaos made for a perfect haven for someone wanting to wipe their trail clean. No travel records were maintained in that country at that time. The government was in a shambles. Christensen effectively disappeared, for a while.

Though PSPD detectives and Riverside County District Attorney investigators believe Andreas Christensen to be the killer and his motive the trust fund inheritance of Edward Hutton, no arrests were ever made. Hutton and Christensen have long since denied any involvement. Yet, here's what the authorities have been able to piece together:

Curtis Wood Hutton and Caroline Hutton, C. W.'s newest wife, were married in 1963. They divorced in 1976, just two years before the murders. Caroline was a great source for the investigators. Caroline and C. W. had lived in Manhattan during their marriage and she recalled meeting Andreas Christensen for the first time in the Lord Nelson Pub. Christensen and her husband became good friends quickly, often going out at night. The longer Caroline got to know Christensen, who was stylish and rambunctious, the more disturbed she became. His past was a mystery, he never talked about it, not even when asked.

When C. W. and Caroline was divorced, her former husband moved to Houston, Texas, and the only contact between the two was on issues of child support and custody battles. She moved to London and when her in-laws were killed, she only learned about it through a friend who lived in Santa Barbara. Her first thoughts were that her husband was somehow involved. She knew about the trust and would often be queried about it by detectives as far away as Palm Springs and as close as Scotland Yard. In each case, detectives would also want to know about Christensen. He was everybody's prime suspect. She also knew that Edward hated his mother and that he was very aware of the inheritance aspects of the trust. She would tell investigators that he talked about the inevitability of the Barbara Hutton trust as something that would eventually come to him, at least half of it, the other half going to his sister Sophia, when his parents were eventually dead.

All very interesting news for detectives but, without any physical evidence to support the motive the police had to move the case to their back shelf, placing it in the Cold Case files of the PSPD and moved on.

In 1979, David St. John, one of the Houston employees of Edward Hutton died from a drug overdose. The apartment he died in was owned by Edward Hutton.

In 1980, the other employee, Anthony Garrido, was killed in Arkansas while hitchhiking.

Then, on June 2, 1981, the police caught a break. They were alerted by Interpol that Andreas Christensen had been arrested in Copenhagen, Denmark on charges of bank robbery. It seems that while writing a traffic ticket for an idling car, the police unknowingly stopped a bank robbery in progress. While an officer was informing the car's driver, Janet Myburgh, 23, a former Zimbabwe police woman, that in Denmark it was illegal to leave a car running for environmental reasons, inside the bank Christensen was pointing a pistol at a teller and demanding money. Before he could leave with his loot, police arrested him and though he called himself Alfred Borg, fingerprints taken while he was in the Danish Army as a young man confirmed that he was indeed Andreas Christensen. It appeared he had returned to Denmark to flee charges of embezzlement he had earned while in Zimbabwe.

By the time Interpol reached out to PSPD, only Tom Barton remained as the original detective, his old partner had retired. The new partner on the case was detective Fred Donnell. Within a few weeks, Barton, Donnell and Riverside County Prosecutor Tom Douglass flew to Denmark to question Christensen while he sat in a Gentofte jail, in a suburb of Copenhagen. They stayed at an old upscale hotel on the waterfront, the Copenhagen Admiral Hotel. The police station was a former brick mansion that had been converted to a government building in World War II.

The detectives described the interviews with Christensen as "torturous."

He was full of himself. He was arrogant. He denied any involvement in the killings. Yet, at times, he let slip little details of the murders. He had an answer for everything.

Christensen admitted, yes, he'd had a pistol like the one used in the killings. He said he'd flushed it down the toilet of a moving train in Germany years ago. He also admitted to being in Palm Springs at the time; although for romantic reasons.

Police believe it more likely that Christensen dumped the pistol somewhere in the desert during his stay in Palm Springs. With no actual way to connect the evidence, police went home more or less empty handed. The Friendly murders went back into the Cold Case files.

Christensen received a six year sentence for the bank robbery.

The case went idle for over 25 years and then the Riverside County District Attorney's office received a phone call from Michael Taylor, a retired San Francisco Chronicle newspaper reporter who had followed the Friendly murders from the beginning. He insisted the case be reopened and that a new forensic technology be applied, whereby fingerprints are lifted off bullet casings to determine who loaded the murder weapon. The District Attorney, Rod Pacheco, complied and an edge of a thumbprint was found. Christensen's prints were all from the pads of his fingers. Therefore, it wasn't a match. A new set of prints would be needed for confirmation. Before any action was taken, Pacheco lost his office in an election and his successor determined the case was unwinnable.

The Friendly murders once again returned to the Cold Case files.

Sources:

John Connolly, A MURDER IN PALM SPRINGS, http://dujour.com/news/a-murder-in-palm-springs/4/.

Brett Kelman, PALM SPRINGS FRIENDLY MURDERS REMAIN UNSOLVED AFTER 35 YEARS, http://archive.desertsun.com/article/20131102/NEWS0801/311 020042/Palm-Springs-Friendly-murders-remain-unsolved-after-35-years, The Desert Sun.com; Nov. 13, 2013.

Ray Ryan, owner of Palm Springs famous El Mirador hotel and a high stakes gambler, was murdered.

The Murder of Ray Ryan

The Ryan Oil Company did well in the 1940s and its owner came to Palm Springs and became a real estate developer and an hotelier. One of his first financial moves was to invest, along with 24 others, in the now defunct, yet still eminently glamorous, El Mirador hotel. The hotel had fallen into a state of disrepair since it opened in 1928. Already closed and reopened twice, as a hotel, bankruptcy, and hotel again, decline. It was then purchased by the U.S. Army for use as a rehabilitation center for returning veterans from WWII. By 1949, the El Mirador was ready for rebirth. Ray Ryan saw opportunity and breathed new life into the grand dame of Palm Springs. After all, he was a solid investor, an inveterate gambler, and he loved both the rewards and excitement of taking risks.

Born in 1904 in Waterstown, Indiana, Ryan was a world traveler and he brought certain flair with him. Besides being married, he also had a girlfriend on the side. Her name was Roberta Linn and she was a young singer working for Lawrence Welk as his Champagne Lady. Ray met Roberta at cancer fundraiser dinner where she was the entertainment singer for the event. He invited her to an after party that night. Roberta's mom said no. Ray was twice her age, and it was the early 1950s. The next day, they went horseback riding. After a few more dates, Roberta was entirely smitten with Ray and him with her.

What Roberta didn't know, was how deeply connected to the mob Ray was. He'd had a marathon low-ball poker game in 1949 with a man named Nicholas "Nick the Greek" Dandolos at the Thunderbird Casino in Las Vegas, which was owned by mobster Meyer Lansky. The game had gone on for nearly a week, playing five to six hours a day. In the end, Ray won over half a million dollars from The Greek. Rumors float that Ray had cheated The Greek and used modern electronic devices and spies to know his opponents cards. Ray's friends defended him saying, Ray was exceptional at remembering and counting cards and was just that good. In many circles Ray was known as an outstanding card player in a variety of games. To pacify the Greek, Ray gave him back $26,000. What seemed to be a small gesture of condolence on Ray's part, years later, turned out to be a deadly mistake that came back to haunt Ray.

To further cement his mob connections and gambling ties, in 1949, Ray was known to give a gold keychain inscribed "D.B. from Ray Ryan" to Las Vegas mafia chieftain Dave "Davie the Jew" Berman. Berman rose to mobster fame when immediately after Bugsy Siegel's murder in 1947, Berman and Genovese family associate Moe Sedway walked into the Las Vegas Flamingo Hotel and Casino and announced they were now in charge.

In the meantime, Roberta got to know her new boyfriend in numerous ways. They travel together, visiting New Orleans and Cuba, where they met up with several mobsters while staying at the Intercontinental Hotel. This was in the pre-Castro days of the island country and it was very posh.

Back in Palm Springs, Ray became very involved with desert charities and hosted the Desert Circus Ball at the El Mirador. His connection helped bring even more publicity to the desert. During this time several gambling establishments had also risen: The Dunes among them. Ray's gambling continued. He mostly won and considered Roberta his good luck charm. She was around often but didn't know the names of the men who discussed politics and crime in Chicago and Italian accents. Being close to danger was exciting and Roberta decided to continue dating Ray even though he was still a married to his Catholic wife, Helen.

Ray helped advance Roberta's singing career, getting her first show in Las Vegas at the New Frontier. The same hotel which had hosted Elvis Presley during his first appearance in 1956, and two decades later, during a Los Angeles court trial, would runveil that the New Frontier was secretly owned by members of the Detroit mafia: Anthony Joseph Zerelli, Michael Polizzi and others through a shell corporation called Emprise. Roberta's opportunity there was incredible. She was immediately surrounded by top-notch production people. Her music arranger was Nelson Riddle, the best in the business. Later, Riddle would help Sinatra on his music. Edith Head designed her gowns and Charlie O'Curran staged her show. With Charlie's help, Roberta would go on to some of the best clubs in the country, including the Copacabana in New York and the Shamrock in Houston. The Copacabana was owned by mob boss Frank Costello and the club had many headliner acts grace its stage.

Once, Roberta and Ray met a friend of Ray's, H. L. Hunt, who at the time was considered the wealthiest man in the world, in New York after her show closed at the Copacabana to watch a baseball game. Hunt had rented the entire top floor of the Waldorf Astoria hotel as his own private suite and he and Ray played Gin for most of the visit. Roberta and man named Mr Venerables watched TV for two hours that night before Hunt exclaimed that there was a woman, April Stevens, hiding in the bathroom because Hunt didn't want word to get out he was cavorting with her. Like Ray Ryan, Hunt was married too. Roberta had her first taste of caviar that night, mixed with champagne. She described its taste as delicious. It turned out that Hunt owned the New York Yankees baseball team and they sat in the owner's box eating tuna fish sandwiches, which Hunt loved, and watched pitcher Don Larsen throw a no hitter.

Years later, a mistress of Lyndon Johnson's would claim that she was in a room where several men including Richard Nixon, Lyndon Johnson and H. L. Hunt were discussing the Kennedy family. Upon departing the location, Johnson told her, "After tomorrow, those goddamn Kennedy's will never embarrass me again." The next day JFK was assassinated.

In the late 1950's Ray Ryan developed two new projects utilizing his Palm Springs connection. One was the Bermuda Dunes Country Club, developed with friend Ernie Dunlevie. BDCC opened its doors in 1958 and actor Clark Gable was the resident celebrity, building a retirement home there on the course. The club became host to the Bob Hope Golf Tournament and was a very popular spot. Roberta and Ray rode their horses over the sand dune landscape many times and breakfasting at the Bermuda Dunes airport diner.

Another of Ray's projects was the Mt. Kenya Safari Club in Africa, where he and actor and African enthusiast William Holden and a few others went into partnership on. The big game retreat and club was a watering hole for hunters as their campsites were moved from spot to spot so they could see and hunt what's known as the "Big 5" of elephant, rhino, lion, leopard and buffalo.

In 1959, Ray tried to get a Teamster's loan based on the value of the El Mirador. The FBI somehow became aware of this and began investigations into Ray and the deal fell through. Through the origins of that loan attempt, Ray made some friends in the FBI.

Ray was seemingly on top of the world. He had a beautiful wife, a gorgeous entertainer girlfriend, extensive investments and powerful friends. In 1963, the ghost of "Nick The Greek" would come back to haunt him when two Chicago mobsters, Marshall Caifano and Charles Delmonico heard about Ryan's payoff after winning his half million ten years back and Caifano and Delmonico decide they want a piece of Ryan's pie. Caifano was the replacement of Johnny Roselli, Sam Giancana's Las Vegas man. According to Caifano's Wikipedia page, to get his position as Don of Las Vegas it's said that, as part of the deal, Caifano had to trade his wife, a Louisville, Illinois, blonde bombshell, to Chicago mob boss Sam Giancana. Delmonico is simply known as a "Roving Ambassador" for the Outfit.

Ryan agrees to meet Caifano and Delmonico at The Desert Inn in Las Vegas for a discussion and ends up being invited for a ride out into the desert after being told he needs to pay $60,000 a year in protection money. Ryan refused to pay and when he was forced into the car; he quickly jumped out the other side and ran away from the two gangsters. He then called the FBI. Based largely on Ryan's testimony, Caifano and Delmonico were convicted and sentenced to ten years and five years.

In 1970, Ray Ryan was investigated by the IRS and was sentenced to three years in prison for tax evasion, and conspiracy to obstruction of justice. He used his FBI connections to admit to giving free Mt. Kenya memberships to mafia chieftains, and other complicities with the mafia. Ray paid a $2.5 million settlement and the sentence was plea bargained away.

When Marshall Caifano was let out of jail in 1972, he ordered a hit on Ray. But, Ryan was protected in Palm Springs because of a neutral territory status the desert has in mob rules, he was afraid and told Roberta to get away from him for her own good.

In her biography Champagne Lady, Roberta Linn states, "I didn't see Ray for a while and something happened. He came home and he was staying at the Desert Inn hotel and for some reason in a game, where he had played with, I think it was, Nick the Greek, or someone like that, some of the fellows from Chicago said he cheated on the game and they were trying to extort money from Ray. So, he called me and told me that I shouldn't be around him because he was having some problems with people and it could be very bad for me. I don't think even then I understood the seriousness of what was going on."

It took a few more years for the mob to catch up to Ray Ryan. On March 8, 1977, he went to the Olympia Health Club in his wife's and his hometown of Evansville, Indiana. He had become concerned about his weight and joined the gym for a three month membership, going routinely on Tuesdays, Thursdays and Saturdays. He was wearing a gold Krugerand necklace and a gold Saint Christopher medal around his neck; the patron saint of travelers. Ryan got into his newly purchased Mark V Lincoln Continental and when he went to start it, the car blew up. A bomb had been wired to the ignition. Local authorities saw the markings of a mob hit.

The murder goes unsolved.

Sources:

Tim Ethridge, BOOK DETALS THE FAST LIFE AND SUDDEN DEATH OF EVANSVILLE OIL MAN RAY RYAN, http://www.courierpress.com/news/book-details-the-fast-life-and-sudden-death-of-evansville-oil-man-ray-ryan-ep-443287054-326182741.html, CourierPress.com, April 8, 2013.

Bruce Fessier, GANGSTERS IN PARADISE, The Desert Sun, November 11, 2014.

Roberta Linn, as told to Eric G. Meeks, LAWRENCE WELK'S FIRST TELEVISION CHAMPAGNE LADY, Horatio Limburger Oglethorpe, publisher, 2007.

Herb Marynell, RAY RYAN – LIFE AS A GAMBLER, http://www.haciendahotsprings.com/RayRyan.htm.

Various contributors, RAY RYAN, https://en.wikipedia.org/wiki/Ray_Ryan_(businessman), Wikipedia.org.

Tom Neal Murdered His Wife

This boxer turned movie actor, often had his good looks compared to Clark Gable, moved to the Little Tuscany neighborhood of Palm Springs with his third wife, Gail Evett, when there was no more denying his once leading man persona was over and gone. It was his home at 2481 North Cardillo Road when on April Fool's Day in 1965 Neal murdered his wife with a .45 pistol after demanding sex and ripping her clothes off her, while accusing his already divorce seeking wife of cheating.

His glory days of WWII stardom began fading 15 years before when he'd committed assault with his fists of fury on then girl-friend Barbara Payton's lover, Franchot Tone. Neal slaughtered Tone. He won the fight but lost Barbara. She married Franchot.

It is believed that as Neal's star fell and he was reduced first to being a Maitre'D at the Doll House restaurant, where he took reservations of former colleagues, and eventually succumbed to land-scaping work to pay the bills, his life became even more inconsolable. After taking one last stab at re-energizing his career with a script based on the gruesome Black Dahlia Murders, he gave up. The script was well received. Neal was not.

In an effort to reconcile with his creditors and Gail, Neal sold his Movie Colony estate, at 1057 East Buena Vista Drive, and moved out to Cardillo Road, then considered the edge of town, where some say he diverted Black Dahlia investment money into his new home before being sentenced to ten years in prison in Indio Superior Court for First Degree Murder. He died in 1972 at the age of 58.

© Public Domain

**Boxer turned actor, Tom Neal,
at the height of his fitness.**

Source:
    Eric G. Meeks, THE BEST GUIDE EVER TO PALM SPRINGS CELEBRITY HOMES, Horatio Limburger Oglethorpe, publishers, 2014.

ORGANIZED CRIME

Mobsters in Palm Springs

They came for the sun, the fun, a time and place to relax, to play golf and to lay out by the pool. Like everyone else who came to Palm Springs, they needed a place to get away from the stress of work and the cold weather back home. Palm Springs fit the bill. So, they came and enjoyed.

The trouble was a lot of these individuals were made men, men on government watch lists who the police wanted to know their whereabouts, men who didn't just argue about market share in a board room, men who sometimes negotiated transactions at knife or gunpoint.

Rules were put in place. Amongst the police, they were kept under as much a watchful eye as could be done. But, eventually, there were so many mobsters living and visiting here that the small police forces of the desert simply couldn't commit to the amount of work a larger city could have done. The mafia men came to find themselves mostly left alone out here and that suited them just fine. And for their part, they made arrangements among the top families and organizations that Palm Springs was to be a neutral territory. No hits could happen here. The Coachella Valley was a safe haven where everyone came to visit in relative serenity, without fear of retribution for what was going on back home in Chicago, Detroit, New York or Cleveland, or wherever else they might hail from. It was a sort of gangster Switzerland; like Miami or Kansas City, where business could be conducted on a discretionary level. Deals might be made in Palm Springs and orders given. But, the desert was not to be screwed with, it's people left along and each mob guy could come here and enjoy a much needed respite from the harrowing work load they might perform elsewhere.

Eventually, the desert became a Who's Who of mafia chieftains. Some even became benefactors, philanthropists and good contributing citizens; joining country clubs, foundations and helping charities. By the 1970s there were enough made men retired in the desert that the FBI, regional, and local police departments coordinate the occasional drive by or surveillance. But, in the end they have to concede that if the gangsters are doing business in illegal trade, they aren't doing it here and if big cities like New York, Chicago and Los Angeles can't control the activities of these individuals how is a sleepy little town like Palm Springs going to do it? Besides, they're behaving just like every other tourist; renting hotel rooms, playing golf, eating in restaurants and shopping in the stores and if they do buy a home and retire here, as many of them have done, again, they are behaving just like everyone else their age as they settle in quietly and comfortably and collect their social security.

The Wertheimer Brothers
and The Dunes Casino

Brothers Al and Lou Wertheimer of the mostly Jewish, Chicago-based Purple Gang saw opportunity in Palm Springs when the El Mirador hotel, which had opened in 1928 and heralded in a new era of celebrity and luxury in the desert. The brothers had been looking for a place to restart after they and their brother Mert had lost their former business, The Colony Club in Detroit, when it was raided by police in 1924. Al and Lou decided on Palm Springs. Mert went to work for Meyer Lansky in Miami, Florida, the Mob's most prominent money man.

The Wertheimers promised more than a dozen Palm Springs city leaders that if they could just get the Sheriff to not interefere, they would fill all the hotels in town. As proof of their proposed plans, the Wertheimers pointed to the legalization of gambling in Nevada and the success of the Agua Caliente resort and Casino in Tijuana. City leader Nellie Coffman, who owned the Desert Inn downtown Palm Springs, lead the anti-gambling fight and ultimately the Wertheimers decided to build their casino in the unincorporated area known as Cathedral City.

Al and Lou were determined to make Palm Springs their new home and ended up building The Dunes; a stylish hacienda type restaurant and casino on Date Palm Drive, near Highway 111. It was on 20 acres enclosed by Tamarisk trees for privacy. Its interior was made of dark wood, crystal chandeliers and heavy velvet drapes hanging around a large round dining room and it had a long dark

**Above: Al Wertheimer (second from left)
and friends gambling at The Dunes Club.
Below: The Dunes Club on Date Palm Drive
in Cathedral City in 1936.**

wooden bar. Customers had to wear dinner jackets and they could play card games or threw dice. The place had class. Locals were discouraged. The Wertheimers understood that if they fleeced the average man in the desert then city leaders would eventually have to close down the joint. They posted a large doorman at the front to prevent just anybody from coming in.

By 1934, The Dunes was doing regular business. It was a who's who of affluence, prestige and celebrity. Al Wertheimer was the patriarch of the brothers and he determined to make good with the town he was doing business in. He had a family too; a wife and two daughters. He's vested in being a positive force in the community. He took up charity causes to put the best face on his desert endeavors and decided to support The Desert Circus, an annual fundraiser, parade and rodeo originally created to raise money for the building of a Catholic church. The Desert Circus quickly grew beyond its religious beginnings and became a fun reflection on Palm Springs western heritage. It became a weeklong even whereby most locals would wear cowboy outfits around town during everyday business and mock courts were established to fine those who didn't participate strongly enough. Often these staged court events were just a way to agreeably set up a media event a means to simply raise funds by city leaders and celebrities. Fines would be laughingly handed out in a fun-styled prepared photo shoot as the participants bailed themselves out of jail. It was all done in cooperative jest. But, the publicity the city received was enormous.

Also in 1934, The Racquet Club opened for business. Actors Charlie Farrell and Ralph Bellamy built their tennis inspired resort in the northern edge of town on a few windy sand dunes and it would quickly become one of the celebrity hangouts in the new burgeoning Palm Springs. The Racquet Club provided a shuttle for guests to go gambling at The Dunes at night and during the day, The Dunes provided racing sheets whereby guests could bet on horse races while lounging at the pool or sitting in the bar back at The Racquet Club.

The Lone Pine hotel, located at 1276 North Indian Canyon Drive (no longer standing), was owned by Musical Knights bandleader Horace Heidt and backed by a separate Chicago based Mob group, known simply as The Outfit. The Lone Pine followed The Racquet Clubs' modus operandi and helped customers out to The Dunes for evening entertainment.

Business was good for The Dunes. So good, other casinos entered the valley: The 139 Club opened its doors on Highway 111 in Cathedral City and The Cove Casino opened literally on the border of Palm Springs and Cathedral City at 67491 E. Palm Canyon Drive (now the Elk's Lodge). Both of these places were closer to town than The Dunes and certainly impacted the flow of clients. In 1936, the Purple Gang wanted a second establishment, closer to the action of downtown Palm Springs, and they constructed The Colonial House (now The Manor House) at 572 North Indian Canyon Drive. It's an expansive, two-story, red tile roofed establishment practically in the heart of Palm Springs. Heavy weight boxer Jack Dempsey was often seen there as the house celebrity and actress Andrea Leeds and her billionaire husband Bob Howard, whose father owned the racehorse Seabiscuit, opened an onsite jewelry store. And, hidden in the basement of the hotel, was a fully functional gambling hall.

Not everyone in town supported the rising new gambling-Mecca environment. They resented the slot machines, punch boards and betting forms found at too many businesses and hotels. In December of 1935, some civic minded individuals asked the Riverside County District Attorney to establish a Grand Jury to help force local authorities enforce the law.

Wertheimer was known to have Riverside County Sheriff Carl Rayburn in his pocket. The Sheriff's raids occasionally confiscated some tables and machinery but, the gambling persisted. The timing of the raids just never seemed to greatly impact the Wertheimer's extablishment. District Attorney Earl Redwine didn't do any better. No one of consequence went to jail or was ever indicted. It wasn't until 1941, when California Attorney General Earl Warren, who would later become the Supreme Court Chief Justice, put some teeth behind state laws, which allowed Redwine and Rayburn's raids to close down the three Cathedral City Casinos.

When the police finally did some real raids, Al Wertheimer was convicted of maintaining an illegal gambling house and was sentenced to a road camp. Because of his age – he was 52 in 1941 – Wertheimer was instead allowed to peel potatoes in a Riverside County kitchen. Not long after his first conviction though, he was found guilty of the same crime which stopped Al Capone: tax evasion. And Al Wertheimer was forced to sell his beloved Dunes.

Mysteriously, The Dunes burned down shortly thereafter.

Sam Giancana
and
Frank Sinatra

The friendship between Chicago's top Mob boss and the singer known as The Voice is too long to tell the whole story here. It could be a book all unto itself. Suffice it to say that they knew each other so well that Giancana was known to wear a solid gold pinky ring given to him by the famous crooner and Sinatra was known to give free concerts for Giancana. Sinatra was known to perform at Giancana's request in restaurants, the opening of nightclubs and at casinos. Sometimes the leader of the Rat Pack would bring along Sammy Davis, Jr. or Dean Martin.

At times, favors went beyond professional entertainment standards. Sinatra helped foster a three-way love triangle between a woman, Sam Giancana and President Kennedy; and Giancana's assistance which helped Frank land his 1950s comeback role in From Here to Eternity was made legendary when Mario Puzo immortalized it – and perhaps aggrandized it – in his book The Godfather.

Instead of detailing every little nuance between these two men, let's instead focus on the times that Giancana came to Palm Springs and stayed at Sinatra's Palm Springs or Rancho Mirage homes, as verified by the FBI surveillance which was maintained on each of them for decades.

Sometime between 1957 and 1960, Sam Giancana was invited to Sinatra's Rancho Mirage home for Easter, where the two played golf and swam in the pool along with Frank's former wife

Nancy Barbato and Giancana's girlfriend Phyllis McGuire. As a thank you to Giancana, Frank gave Miss McGuire a role in his film Come Blow Your Horn, which was released in 1963. As a thank you to Sinatra for her part in the movie McGuire gave Sinatra a set of crystal Steuben glasses; an unwelcome gift as it turned out. At a dinner one night at Frank's house, Phyllis McGuire noticed that the stemware Sinatra was using was not the real thing. She even said so to Frank. He denied it, claiming his glasses were Steuben. McGuire even turned her glass over to prove it to him, saying, "It's not Steuben unless it says it," which Frank's did not. At dinner he kept denying the suggestion and never thanked her for the glasses she sent him. Sinatra was known as a man with a legendary temper, who would never apologize and never forget.

December 6, 1961: Sam Giancana and Johnny Roselli, shortly after Roselli's stay with Sinatra in Rancho Mirage, are overheard on an FBI wiretap discussing Sinatra's failing relationship with the Kennedy's. Sinatra had convinced Giancana to support JFK in the presidential election with campaign contributions and gathering votes via union affiliations and ballot box maneuvers. Giancana was ultimately not happy with the outcome of the election as Bobby Kennedy soon thereafter began his crusade against the mafia.

February 7, 1962: Bobby Kennedy is given a 19 page memo from J. Edgar Hoover, detailing calls from a Judith Campbell to President Kennedy's personal secretary at the White House and also calls from Miss Campbell to Sam Giancana. Sinatra had introduced both JFK and Giancana to Campbell and in about a month; the President was to stay at the Sinatra compound in Rancho Mirage. Sinatra was making additions of a helicopter pad and cottages for the Secret Services in expectation of the President's arrival. Peter Lawford was dispatched to tell Frank that the President had changed his mind and would be staying elsewhere. Sinatra never talked to Lawford again and dropped him from the Las Vegas Rat Pack shows and movie roles immediately.

March 24-26, 1962: JFK stayed at Bing Crosby's home in Thunderbird Country Club instead of Frank Sinatra's, where the Kennedy had his famous rendezvous with Marilyn Monroe.

Easter 1963: Sam Giancana again visited Frank Sinatra's Rancho Mirage home to get away from the cold and snow of Chicago and bask in the sunshine while playing golf and relaxing by the pool. FBI surveillance of Frank and Sam was so heavy that Sinatra and Giancana would send out multiple dummy cars when would leave the compound as a way to confuse the FBI agents trying to follow them. Later that year, Giancana filed a harassment lawsuit against the FBI and agents were forced to remain at least a block away during their tails of Giancana and had to remain at least one hole behind him on the golf course.

Fun fact: Sam Giancana was nearly a scratch golfer, often scoring in the low 80s.

February 17, 1970: Frank Sinatra testified to the New Jersey State Commission on Investigation into his involvement with the mafia syndicate Cosa Nostra. He denied knowing any of the mobsters in the syndicate. He testified for an hour and fifteen minutes, under hard questioning into his relationships with Sam Giancana, Joe Fischetti, Lucky Luciano, and more top name mobsters. The investigative committee got nothing worthwhile from Frank even though it has been proven many times over that he was friends with all these men.

Eventually, Sam Giancana bought a home in Indian Wells as a permanent residence and owned it till he was gunned down in his Oak Park, Illinois home on June 19, 1975 despite the fact the he was in police protective custody at the time.

February 11, 1981: Frank Sinatra testified to the Nevada Gaming Commission and covered up his friendship with Giancana even though there were numerous documents detailing meetings between the two. These documents were not available to the Commission at the time. Due to the lack of subpoena power, the Commission was helpless to interview all the necessary people to conduct a full investigation into Sinatra's gangster past; which would have ended Sinatra's possibility of owning a casino. Frank's attorney, Mickey Rudin, set up interviews for the Commission with individuals who would only flatter Frank before their eyes. Ava Gardner was one such interview. She met the investigators in London and wined and dined with the men, all the while conveniently avoiding telling them of the numerous times she had personally met Sam Giancana and other Made Men at Sinatra's desert home. Frank was ultimately approved for a Special Employee license to be a part owner of Caesar's Palace.

© Public Domain/FBI File Photo

Al Capone on February 26, 1931, when he was arrested on a vagrancy charge and held by the Chicago Division of the Federal Bureau of Investigation.

Al Capone

Two Bunch Palms resort in Desert Hot Springs laid the foundation for mob stories in the desert, although their claim to gangster fame probably isn't true.

It's said that mob boss Al Capone stayed there in the 1930s. It even has an Al Capone suite but, former Mayor Frank Bogert told his own tale behind the Capone legend. He said that in 1931, then owner Billie Lipps asked him to dig a hole on the property to bury a dog – a real four-legged dog, not some euphemism of a rowdy gangster type person – and to dig the hole deep so coyotes wouldn't unearth the buried animal. It was during Bogert's digging this grave that the hot water spring was discovered. Subsequently, the property was renovated, rooms were added, and the hotel was founded.

1931: the same year Frank Bogert dug the dog's grave, discovered a hot springs, and helped renovate a home into a hotel, was the year that Capone went to prison for tax evasion. In the earliest part of the year Capone was in the Cook County Jail in Illinois on contempt of court charges. Al Capone wouldn't get out of jail till 1939, when he went into the Union Memorial Hospital in Baltimore, MD, to treat paresis (caused by late stage syphilis). Once out of the hospital, Capone moved to Palm Island, Florida, where his health continued downhill as he battled what we today call Alzheimer's disease. On January 21, 1947 he had a stroke and died four days later in his home.

Looking at the factual timeline of Al Capone's later days, it is very unlikely that he would've come out to Palm Springs, CA, during this stage of his life, and if he did, he would've done so as an invalid and not a great mob boss.

Johnny Roselli

Johnny Roselli

"Handsome Johnny" as he was known, born Filippo Sacco, July 4, 1905, moved to Los Angeles in the 1920s and changed his name to escape a murder investigation in the Chicago area. In LA he became heavily involved in the movie industry; was credited as a producer on some Brian Foy gangster films; and later moved up to union organizing and shakedowns involving 20th Century Fox Chairman Joseph Schenck who conveniently surrendered his Palm Springs Movie Colony home in a card game to Darryl Zanuck rather than having the IRS confiscate it. Roselli was a known early visitor of Palm Springs staying at both the Racquet Club and the El Mirador hotels and often visiting The Dunes. Once, at the Racquet Club, Roselli got into a bar fight with Hotel Manager Frank Bogert, who had deservedly earned a reputation in town as a real cowboy. Bogert ended up chasing Roselli and his bodyguard out of the bar and off the property. A few nights later, owner and actor Ralph Bellamy received a phone call from The Dunes floor manager threatening that if Bogert isn't out of town by nightfall he'll be dead. Bogert wasn't worried and in the end nothing happened.

Johnny Roselli was connected to Frank Sinatra in more ways than one. Supposedly, it was Roselli's friendship with Columbia Pictures President Harry Cohn that helped Sinatra get his coveted comeback role of Maggio in From Here to Eternity, a move that was cemented into American literary history when Mario Puzo immortalized the event by paralleling it in his book The Godfather.

Roselli was known to stay and attend parties at Frank Sinatra's home on several occasions in the 1950s and 1960s and Roselli was in the FBI report given to Bobby Kennedy which determined that JFK should not stay at the Sinatra compound during his March 1962 visit to Palm Springs.

In 1973, Roselli visited Palm Springs for the last known time, when he attended a meeting of mobsters Tony "Big Tuna" Accardo and Tony "The Ant" Spilotro. The entire conversation is unknown. However, it is speculated that Roselli was there to either discuss Spilotro's promotion in the mob or to discuss Roselli's planned retirement to Florida.

Johnny Roselli was eventually murdered. He had been both strangled and shot. His legs had been cut off and then he was stuffed in a steel drum and found floating in Dumfoundling Bay, near Miami, Florida on August 9, 1976.

Anthony "Big Tuna" Accardo

From the 1960s till only a few years before his death, this Chicago mob boss owned a home in Palm Springs on Alhambra, in the Canyon Country Club. Born April 28, 1906, Antonio Leonardo Accardo was the son of an immigrant Sicilian shoemaker and joined the crew of Jack "Machine Gun" McGurn in 1926, when he was only 20. The first nickname Accardo earned was "Joe Batters" after hitting three gangster traitors with a baseball bat at a dinner Capone held. Accardo grew to hate this nickname. He was renamed "Big Tuna" after going on a fishing trip where he caught a giant tuna. Accardo was sent to prison in 1932 for 11 years for tax evasion. He was best known for his being a shooter at the St. Valentine's Day massacre, the murder of rival crime boss Frank Yale, and north side Chicago gang leader Hymie Weiss.

In the 1940s, Tony Accardo became underboss of Chicago, while Al Capone was imprisoned. Under Accardo's leadership, the crime syndicate was able to reorganize into new channels of commercialism. For instance: they moved into slot machines and vending machines, which were placed in gas stations and restaurants in the Outfits territory. They also increased production of counterfeit cigarettes and liquor stamps, boot legging into dry states, and expanded narcotics smuggling. In Las Vegas, Accardo made sure that casinos ran or owned by families under his influence used his slot machines and he converted the gang's brothel businesses into call girl services.

Tony Accardo is not confirmed as having purchased a home in Palm Springs although, he was known to visit the desert many

© Public Domain

Chicago crime boss Tony Accardo

times; especially after his retirement from The Outfit.

In 1957, Accardo stepped down as boss, removing himself from the day to day operations of the crime world and earned the title Consigliere and passing the reigns over to the more flamboyant Sam Giancana, who still had to defer to Ricca and Accardo for major decisions. Ricca was the official boss until he died in 1972, at which time Accardo became Chicago's top mob boss. Accardo died May 22, 1992 at the age of 86.

Joseph Aiuppa in 2007.

ERIC G. MEEKS

Joey "The Dove" Aiuppa

Joseph Aiuppa, (pronounced I-U-PA) born December 1, 1907, was a former boxer turned protector and, in the 1920s, became a driver in the ranks of the Chicago Outfit headed by Anthony Accardo. By the 1940s, he would run underground gambling establishments for the Outfit. His cover job was managing furniture manufacturer Taylor & Company, which actually was a front for a slot machine company.

In 1966, Aiuppa was convicted of illegally transporting Mourning Doves (actual birds) across states lines under the Migratory Bird Act of 1918, as part of Robert Kennedy's crackdown on the mob. He was sentenced to a 3 month prison term and fined $1,000. Thereafter he was known as Joey "Doves".

In June, 1975, Aiuppa conspired with Johnny "Handsome Johnny" Roselli to kill Sam Giancana. Motive for the murder varies from Giancana's refusal to share south of the border caisson profits with his lesser gang members to Giancana's involvement with an alleged CIA conspiracy to assassinate Cuban leader Fidel Castro.

Shortly after Giancana's death, "The Dove" bought a home in Palm Springs, CA, where he came frequently until his conviction, in 1986, for skimming Las Vegas casino profits. That same year, another gangster: Tony "The Ant" Spilotro and his brother Michael, were beaten to death and buried in a cornfield near Aiuppa's Morocco, Indiana, home as retribution for The Ant's involvement in Aiuppa's conviction. Michael was killed to minimize further revenge. The beating and burial were recreated in the movie Casino starring Joe Pesci and Robert DeNiro. Aiuppa was sentenced to a 28 year prison sentence, of which he served 10.

He was released in 1996 and died of natural causes about a year later, in 1997, at the age of 87.

ERIC G. MEEKS

Vincent Dominic "Jimmy" Caci

Born August 1, 1925, Caci grew up in Western New York and owned a construction company in Erle, Pennsylvania, and supposedly owned restaurants in both New York and California. In the 1970s he was sent to Attica prison for armed robbery and while there became friends with Stephen "The Whale" Cino.

By the late 1970s he'd moved to Palm Springs where he worked for the Los Angeles based crime family, The Milano's, as a loan shark and was given the title Caporegime. Caci became street boss of the Los Angeles family for a short time in 1988 when Peter Milano went to prison in 1988.

In 1996, Caci was sent to prison for 3.5 years himself for conspiracy, wire fraud and interstate transportation of illegally obtained money in connection with a telemarketing scheme. The telemarketing scheme was done in connection with another local gangster named "Fat Philly" who hung out a restaurant called Tony's Pasta Mia downtown Palm Springs. I had several friends who worked at Tony's and during the early parts of the trial concerning the telemarketing crime a comment of Philly's was repeated to me. Philly was at Tony's bar, drinking and boasting loudly about his exchanges with authorities who were investigating him. Philly was asked if he wanted the number of a good lawyer to which Philly replied, "Hell, I don't need to pay no fucking lawyer. I just need a D.A. who'll make a deal. I'm fucking guilty."

After Caci's prison term, he lived another ten years in the Palm Springs area. He died on August 16, 2011, at the age of 86, at Eisenhower Medical Center in Rancho Mirage.

Frank Buccieri

Frank "The Horse" Buccieri

Though a lifetime criminal, his only conviction came as a boy of 17, when, in 1936, he was found guilty of petty larceny. Frank's brother, known hit man Fiore "Fifi" Buccieri asked the judge if the family could punish young Frank instead of having the charges sent to a grand jury. The judge agreed and Frank was given five lashes with a bent rubber hose by a family member.

Also known as "Frank Russo" or "Big Frank", this Chicago mobster earned his stripes as a manager of illegal gambling and loan sharking on Chicago's West Side in the 1960s. He bought a home in Palm Springs in the late 1970's.

In 1981, Buccieri was appointed a Capo, or a Captain, by the New York based Lucchese crime family to run the Outfits California based criminal enterprises. Frank "The Horse" died on March 8, 2004, of natural causes.

Michael Rizzitello

Also known as Mike Rizzi, Rizzitello was born in Canada on March 29, 1927 and later moved to New York City where, in the 1950s, he worked for "Crazy Joe" Gallo as a member of the Profaci crime family. After a failed attempt to take over the family by force in 1956 – Rizzitello was a gun man – he moved to Southern California and began to work for the Los Angeles crime family, which at the time was run by Frank DeSimone. Rizzitello became involved in illegal gambling, loan sharking, fraud and extortion and in 1962 was arrested for series of armed robberies in Hollywood. He served nine years in chino prison, where he met his new best friend William Carroll.

In 1976, Rizzitello became a made man alongside consigliere Frank Bompensiere, acting boss Aladena "Jimmy the Weasel" Fratianno and co-acting boss Louis Tom Dragna. A year later Rizzi became a Caporegime, the same year he was convicted in a mail-billing scheme and sentenced to three years. In a separate case, he pled no contest to extortion and filing a false insurance claim and in May of 1977 was sentenced to 2-3 years in state prison. When Rizzi was sent to pressure a casino owner to give the Chicago Outfit $1,000,000, it was "The Weasel" Fratianno who turned state's evidence and ratted out Rizzi. In response, Rizzi was sent to kill Fratianno but the FBI intervened and protected Fratianno in exchange for his testimony. Rizzitello was put on trial for attempting to kill a government witness, but was acquitted. Finally, in 1978, Rizzitello was convicted of racketeering and extortion and sentenced to five years in prison, which coupled with his other conviction, landed him behind bars till 1986.

Less than a year later, Rizzitello attempted to kill his former best friend, William Carroll, for not sharing profits in The Mustang Club, a strip joint in Santa Ana, CA. Rizzi shot Carroll in the back of the head three times while saying, "This is for not letting us eat." Carroll did not die, although he did become blind in one eye and co-operated with the FBI and police, naming Rizzitello and Joey Grosso as his attackers. In 1988, Rizzitello was blacklisted by every casino in Las Vegas due to his connections in crime. Rizzitello was convicted of attempted murder and sentenced to 33 years in prison. In 2005, Rizzitello was still in custody and died while in Palm Springs. He was interred at Forest Lawn Cemetery in Cathedral City.

PALM SPRINGS TRUE CRIME

James "The Turk" Torello

Born December 15, 1930, his first arrested in 1945 and would eventually have a rap sheet that included Auto theft, armed robbery, burglary, and hijacking and violating federal firearms laws; ending in a conviction, for which Torello would serve two years in prison. On one occasion, Sam Giancana sent Torello and mobster Jackie Cerone to kill another Outfit member, Frank Esposito, in Florida. Due to an FBI wiretapping operation in place at the time against Giancana, Esposito was tipped off and he successfully evaded his being cut into tiny pieces and fed to the sharks off Florida's coast. In 1973, "The Turk" became the chief enforcer of The Outfit and made money with loan sharking, illegal gambling and pornography.

Like many of the Chicago gangsters he'd spent many winters in the desert enjoying the safe haven decreed by the families and, in the late 1970s, after a lifetime of crime, Torello bought a home in the Palm Springs area. Unfortunately, he was a heavy smoker "The Turk" died of cancer in April 1979 at the ripe young age of 46.

Tommy "Fatso" Marson

Marson was a member of the Chicago Outfit and the Gambino crime family, who was told to get Frank Sinatra to play the Westchester Premier, owned by several mob members and other investors. The phone call for Marson's involvement came while he was staying at The Ingleside Inn in Palm Springs. Owner Mel Haber was nearby when Marson was given the house phone as he lounged poolside at the inn. Marson received one call from Chicago and his next was to Frank Sinatra who at first claimed he was busy. Marson told Sinatra this was not a request. Sinatra played the Westchester May 2 and 3, 1976. A photo was taken backstage on one of the nights that showed Sinatra sling and with his arms around just about every Chicago mob boss alive at the time. It was this photo that haunted Sinatra till the end of his days, making him guilty by association of being a friend of the mob.

Marson would eventually become a Rancho Mirage home-owner after purchasing a Tamarisk Country Club estate near Sinatra. In the early 1980s, it would be Tommy Marson who would loan $50,000 to John Nichols, the administrator of the Cabazon Band of Mission Indians, as a started fund to open the first Indian Casino in the USA.

Sources:

Bruce Fessier, GANGSTERS IN PARADISE, The Desert Sun, November 30, 2014.

San and Chuck Giancana, DOUBLE CROSS: THE EXPLOSIVE INSIDE STORY OF THE MOBSTER WHO CONTROLLED AMERICA, Warner Books, 1992.

Kitty Kelley, HIS WAY: THE UNAUTHORIZED BIOGRAPHY OF FRANK SINATRA, Bantam Books, October, 1986.

Ronald Koziol, MAFIA BOSSES MET AFTER SPILOTROS SLAIN, Chicago Tribune, July 1, 1986.

Ronald Koziol and Ronald Yates, ELITE PALM SPRINGS BECOMES A GANGSTERS PLAYGROUND, The Chicago Telegraph, The Evening Independent, May 9, 1978.

John William Tuohy, GONE HOLLYWOOD: HOW THE MOB EXTORTED THE HOLLYWOOD STUDIO SYSTEM, AmericanMafia.com, May 2002.

Various contributors, TONY ACCARDO, https://en.wikipedia.org/wiki/Tony_Accardo, Wikipedia.org.

Various contributors, JOSEPH AIUPPA, https://en.wikipedia.org/wiki/Joseph_Aiuppa, Wikipedia.org.

Various contributors, FRANK BUCCIERI, https://en.wikipedia.org/wiki/Frank_Buccieri, Wikipedia.org.

Various contributors, JIMMY CACI, https://en.wikipedia.org/wiki/Jimmy_Caci, Wikipedia.org.

Various contributors, SAM GIANCANA, https://en.wikipedia.org/wiki/Sam_Giancana, Wikipedia.org.

Various contributors, MICHAEL RIZZITELLO, https://en.wikipedia.org/wiki/Michael_Rizzitello, Wikipedia.org.

Various contributors, JOHNNY ROSELLI, https://en.wikipedia.org/wiki/John_Roselli, Wikipedia.org.

Various contributors, JAMES TORELLO, https://en.wikipedia.org/wiki/James_Torello, Wikipedia.org.

ARSON

Burning Down Paul D'Amicos Restaurant
and
the Killing of his Bookkeeper

In the late 1990s, Paul D'Amicos restaurant in Palm Springs was having some financial difficulty. The place was known as classy and with good food. It was also considered to be a mob backed joint, probably laundering money for the mob. Yet, it wasn't making enough money for whomever or whichever mobster had a controlling share and one night it almost burned down. Palm Springs Fire Department got there too soon and the building remained intact enough for its insurance company to not consider the place totaled and therefore the payout wasn't going to be enough. It would be rebuilt.

A month or three later, the head accountant for the restaurant was killed in broad daylight in Palm Springs with a single bullet to the head while he walked in a parking lot. Again, rumor has it that he was skimming profits from the restaurant and not sharing properly with the appropriate mobster.

Within a couple months after that, the restaurant burned again. This time when it went up in flames there was no stopping it. According to an arson investigator at the time who was a frequent shopper at my bookstore in Palm Springs, 'When the fire trucks rolled up to fight the blaze they went to attach their hoses to the closest fire hydrants and found that they had been stuffed with cement.' All the fire department could do was standby and watch as the building burned to the ground.

Source:
 The memory of Eric G. Meeks

FRAUD
AND
OTHER SCAMS

PALM SPRINGS TRUE CRIME

Darryl F. Zanuck

Joseph Schenck

Zanuck conspired with Schenck to defraud the IRS by
Zanuck winning this 10 bedroom, 9 bath, mansion
at 346 East Tamarisk Road, in a card game.

Darryl Zanuck and Joseph Schenck
IRS Swindle

In 1935, Joseph Schenck was on top of the world. He was 42 years old and wealthy as the head of United Artists movie studio. He had just partnered with one of his best friends, Darryl Zanuck, to create a new studio: 20th Century Fox. Sure his marriage to actress Norma Talmadge was over and done with; the divorce now final. To celebrate, he had built a beautiful new Palm Springs mansion at 346 East Tamarisk Road. What could go wrong? Well, there was that one other problem but, Schenck was sure he could handle that. Pretty sure, anyways...

The problem was with the IATSE, the International Alliance of Theatrical Stage Employees, which was basically the Union which negotiated for all the stage crew on film productions. The IATSE was run by the mob and it's local concerns were its President George Brown, a former shakedown artist, pimp, and Chicago mob low-life and his partner with the title of "Special Representative," Willie Bioff, who was also a former pimp and shakedown scammer, who always wanted his fingers in not only Schenck's cash register; but all the Hollywood bosses tills.

In some way, the studio chiefs didn't mind the mob being involved. Since the early 1930's they'd been a strong enough influence over the organization that they efficiently controlled the 12,000 union members, preventing strikes or work slowdowns. The mob kept wages at a level where the studios could control production budgets and make profitable films and most importantly, the mob had helped raise prices for live theatre, operas, and plays that were the movie industry's main competition. The mob had actually helped make the movie business more profitable through lower wages and less competition. The problem was that although the mob generally kept their word once a payoff was made, this "Special Representative" Willie Bioff had a very hungry appetite for more and more money.

Something had to be done and all the studio heads agreed.

Joseph Schenck was a patriarch of Hollywood. His brother, Nicholas Scheck, was selected to figure out a strategy, a plan, to satisfy the mob and the studios. He was given a combined budget of up to $1 million to handle the situation. After assessing who needed to be paid off, Schenk decided that the only man who really needed to be bought was Willie Bioff, and that he could be had at a one-time price, for far less than a million dollars.

So, here's how the deal went down: In April of 1936 Nicholas Schenck told Willie Bioff that the DuPont Chemical Corporation wanted to increase their foothold on the raw film business in Hollywood. That's the production of the actual film rolls themselves. At the time, Eastman Kodak was the country's number one producer of raw film. To switch film manufacturers, Schenk needed the IATSE to help convince all the workers and the studio bosses that the DuPont products were the right ones to go with and as an incentive to Willie Bioff, Schenck would see to it that Bioff would earn a 7% commission on the various studio's new purchases of the raw film from DuPont. It could all be done very legitimately and Bioff would end up earning some $159,000 (nearly $3mil in today's dollars) as a "Sub-Agent" on the deals. To sweeten the deal and ensure Bioff's participation, Nicholas Scheck had his movie mogul brother, Joseph Schenck; give Bioff a check for $100,000 up front. Bioff was thrilled and the studios switched over to DuPont Chemicals raw film that year. Bioff had one condition though: Johnny Roselli, a Hollywood enforcer and IATSE organizer for one of the other east coast mob families, could not find out about his, Bioff's, commission deal.

Bioff however had a hard time playing down his newfound wealth. He bought expensive suits, a new car; even a ranch house and he caught the attention of not the mob families, but the President of the Screen Actors Guild: Montgomery Clift, and somebody had given Clift a copy of the $100,000 check Schenck had used to bribe Bioff. Clift immediately informed the IRS of the transfer of funds, which of course had not been recorded or reported anywhere and an audit of Schenck ensued.

The audit resulted in an indictment against Joseph Schenk for tax evasion, the same crime that brought down Al Capone. Within a few years, Joseph Schenck would be found guilty, receive a hefty fine and be sentenced to five years in federal prison. In the interim, he would successfully maneuver some of his assets away from his own portfolio and into the hands of Darryl Zanuck. Zanuck went from Vice-President to President of 20th Century Fox Film Corporation and somehow, in a stroke of either luck or strategy, Zanuck conveniently won the title to Schenck's Palm Springs Movie Colony mansion in a poker game before the IRS could get their hands on it.

Schenck, a business man true and through, made a deal to lessen his penalties by agreeing to cooperate with the government in other investigations of the mob, Union organizations and Hollywood. Schenck told them everything he knew and he ended up only serving one year in prison.

Based on Joseph Schenck's testimony, grand jury indictments were issued for all the major studio bosses and the Union mobsters. Nothing was coming together for the FBI investigators until Harry Warner testified and completed the picture. Warner's subsequent testimony put the mob behind bars. On May 23rd, 1941, indictments were handed out for a slew of made men, including: George Brown and Willie Bioff. Over the next two years trials commenced which landed more than a half a dozen mobsters with guilty verdicts and penalties of $10,000+, liability for back taxes and an average of ten years in prison.

PALM SPRINGS TRUE CRIME

Schenck's and Warner's testimonies effectively ended the mafia's control of the IATSE and seriously loosened the mob's grip on Hollywood...at least for a while.

Sources:

© Public Domain

Jim and Tammy Faye Bakker

Jim and Tammy Faye Bakker

Two bible college sweethearts, who left school early to chase their dream of becoming televangelists, Jim Bakker and Tammy Fay LaValley had already been married five years when they went to work at the Pat Robertson Christian Network in 1966. They helped turn The 700 Club into one of the country's most watched Sunday morning evangelical shows and raised Pat Robertson to a household name. At the same time, they raised themselves to national attention too with The Jim and Tammy Show aimed at young children's religious beliefs and filmed from their Portsmouth, Virginia home.

In the early 1970s, they decided to strike the big time themselves and moved to North Carolina and hosted Christian telethons on Ted Turner's cable stations. They then moved to California to found the Praise The Lord (PTL) gospel show under their new corporate structure of the Trinity Broadcast Network. In 1976, they moved back east, this time to Fort Mill, South Carolina, bringing all the momentum of their successful TV ministry and created The Heritage Village Church and Missionary Fellowship.

The Bakker's church was called The Assemblies of God and they accepted anyone into their new Christian style of faith. No discrimination of race, creed, sexual orientation, criminal record or even religious denomination was allowed under their holy roof. All were welcome. This became the bedrock upon which their empire was built.

And, in the style of how Jim and Tammy Faye became one of America's richest televangelist, "if you act now to send in your

$29.95 God wants you to have this crystal pendant similar to the style the early Christians wore at the time of Christ's crucifixion. You can wear this symbol of hope recognized by God's children both here and afar as you say your daily prayers. God wants you to benefit from today's availability of worshipful gems."

Like snake oil salesmen from centuries before, they sold worthless religious trinkets to the sullied souls of men and women across America. Yes, anyone was welcome in their church. However, to get a special place within their haloed halls you had to buy stuff. Jim Bakker looked professional, clean and wholesome under the bright lights of their TV ministry and with Tammy Faye, garbed on flowing gowns and heavy mascara, crying at his side, tear streaming in multi-color Jokeresque reverie, the two were invincible. The telephones rang with orders for prayer beads, specialty crosses, and more. They became wealthy.

By the mid-1980s, the prosperity of the Bakker's was tremendous. Their church had grown to a 2,300 acre religious themed amusement and water park, called Heritage USA, where believers could ride roller coasters, Ferris wheels, water slides and carousels, all in the name of Jesus Christ, Amen. It was attracting some 6 million visitors a year and at the height of their enterprise, the Bakker's were grossing some $128 million annually. Their church had grown into the third most popular attraction in the country; only surpassed by Disneyland and Disney World.

Their prosperity was not meant to last. Apparently, the good lord had other plans for Jim and Tammy Faye. In 1984, the Charlotte Observer newspaper began investigating the sale of "Lifetime Memberships" (timeshare) at the Heritage USA theme park hotel, which guaranteed 3-day stays for those willing to pay for a little slice of heaven on earth. Over the next three years, the Observer found enough prosecutorial evidence to lead to a court trial against Jim Bakker, who was the CEO of the entire organization and solely made nearly all corporate level decisions. It was proven that he had y oversold the 500 room hotel twice over while simultaneously paying himself $3.4 million in bonuses. To keep track of his illicit activities, Bakker had kept two sets of accounting books.

In March of 1987, during the Charlotte Observer's investigations into the claimed non-profit status of the church, reporters discovered a $279,000 payoff to Jessica Hahn, who was originally called a church secretary and then was later merely described as a woman introduced to Bakker by a friend. The hush money was meant to buy Hahn's silence over her accusations of rape by Jim Bakker while on a sabbatical to Clearwater Beach, Florida.

Jim and Tammy Faye Bakker's first Palm Springs hideaway at 688 East Vereda Sur.

That same month, leaving his business and religious enterprises in the hands of Reverend Jerry Falwell, Jim Bakker stepped down from his positions at his church and his corporations and moved as far away from his flock of followers as he and Tammy Faye could. They moved to Palm Springs, CA, to a $600,000 home in the Movie Colony neighborhood at 688 East Vereda Sur so they could gather their thoughts, circle their wagons, and prepare for the legal and media onslaught that was sure to come.

And come they did.

The home was thronged by news vans and prying reporters who made the Bakker's comings and goings national news on a nearly daily basis. The excesses of wealth did little to improve the Bakker's image as the 5 bedroom, 6 baths, 4,097sf home was declared a mansion in the press, who found it easy to write about the gold faucets in the home and the air-conditioned dog house outside. In the dog's defense it does get pretty hot in the desert in the summertime.

By July, 1987, as South Carolina Justice Department Investigators helped Prosecutors define about $92 million in accounting irregularities, the Bakker's had had enough of Palm Springs and the relentless reporters. The now infamous couple pasted on happy faces as they left their Palm Springs home, Jim waving goodbye from behind the wheel of a convertible Cadillac and Tammy sitting alongside him blowing kisses to the media people crowding the street. A rented moving truck followed behind and the small convoy headed east again, this time to Tennessee.

As soon as the weather cooled Jim and Tammy Faye were back again, this time to a more secluded home in the Mesa neighborhood of Palm Springs, located at 366 West Camino Alturas, a more reclusive 4 bedroom, 4 bath, 2,833sf home on a dead end street – pun intended. It was in this home that in January, 1988, the Bakker's tried a strong offense as their best defense and held a press conference where they claimed, with God's help, Jim would triumph over his detractors and the Judas's of South Carolinian courts to build a new west coast theme park right here in the Coachella Valley. They intended to build a new empire and felt Southern California and Palm Springs in particular was just the right place to do it.

Unfortunately, South Carolina prosecutors and the IRS did-

Jim and Tammy Faye Bakker's second Palm Springs home at 366 West Camino Alturas was most likely chosen for its lack of photographic curb appeal.

n'tagree and God didn't show up to help Jim Bakker in his defense. In 1988, Jim was indicted on eight counts of mail fraud, fifteen counts of wire fraud and one count of conspiracy and by the first week of October 1989, he was found guilty on all 24 accounts. He was sentenced to 45 years in a federal medical prison and given a $500,000 fine. His cell mate was the anti-government conspiracy theorist Lyndon LaRouche.

Jim left the PTL some $65 million in debt. Tammy continued to live in Palm Springs. She apparently loved the area. I would occasionally run into her at thrift stores in the desert where she was buying the odd item for home decoration or selling pieces of her colorful and expensive wardrobe. She divorced Jim in 1992 and remarried in 1993 to Roe Messner, a family friend and real estate developer who had helped finance and build Heritage USA. He must've been a really good friend, because it was Messner who paid the $279,000 to Jessica Hahn, for which he was eventually found guilty of fraud in relation to the PTL Club scandals. Messner was also supposedly dispatched to their Palm Springs home during the financial and sex scandals by Jerry Falwell to find make an offer for the Bakker's to keep quiet and allow Falwell to take over the PTL and its subsidiaries. Falwell denied any such actions on his part. Supposedly, Tammy Faye wrote on a napkin, saying she wanted $300,000 a year for life for Jim and $100,000 for life for herself. When Jim was asked what he wanted, Messner said that Jim stated 'he didn't want anything from the PTL.' Messner ended up filing for bankruptcy protection due to the PTL ministries owing him an outstanding debt of some $14 million and him owing his own creditors some $30 million. Messner and Tammy Faye simultaneously divorced each of their spouses, Tammy Faye from Jim behind bars and Roe from his first wife, and then remarrying each other. They made their home together in Rancho Mirage.

Jim was moved to a minimum security prison in 1993 and then thanks to a rehearing of his sentencing was released on December 1, 1994. Merry Christmas.

In 1996, Roe Messner was found guilty of bankruptcy fraud charges and ended up serving three years in federal prison.

In October, 1996, Tammy Faye released her biography Tammy: Telling It My Way and I got to attend a presentation by her at Temple Isaiah in Palm Springs. She stood at the pulpit in the Jewish temple and spoke at length about her troubled times. Her mascara was freshly spackled and she was the most amazing public speaker I've ever heard. Tammy Faye had this way of making eye contact to many people in the crowd and then walking out among the audience and extending a hand shake to people that endeared her to each and every listener. It is easy to understand how she was so able to woo millions of people to attend her church, buy her gospel products, and marry two men, both of whom went to prison while she did not. I bought ten of her books that day and put them in my bookstore for sale. They all quickly sold. She lived on another 11 years, visiting thrift shops around Palm Springs and periodically ending up on talk shows and religious revival shows. She even went on Larry King, weak, thin and weary, though once again wearing heavy make-up, shortly before she died of cancer in 2007.

Roe Messner is still alive. He calls himself a master builder and is credited with being the biggest builder of churches in the country, having constructed some 20 churches of different denominations. You can visit his website at http://www.roemessner.com/. In 2003, he published his book Church Growth by Design: A Complete Guide for Planning and Building Churches to God's Glory.

Jim Bakker published his biography in 1996 entitled I was Wrong. He remarried in 1998 to Lori Graham and he now preaches at Morningside Church. In 2003, he began daily broadcasts of The Jim Bakker Show from its studio near Branson, Missouri to a much smaller audience than he ever did with Tammy Faye. On July 1, 2015, according to Wikipedia, Jim Bakker's ministry purchased the trademark to former the PTL Television Network name and logo and announced their network would be rebranded the PTL Television Network, carrying current Jim Bakker programming and classic episodes old PTL Club footage, the Jim and Tammy Show, and other television shows produced at the former Heritage USA studios. He is now 75 years old and looking to make a comeback despite the $6 million he still owes the IRS.

Sources:

Bill Higgins, EIGHTEEN YEARS AGO, JIM BAKKER WAS FOUND TO HAVE SIPHONED OFF $3.7 MILLION FROM HIS MINISTRY FOR, AMONG OTHER THINGS, HIS AND HERS ROLLS ROYCES, http://www.hollywoodreporter.com/news/throwback-thursday-jim-tammy-faye-801595, The Hollywood Reporter (.com), June 11, 2015.

Louis Sahagun, BAKKERS MOVE OUT OF PALM SPRINGS HOME, HEAD EAST, Los Angeles Times (.com), http://articles.latimes.com/1987-07-29/news/mn-4392_1_palm-springs , June 29, 1987.

William E. Schmidt, FOR JIM AND TAMMY BAKKER, EXCESS WIPED OUT A RAPID CLIMB TO SUCCESS, New York Times, May 16, 1987.

Various contributors, JIM BAKKER, https://en.wikipedia.org/wiki/Jim_Bakker#Later_career, Wikipedia.org.

Various contributors, ROE MESSNER, https://en.wikipedia.org/wiki/Roe_Messner, Wikipedia.org.

Various contributors, TAMMY FAYE MESSNER, https://en.wikipedia.org/wiki/Tammy_Faye_Messner, Wikipedia.org.

Various contributors, PTL SATELLITE NETWORK, https://en.wikipedia.org/wiki/PTL_Satellite_Network, ikipedia.org.

Unknown author, WHERE ARE THEY NOW?: JIM BAKKER, http://www.charlottemagazine.com/Charlotte-Magazine/August-2010/Where-are-They-Now/Jim-Bakker/, Charlotte Magazine (.com), August 2010.

The 1990's Pyramid Scandal

Somewhere in late 1995, in much the same way as other folks might host Tupperware parties, Diana Hodgkins and Kathleen Rector, two very pretty ladies who worked as concierges at the Marriott Desert Springs Resort in Palm Desert, started hosting pyramid parties at their desert homes. Before a year was up, they made several hundred thousand dollars selling shares in what law enforcement officials call an Endless Pyramid Scheme. More than a thousand people participated in the pyramid and more than a million dollars exchanged hands.

The group called themselves "Friends Helping Friends" or "The Gift Exchange." Yet, the only gifts exchanged was the $2000 entry fee it cost to participate. The secret to their success was getting some very influential people involved at the top of the organization. In July, 1996, the following people were indicted by the Riverside County District Attorney's office:

David George: President of College of the Desert for about 10 years. He resigned a month after the indictment was delivered.

Dolores Ballesteros: Superintendent of Desert Sands School District. She was fired after acknowledging her involvement in the scandal.

Matthew Monica, Jr.: A College of the Desert guidance counselor and Desert Sands school board member and his wife Mary Ann, a college secretary. Matthew was censured by his school board members. Yet, he still serves today on the school board with full rights like any other elected member.

Nancy Dolensek: Executive Director of the McCallum Theatre, and Vickie Brown, the theatre's Controller. Nancy resigned from her position.

Marianna Dorson: A retiree who took up working the pyramid as a full-time income source.

I sometimes wonder why I wasn't asked to participate. As the scheme unraveled in the local newspapers and courtrooms, several friends – a Palm Springs Planning Commissioner comes to mind, a local magazine publisher, a high end retail clerk among them – came forward to share with me how they had made $16,000 to $64,000 and ran the gamut of tiers several times as they easily made money. At the time, I owned a bookstore downtown and was very active politically in Palm Springs, well connected, had unsuccessfully run for City Council two years before and then was selected by the Palm Springs Chief of Police to sit on a Police Advisory Board. Maybe the people participating thought I might be a whistle blower and you know what? They would have been right.

Some of the people who participated could afford a couple thousand dollars to join and had plenty of friends who could come in after them to prop up their personal pyramid. As those involved sifted down from the executive levels, through administrative and managerial personnel, involvement finally slinking into blue collar employees; and these were people who really needed that $2,000 to pay their rent, their groceries, their gasoline, and other day to day expenses, under the false promises of making 8 times their money or more; as these people got involved and there was no one else to come in behind them and pay for the next, and lower, tier of squares; the pyramid fell apart. Those at the bottom – and I knew a few: a maid and mother of three, a hard working gas station attendant pulling double shifts, a single mother retail clerk, a hotel bellman – knew of no one else to join under them and the endless scheme came to a halt. Those at the bottom cried foul and rightfully so. I can just imagine these working class people being convinced by their bosses or their bosses boss or some other person of reputable position to put up their hard earned money under the false pretense of easy returns and then having it just vanish and those same reputable people not being there to answer their phone calls or help them get out; their savings and invested money really no more than handed over to these influential's, the very people they thought they could trust.

I remember how, at the time, a bookstore customer came in one day and offered me a complete packet of information on the pyramid scheme. He wasn't trying to get me involved. It had already been plastered all over the news that it was illegal and people were getting arrested. No, he offered me it for informational purposes and knew that I was a rabble-rouser that would do something interesting with the documents. He was right. I started running radio ads on the local talk radio shows, saying, "Come into Celebrity Books and buy anything and I'll give you a copy of exactly how the Pyramid scandal works, actual documentation from the people who ran the scandalous scheme themselves." It was the best advertising campaign I had ran up to that time. Many people came in. One was even a District Attorney investigator who flipped his badge at me and demanded that I give him a copy of the documents. I told him the rules are that he had to buy something and suggested that he get himself a soda. They were only seventy-five cents at the time. He did so and I gave him a copy. The copy he received had at least one of the indicted nine hand-written names on the pages.

Here's a copy of some of those same documents used to create the pyramid. I will not give you everything they used. Those are kept on file at home in my private file cabinets. I am not promoting that you use these to start a pyramid.

EXCHANGE CLUB.......

Enclosed is some informa~~~   ~~~xchange Club.
We are all extremely excite~~~   ~~~l collected
(or are about to collect) $16,~~~   ~~~ollected
has rejoined the group and will~~~   ~~~when
they get back to the top (in abou~~~

The concept is that you put in $2,000 ~~~
partner for $1,000 each or 4 people with~~~
up the tree as people come in until you rea~~~
$16,000. If you were to reserve your space w~~~
the bottom you would immediately move up to the~~~
soon as all 8 places were filled, which would be ~~~
Please note that your money would not be needed unti~~~
places have been reserved.

The nice thing is that you never lose sight of what is happ~~~
with your money, or your particular group, since there are
meetings three times per week. If you cannot attend all the
meetings, no problem, one of us will be happy to keep you
informed. The main goal is to bring in as many new people a~~~
possible, (then we all benefit), however the rules say you ~~~
need to bring in a minimum of one person before you reach t~~~
top. It's fun to work with people in your group. Some of ~~~
time you will know quite a few of them, but even if you d~~~
know anyone but the person who brought you in, you're al~~~
for a common goal, so it's a very friendly atmosphere.

Another very important concept is that you do have a w~~~
you so desire. When you get up to the second from th~~~
can sell your square (probably for more than $2,000 ~~~
person in our group who has been offered $4,000 for~~~
position).

About 500 people have received $16,000 since the E~~~
was introduced in the desert during the summer a~~~
time, it is in full swing. It takes about 6 w~~~
sooner or later than that depending on the s~~~ ~~~ple
join) to go from the bottom to the top. T~~~ ~~~ple
who have gone through 3 or 4 times. If ~~~ ~~~
regarding the legality, please read the~~~
information, there is a policeman in~~~

Hope you will consider coming to ~~~
will have all your questions an~~~
greater comfort level when yo~~~
involved, (upstanding citiz~~~
moving. Now is definitel~~~   ~~~ngs are
Mondays, Wednesdays and ~~~   ~~~45 minutes.
We will let you know ~~~   ~~~ll look forward
to seeing you the~~~   ~~~s no obligation
- you can jus~~~

THE EXCHANGE GIFT PLAN

Participation Guide

1. You must be invited by a participant or a retired participant in good standing.

2. To participant, you must reserve in your name with your phone number a position in a group.
Once you have reserved a position you should be prepared to give a cash-only gift at the next meeting.

3. You need to understand that it is your responsibility to introduce a minimum of one person with his/her gift by the time you reach the position of Trustee or your money could be refunded and your position sold (at the discretion of the Beneficiary of that group).

4. All participants are required to attend every meeting. If you are unable to attend, you must contact the Beneficiary and make sure you have a proxy in your place. Your attendance is important to support your group. You must attend at least two meetings or your money will be refunded and your position sold (at the discretion of the Beneficiary).

5. The Beneficiaries are responsible for arranging the day, time and location of the meetings. NO ALCOHOLIC BEVERAGES ALLOWED.

6. All gifts must be announced by the groups Beneficiary and distributed in the participants.

7. The Beneficiary is responsible for contributions can

. . . . the

. . . when all eight Benefactors positions are reserved and

Once the Beneficiary has retired the group splits and all participants move up a position. This creates two new groups each with a new Beneficiary. The retired Beneficiary should keep in touch with the eight participants who gave him/her the gifts to see if their groups are going well.

8. **THE PHASING OUT PERIOD:**
Each person who becomes a participant after October 1, 1996, is required, once they make it to the position of Beneficiary, to collect 75% of the value of the gift they gave upon entry into the plan . . . of their eight Benefactors. This holds until the gift required for entry rounds off to $0.00, . . . nearest cent. This constitutes the **end to The Gift Plan.**

Q: *How do I become a participant?*
A: *Participation is by invitation only. Your must be invited by . . . close friend who is a current participant or a past participant in good sta . . .*

Once you become a participant, you must follow the rules of the plan or your money will be refunded and you will be excused from the plan.

The Gift Plan continued;

Q: *If I should change my mind, would I receive a refund?*
A: When you change your mind at the entry level (Benefactor) your Beneficiary will refund your money and your position can be sold by the Beneficiary to another person. If you should change your mind after the group has split and you are on a level of Protector or above, you can sell your position within your group.

Q: *Is this a pyramid?*
A: Absolutely not! There are a few differences:

In a pyramid;
1. There is no specified ending date or a completion to the plan.

2. Most money continually goes up to the same people at the top. There are ~~people ever "retire" their positions.~~

Once each group in this gift plan ~~...~~ retire and the remaining participants split into two new groups, with every participant moving up one level.

Q: *What happens if the Beneficiary retires before collecting all of his/her monies?*
A: This would be a rare situation. However, the two Trustees would divide the remaining money due the Beneficiary once all eight Benefactors positions ~~are~~ filled. Then the group would split and all participants ~~move~~ continue as usual.

Q: What ~~are~~ ... gift. The ... participants and the spirit of

~~Whom~~ should I invite to become a participant?
A: Be choosy about whom you invite. The people you invite should meet the following guidelines.

1. You should know them very well, the plan works if participants know each other this builds a level of trust. We provide name tags and phone numbers of people involved in the plan.

2. A person who needs help financially. A friend or family member who has lost his/her job, is struggling to pay bills, saving to by a car, about to lose a home... all of these people are good candidates. A person who has the initial gift money.

3. Someone motivated to bring in new participants. The gift plan is only as strong as its weakest participant, it is important that you give thought to the people you are bringing in.

Everyone counts on each other, without serious participants, the gift plan simply dies out. There are no free rides, the rules are designed to prevent people from taking a free ride to the top and will help ensure that every participant who joins benefits.

Q: *Is this illegal?*
A: Pyramids are illegal and *this is not a pyramid.*

The gift plan is not an *endless chain* since the gift plan splits every time there are 15 participants and the Beneficiary retires.

A pyramid has no ending, The Gift Plan has a phasing out period beginning October 1, 1996 and ending about December 31, 1996.

Q: *What about the IRS?*
A: The government says that you must report all income to the IRS. This may fall under the Annual Exclusions from Gift Taxes. You should consult your tax advisor to be certain you fall into the proper reporting guidelines.

The basics of the Annual Exclusions ...
The amount ...
... gifts in
... can be money of other assets,
..., real estate, life insurance, jewelry, and works of art.
The exclusion figure went from $3,000. (an outdated figure that remained unchanged from 1942 through 1981) to $10,000.

These exclusions permit you to pass along as much as $10,000. to each of as many children, friends, or relatives as you like, provided none of them receives more than $10,000. The $10,000. figure doubles to $20,000. when your spouse consents to "gift splitting," which treats property owned by only one spouse as though half was given by the husband and half by the wife.

Eric G. Meeks

Results of Some Research Done

IRS
(Internal Revenue Service)

First and foremost, we are not advocating that anyone not pay their taxes!!

The best person to advise you is your tax consultant or financial advisor.
Depending upon whom was asked at the IRS you receive several answers as to how the gifts you receive are taxable.

District Attorney & the law

On Thursday, June 22, 1995, the Redlands branch of the District Attorney's Office was contacted regarding the legality of The Exchange Gift Plan. The spokes person simply replied, "We have no comment?" When pressed further, stating that there were law-abiding citizens who wanted a straight answer on this issue and needed to know specifically what might be wrong with this type of plan, the spokes person would only repeat, "We have no comment."

Following this phone call, the San Bernardino District Attorney's Office was contacted. The spokes person indicated there was no investigation going on at this time, that erhaps the Fontana branch of the D.A.'s office would have some information.

e investigator at the Fontana D.A.'s office was unavailable for comment.

further investigation, it appears that there is no case law dealing with this issue. is no precedent, that's why there are no straight answers. Penal Code 327, the t is most often cited regarding the legality of this type of organization, was ed to deal with the pyramid schemes of the 1970's. Penal code 327 addresses o set-up or operate an "endless chain." The Gift Plan, with Beneficiaries that e their participation, groups that split in half, and a phase out date, clearly is dless chain."

At a participant asked her neighbor, who just happens to be a judge, to look it o id it looked good, go for it!

Anoth pant has an attorney on retainer. The initial reaction to the paperwork was, " mebody's really done their homework on this."

There h nd continue to be attorneys, a member of the District Attorneys office in lifornia and members of law enforcement participating in the Gift Plan. At none of them have found any legal irregularities or problems with the plan. st part law enforcement is more annoyed by the inquiries in reference to ty of these groups The integrity of the participants is paramount in protecting

REMEMBER I JR RESPONSIBILITY TO BE COMFORTABLE WITH YOUR PARTIC AND ITS LEGAL ASPECTS.

PALM SPRINGS TRUE CRIME

Gift Exchange Program

★ **BENEFICIARY** ★

FIRST NAME

TELEPHONE

SPONSORED BY

TRUSTEE

FIRST NAME

TELEPHONE

TRUSTEE

PROTECTOR

FIRST NAME

TELEPHONE

SPONSORED BY

PROTECTOR

FIRST NAME

TELEPHONE

SPONSORED BY

PROTECTOR

FIRST NAME

TELEPHONE

SPONSORED BY

BENEFACTOR

TELEPHONE

SPONSORED BY

BENEFACTOR

TELEPHONE

SPONSORED BY

BENEFACTOR

TELEPHONE

SPONSORED BY

BENEFACTOR

SPONSORED BY

BENEFACTOR

FIRST NAME

SPONSORED BY

BENEFACTOR

FIRST NAME

SPONSORED BY

BENEFACTOR

FIRST NAME

SPONSORED BY

BENEFACTOR

FIRST NAME

SPONSORED BY

CRIME SCENE - DO NOT CROSS

CRIME SCENE - DO NOT CROSS

BENEFICIARY
RESPONSIBILITIES

* Keep your group informed:
  -Call between meetings, and remind them of the next meeting.
  Be sure they know where it will be.

  Provide copies of your groups chart status

  _____ ~our group, help them with any problems they might

* Keep _____ _____ ~es and help with planning
  meetings an_ _

* Share the cost of the meet___ _____ ___ while
  you are at the top as Beneficiary. _
  _____, on Monday of each week. _ __
  envelope with your name on it. If you won't be there on Monday pa_
  give it to your proxy to bring.

* Water is the only refreshment that will be available at the meetings
  The Hotels do not allow us to bring in our own food and beverage.
  Since the meetings do not last long this should not be a problem.

* Please be certain your group vacates the meeting room no later than
  8:00 pm, as that is the time we have the room reserved for.

* Sorry, No one under 18 is allowed at the meetings.

Notes to help your group keep moving:
-Encourage attendance, as it helps the group stay focused and working together.
-Stay "POSITIVE" there is no set time frame for the groups to split just keep at it
and it will happen.
-Help people get involved if you can, arrange partnerships, help people focus on
how to invite friends and family. Sponsor someone if you can and want to.
-Caution people against taking too many places in a group, unless they can
introduce lots of people to the plan. Groups work better with lots of different
people in the places.
-Explain how holding back on inviting friends and family can slow things d__
overall because it always takes time for people to m_k_ _ __ _
involved and if you wait to invite ___
-Explain ho_ _ __
___ __ _ g_oup is their responsibility when it
____cu_ion when they reach the Beneficiary position.

*** All money collected from Beneficiaries is used for meeting expenses only. Receipts*
are required.

GIFT CLUB

How can it be successful for you:

-Think of friends, family or business people that you trust

-Make a quick list of 10 of these people

-Call them, make a simple and short invitation

* Don't be discouraged if they say NO! or That's a Pyramid!, once you keep seeing the gifts being presented and telling them about it they will begin to ask you more about it. It may take a few weeks to get them there, but they will come. As you move up they will come and see how it works.

-Be excited, and they will catch some of the enthusiasm

-Don't hold back, invite often and now! It takes a little while for people to work it into their schedules and budgets.

I want to see receive a gift:

1.
2. _____ _____
3. _____ _____
4. _____ _____
5. _____ _____

9. _____ _____
10. _____ _____

Be Creative !!!
-Put a few of your friends together in a spot
-Help a friend if you can, they can help bring others in
-Regenerate your gift once you reach the top

Sample Invitation:
You'll never guess what I have gotten involved with!! It's one of the funniest things I have ever done and I am going to receive money from it. It's called the Gift Club, and its a close circle of friends and business people that are together to help each other. You don't have to sell anything. It would be great if you could come with me some time, its the best way for you to see how it works. It's so wild! But it is working!!! It only takes about an hour of your time to hear about it and no one pressures you.

** SPEND JUST 5 MINUTES A DAY TALKING TO PEOPLE AND IT WILL WORK!!**

Sources:

Tom Gorman and Diana Marcum, ALLEGEED PYRA-MID SCHEME BOASTEED IMPRESSIVE CAST, Los Angeles Times (.com), July 14, 1996.

Diana Marcum, 9 PROMINENT COACHELLA VALLEY RESIDENTS PLEAD NOT GUILTY IN PYRAMID SCHEME, Los Angeles Times (.com), July 3, 1996.

© PSPD File Photo

Cliff Lambert was a wealthy retired Palm Springs
gentleman who fell victim to a group of Grifters,
called The Boiz. They killed him and stole
his money, his car, his art and more.

ERIC G. MEEKS

Cliff Lambert and The Boiz

Introductions

Cliff Lambert's demise began in April, 2008, when he offered Danny Garcia, 25, a nice young man he'd met on the internet, to come down to Palm Springs for the weekend. From time to time, Cliff invited young men into his home as a means to add some enjoyment into his lonely life. Cliff was wealthy, in his early 70s, and lived alone. His marriage had ended decades ago. He had no children. His former lover left him a few years back and then died in a tragic pool accident. Now all Cliff had was his money, his art, his jewelry, his cars, his home and a small dog.

Unbeknownst to Cliff at the time, Danny was not a nice young man. He was part of a group of shysters who preyed on people to extort huge sums of money by fraud or larceny. Danny was a Grifter. He was relatively good looking, in his twenties, and he and his friends called themselves The Boiz when they got along. Often times they did not get along and they would find themselves literally at each other's throats as some of them went in and out of prison for their nefarious crimes and each laid claim to the others money, their friends and anything else they could lay their hands on.

Danny's known criminal past began in 2004, when he and attorney David Replogle, 69, fraudulently filed a lawsuit against a wealthy gay San Francisco man, Thomas White, claiming that Danny had been sexually molested by White while he was still underage. It was a very public trial and got involved in state politics because the attorney who represented White was married to the head of Califor-

103

© PSPD File Photo

© PSPD File Phot

Danny Carlos Garcia was Cliff Lambert's first contact with The Boiz.

nia's State Board of Equalization: the Franchise Tax Board. White lost the case and had to pay out over half a million dollars to Danny and David, which they then split fifty-fifty.

After that case was won, David Replogle went down to Puerto Vallarta, Mexico, and found some fifty young Mexican boys whom he bribed into filing similar lawsuits against Thomas White in Mexican courts. Based on these trumped up charges, White was arrested while doing charity work for orphans in Thailand and extradited to Mexico where he stood trial and lost again. The fact that some of the young boys later recanted their accusations against Thomas White was not sufficient for the Mexican courts to reverse its decision. He is still incarcerated in a Mexican prison with a life sentence.

These are two of the people Cliff Lambert let into his life when he invited Danny down to his Palm Springs home in 2008. Another was Danny's cousin Dennis who, most of the time, would act as Danny's chauffer. Dennis really wanted nothing more than to grow his thriving northern California marijuana business. However, because the money was so good when Danny's schemes worked out, Dennis seemed to always get a little too involved. He was also a big guy who could be Danny's muscle when needed.

The worst of Danny's friends, the worst of The Boiz, was a short, wiry, little Nepalese homosexual named Kaushal Niroula. Kaushal liked to pretend he was the exiled prince of Nepal, stranded in America with spotty finances after a political coup forced his family to flee Nepal and their bank accounts were seized. This guise allowed him the perfect cover as to why at times dirt poor, when he was in between heists, and why at times he would be famously wealthy, when his fraudulent schemes paid off. At these times, he would claim one of his family's accounts had been unfrozen.

In actuality, Kaushal was a foreign exchange student from a very poor family in Nepal. He had over stayed his Visa when he quit going to college a few years back. He and Danny had first met in

2004, when Danny and David were filing their lawsuits against Thomas White for molesting Danny. Kaushal tried to get Danny to give him White's personal banking information on the grounds (a lie

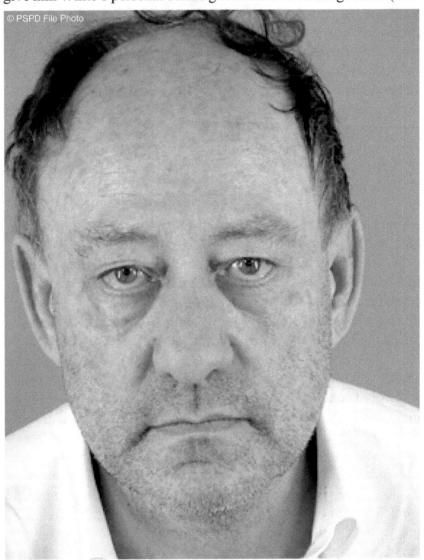

© PSPD File Photo

The Boiz attorney and co-conspirator, David Replogle.

to justify Kaushals being near broke at the time) that White owed Kaushal's family millions of dollars from the coup which had occurred in Nepal and ousted his mother and father from their royal positions.

Danny did not give Kaushal Thomas White's information at that time. Later he would.

The second time Danny met Kaushal was in late 2006, just after Kaushal had swindled some $400,000 from a Japanese woman wanting to own property in Hawaii. She didn't have the necessary Visa to stay long enough in the United States and enjoy the island home even if she could purchase it. Kaushal befriended her, saying he had an attorney, David Replogle, who could get her the necessary papers (all a lie). While helping her, he stole checks from her and then stole her money. Kaushal left a paper trail which led the police to him and he ended up in jail. He made bail, but in doing so used nearly all of his cash. While awaiting trial, Kaushal then stole jewelry from another friend. He again left a trail and was again thrown in jail. In between these two scams, using sex, he befriended a man who was a respected art dealer and scammed the sale of unique art pieces of which he claimed he had access. Before this grift was done, Kaushal had stolen $237,000 from the art dealer and blown all the money on a weeklong stay in the Presidential suite at the Bellagio hotel and casino in Las Vegas, where he and Danny cemented their friendship with champagne, casino chips galore and lots of sex.

When Kaushal was again short of money he gave Replogle sex and a promise to pay later. With Replogle's help, Kaushal made bail a second time on the jewelry heist trial and then had immigration knocking on his door. Now Kaushal was on the run, afraid of any police entity which might roust him from sleep and in need of large sums of cash to pay court and attorney fees to fight his legal cases. Kaushal was desperate and afraid he was going to be either sent to prison for a long time and/or deported back to Nepal where he was known as a low life and would not be able to continue the fraudulent

**Kaushal Niroula, aka The Prince of Nepal,
would prove to be the worst of The Boiz, and
ultimately orchestrated the murder of Cliff Lambert.**

scams which provided him the extravagant lifestyle he ever-so-much enjoyed in the United States.

The Boiz, lived in and around San Francisco's gay Castro district, frequenting the same bars and restaurants, and living it up while pretending to be successful entrepreneurs who could afford to tip big. The Boiz often attracted other men to have sex with them; some just because they were handsome and others because they could be preyed upon financially. Danny and Kaushal and David always had at least one scam they were soliciting. Sometimes they were running two to three at a time, and they were about to rip Cliff Lambert's life apart.

The Set Up

From the first weekend in 2008 when 25 year-old Danny Garcia went to visit Cliff Lambert in his Las Palmas neighborhood home in Palm Springs, bad things began to happen to Cliff.

Cliff's home was well appointed. It had beautiful watercolor original paintings, expensive framed lithographs – one even signed by Picasso. There was an ancient Peruvian statue and a large Tiffany clock. Lying about on the end tables and coffee tables were gold cigarette cases and other valuable knick-knacks. In the garage were both a silver Mercedes convertible and a blue Rolls Royce Cornice. Cliff dressed in designer clothes and kept his home secure by an electronically monitored system of locked doors, windows and gates, which had to be opened by remote control. He was fairly secure financially although, the family of his deceased lover was pursuing Cliff for palimony money.

Cliff had several staff people: maids, pool service, gardeners, etc., to maintain his home. His number one assistant was Lester, a twenty-seven year-old African-American, who ran daily errands for Cliff, filed paperwork and helped pay and manage the other staff people. Cliff and Lester were good friends and Lester, along with another good friend of Cliff's, Cody, often helped Cliff interview the prospec-

109

tive young men Cliff invited into his home at 317 Camino Norte West.

Danny was welcomed into Cliff's home. He met Cliff's friends and staff and saw the luxurious lifestyle Cliff enjoyed. During his first weekend stay, Cliff and Danny went out to an uptown art gallery, made dinner at home one night, went out another, relaxed by the pool and generally made a pleasurable weekend of their time together. Yet, overall, Cliff was not enamored with Danny, who mentioned more than once about an investment opportunity in a waste management and alternative energy company called Startec which Danny had an interest in and at the end of the weekend the two parted as friends, but not lovers.

From the moment Danny left Cliff's home, problems started. The first, was when Danny went to upgrade his plane ticket from coach to First Class. The ticket was paid for by Cliff's credit card and while the cost of the upgrade was only $16, Danny's gall at doing this without permission infuriated Cliff, who immediately cancelled the payment of the entire ticket and left Danny stranded at the Palm Springs airport. Cliff refused to answer Danny's calls for help and the stranded Danny called Dennis to drive down to the desert from northern California and pick him up. That same evening, Cliff began having computer problems. Unbeknownst to Cliff, Danny had passed on information concerning Cliff to a computer hacker friend in Utah, Alec Shabazian, another one of The Boiz, who had accessed Cliff's most personal banking information and was locking Cliff out of his own computer. Thirdly, Cliff's home was burglarized a few weeks later and a significant portion of the artwork and other items were stolen. Cliff told the police he thought the burglary was the work of a maid he had recently fired.

Danny tried to sell the artwork to a reputable dealer in San Francisco. He was given $15,000 up front and a promise of more if the art demanded it. Upon greater inspection, the dealer deemed the art not worth his original estimate and demanded his $15,000 back.

Instead, Danny brought him other expensive household items: silver bowls, a pre-Colombian gold piece, a diamond ring, a large Tiffany clock, etc. The art dealer had no use for these things and instead of helping Danny; he inserted him into a shared database with other reputable dealers and the police, stating that Danny was suspected of attempting to sell stolen items. Danny, with nowhere else to go turned to another older gay man whom he frequented as a fence for the miscellaneous items.

A few weeks after Cliff's cancelling of the plane ticket, Danny returned to Cliff Lambert's door, flowers in hand, attempting to reconcile. Cliff was surprised at Danny's unannounced visit and told him so. Danny was cautiously invited in and said he wanted to apologize. He claimed to be in the desert visiting another friend and hoped Cliff didn't mind his stopping by like this. Danny thought it an opportune moment to make up for his misbehavior, thanking Cliff for his hospitality and company, regardless of whether or not Cliff invested in Startec.

Cliff was pleased with Danny and again invited him to stay at his home during his visit.
Another burglary occurred during Danny's stay and this time the burglars took all the art.

Between Danny's visit and the fall of 2008, Cliff's home was burglarized two more times; making it four times in total he was robbed.

* * *

In early December 2008, Cliff Lambert was hanging Christmas lights on his home with the help of one of his staff, when he received a phone called from New York attorney Samuel Orin (really Kaushal) claiming that Cliff had been left a substantial amount of money and artwork by a deceased wealthy friend. Apparently, the first Will she had left behind after she died had become clouded by the appearance of a second Will and it had taken some time to clear the matter up. Cliff had been named in the second Will who eventually had superseded the first. He was to be made wealthy again. Cliff's friend Cody thought it all a scam. Cliff had to find out if it was real.

Behind the scenes, David and Kaushal were working on a plan to steal all of Cliff Lambert's possessions. They had conspired with Russell Manning, the art dealer who'd been set up by Kaushal to take the fall for the stolen art and money. They told Russell would receive $500,000 if he would be the Power of Attorney for a client of David's who was going to offer a substantial settlement to Kaushal. David said the client was going to settle with Kaushal because the client had, unfortunately, given Kaushal AIDS. Russell didn't trust David and Kaushal but, the money was too much to pass up. Russell agreed.

Miguel Bustamante was a muscular bisexual twenty-six year-old who attended college, shared an apartment with his girlfriend, and tended bar at a gay club called JET to pay the bills.

The plan was for Craig and Miguel to break into Cliff's home and kill him after he'd had dinner with Kaushal, who would be masquerading as attorney Samuel Orin who had papers for him to sign concerning the false Will. David and the computer friend in Utah, Alec, would make sure the alarm system was remotely disabled so Craig and Miguel could gain entry. According to testimony later on, Miguel was fully aware of the murder plan from the start. Craig, however, thought he was just being brought along as part of a robbery, to do the heavy lifting of moving the merchandise from the home.

On December 2, 2008, Kaushal, Craig and Miguel flew into Palm Springs and got a room at the Hyatt downtown. Kaushal had fraudulent legal documents, from the Law Offices of Samuel Orin, showing Cliff was to receive a large inheritance. David had prepared the documents and prepped Kaushal on his role.

Danny and Dennis drove into Palm Springs and didn't want

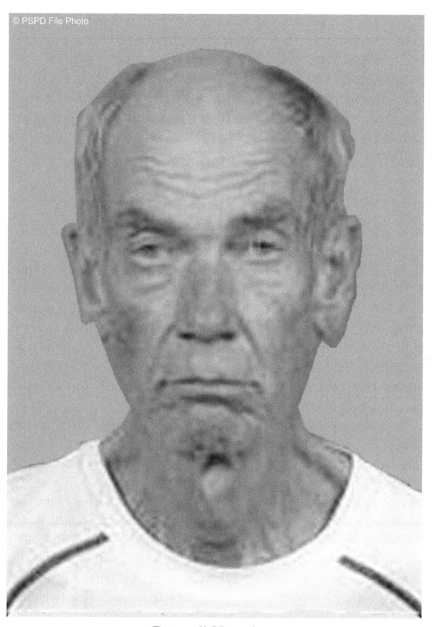

Russell Manning

Kaushal or Miguel or Craig to know where they were staying, just in case something went wrong. Danny and Dennis were available to assist with a quick getaway and could be called on a burner cell phone Kaushal had acquired for the heist. Dennis thought the whole scam, murder, and robbery was bullshit and didn't think Kaushal would go through with it. Dennis was very mouthy anytime Kaushal's name was mentioned and wanted to go back to northern California the entire time.

*　*　*

Two days later, on Thursday December 4th, 2008, The Boiz were determined to play out their caper. Kaushal, acting as Samuel Orin, met Cliff Lambert at Dink's restaurant and bar, while Craig and Miguel broke into Cliff's home. Danny and Dennis were look outs, driving between Dink's and Cliff's home to keep an eye out for anything going wrong. When Dennis drove past Cliff's home, he flicked his high beams to splay bright light on the house. Danny asked him why he'd done that and Dennis replied, '…to Fuck with'em.' Danny and Dennis then parked outside Dink's and watched first Cliff and then Kaushal walk into the restaurant.

When Cliff arrived at Dink's he saw his friend, Dink's owner Denny Edwards, and mentioned he was meeting an attorney for dinner who was bringing information about an inheritance worth $150-$200 million in rare art.

After Kaushal walked into the restaurant, Dennis blew his top at Danny while sitting in the car outside, claiming this whole scenario was bullshit and saying Kaushal would never see it through and that even if he did, Dennis didn't want any part of it. Dennis decided right then and there to start driving north and left Palm Springs, against Danny's protests. Danny did not get out of the car though.

Inside Dink's, Kaushal and Cliff ate chicken noodle soup and crabmeat. They started the dinner with just water but, as they grew

Craig McCarthy, was part of The Muscle in the Cliff Lambert murder.

Miguel Adolfo Bustamante, the other half of The Muscle hired to kill Cliff Lambert and the first to crack under pressure from the police .

more comfortable with each other, moved on to Chardonnay wine and then to Dewar's mixed drinks. The bill came to $126 for the two of them. Kaushal paid the waitress $220 and told her to 'keep the change.'

During the meal, Craig and Miguel had inserted themselves into Cliff's garage and chosen dark corner vantage points to attack from once Cliff parked his car. After crouching in the dark for only about 15 minutes, when Cliff came home they both froze. They each had hoped the other was going to attack first. Cliff got out of his car and waltzed into his own home unmolested. In hushed whispers, Craig and Miguel discussed their roles in this crime and came to the conclusion it was too serious for their blood. They removed themselves from the garage and walked to a nearby Pizza Hut, where they called two girls Miguel had met the night before. The girls came, picked them up and dropped the Miguel and Craig off at their hotel.

When Craig and Miguel got there, Kaushal was sitting in the lobby and was furious at their not having done their part. Kaushal dismissed Craig to go to the room, who admitted he wanted nothing to do with the crime. Kaushal gave Miguel a real dressing down, verbally battering him until Miguel agreed they'd try again tomorrow night.

317 Camino Norte, in Palm Springs Las Palmas neighborhood was Cliff Lambert's home.

The Murder

December 5, 2008. It was the day before the Festival of Lights parade in Palm Springs and Cliff was looking forward to going with his friend Cody.

Craig and Miguel spent the day arguing about whether or not to do the job. Craig just wanted to go home. Miguel, persistent because of the money he was to receive and kept pressuring Craig. Miguel had been promised $30,000 by Kaushal. Craig $2,000. Finally, Miguel got Craig to recommit to help by confirming all Craig had to do was move stuff.

At 5:30pm that night, Craig and Miguel got a text message from Kaushal telling them it was time to take a taxi cab from their hotel in Palm Springs to a couple blocks away from Cliff's house. They walked the last little bit to the home, climbed over the fence and quietly went to the sliding glass kitchen door. Kaushal had returned to Cliff's home earlier, again, under the guise of attorney Sam Orin. Cliff had welcomed him in so the two could finalize the paperwork concerning Cliff's artwork inheritance. When Miguel texted Kaushal saying he and Craig were ready, Kaushal excused himself from Cliff, saying he had to go to the bathroom. Instead, Kaushal went into the kitchen and let Craig and Miguel inside.

Cliff was in the living room. He heard voices in the kitchen and went to investigate. When he did, he saw Kaushal talking to a muscular Hispanic man and immediately questioned both as to why the man was inside.

Miguel yelled at Cliff while simultaneously Craig rushed him from the side. Both grabbed large knives from the chopping block on the kitchen counter. Craig had overcome his earlier reservations about his role in the caper and held a knife to Cliff's throat as the two struggled. Cliff was no match for the young black marine. Miguel grabbed Cliff from Craig and stabbed him in the back of the head. Cliff howled from pain and dropped to the floor. Miguel

117

pounced on the fallen older man and stabbed him repeatedly through the back of his shirt; over and over again. Cliff curled into a ball as his only means of protection. Miguel kept stabbing, more times than he could count, until Cliff stopped moving and blood was oozing over the floor.

Kaushal left the room during the initial attack. When the noise from the struggle subsided, he came back into the kitchen and asked if it was done. Miguel was in a daze as he stabbed Cliff, yet again. Then one time more. Cliff took his final breath and died there, on the floor of his kitchen. Blood was everywhere. When Kaushal saw the deed was done, he ordered Craig to remove Cliff's jewelry and ransack his pockets. Craig found a gold ID bracelet, a gold ring, and a money clip. Kaushal snatched these away from Craig, claiming he needed these items so Miguel and Craig could get paid.

Craig grabbed some paper towels and tried futilely to mop up the mess. Kaushal disappeared for a moment and returned with bath towels and a blanket. He order Craig and Miguel to clean up the mess with the towels and then to wrap Cliff's body in the blanket. He also told them to put the body in the trunk of Cliff's silver Mercedes, which they did but, not without breaking Cliff's leg to make him fit. Kaushal threw a bag with the knives and the bloody towels into the back seat of the car.

Cliff's little dog was in the garage with them. Kaushal gave the keys to Cliff's Mercedes to Miguel and said they should take the dog and get rid of it with the body. Kaushal said he'd meet them in San Francisco. They should get going. He'd check out of the hotel and catch a plane back.

By 9pm that night, Craig and Miguel were headed north on the interstate. About an hour later, somewhere around Fontana, they exited the freeway and got a room at America's Best Inn & Suites. They put their dirty clothes into a washing machine at a Laundromat and then bought some food at a nearby convenience store to snack on.

Kaushal was determined to leave Palm Springs. However, he'd found out that at this time of night there were no planes departing for San Francisco. He texted Danny saying the deed was done and then called another friend, Sami, his San Francisco limo driver, to come pick him up the next morning at Le Parker Meridian hotel in Palm Springs.

Danny and Dennis couldn't believe Kaushal had killed Cliff. It was more likely Cliff was being held captive somewhere. Danny wanted to leave immediately. Dennis was tired and said they'd go in the morning.

*   *   *

The next day was Saturday, December 6, 2008, and despite his grumblings, Dennis picked Danny up well before sunrise, from his boyfriend Matthew's apartment in Sacramento and they headed south,.

At 6:45am Sami arrived with his limousine to Le Parker Meridian hotel and texted Kaushal to come out front. Kaushal replied he was not at Le Parker. He was at the Holiday Inn, about a mile away. Sami got back in his limo and went. As they headed out of town, Kaushal informed Sami he was to meet his friend Danny at the Casino Morongo, about 30 miles outside of Palm Springs.

At the casino exit, there was a gas station and Danny spotted Sami filling his limo up with fuel. Danny parked on the far side of the station and texted Kaushal his location. Kaushal told Sami he'd be back in a minute, grabbed his attaché case and walked around to meet Danny and Dennis. There, Kaushal gave Danny Cliff's laptop and told him to hack into it. Inside would be all of Cliff's personal banking information. He also told Danny to go Cliff's house and prepare it to be listed for sale. Danny said he would. However, when Kaushal left, Danny got into Dennis's car and told his cousin to head north. While texting back and forth with Kaushal, Danny continued the charade, pretending to be inside Cliff's house until he finally said everything was handled and claimed to have left.

That same morning, Craig and Miguel checked out of their budget hotel near Fontana and also headed north towards San Francisco. Along the way, they stopped at a Home Depot and purchased shovels, then went north again until Miguel spotted a secluded residential neighborhood. They got off the freeway and drove through it, went up a hill. They were searching for somewhere to dump the body. Finally, Miguel saw several mounds of dirt at a roadside construction site. Being the weekend, no Caltrans workers were around. They pulled between two large mounds of dirt so the car was well hidden from the road and got out the shovels and started digging. When it was deep enough they put Cliff's body in it. Craig looked in the back seat for the murder weapons and towels. Miguel said he'd thrown it in the dumpster back at the hotel. They filled the hole with dirt and drove north again. Craig kept the dog.

Ransacking Cliff's Estate

Back in Palm Springs, Cliff's friend Cody was wondering what happened to Cliff. The two were supposed to meet up and go to the Festival of Lights parade but, Cliff wasn't returning his phone calls. The last time he'd talked to Cliff was mid-day on Friday. He should've called back by now. It was late afternoon and the crowds were gathering on Palm Canyon to grab the prime viewing spots for the parade. It would start around sundown and it wasn't like Cliff to just disappear without relaying a message. Cody called Cliff a total of 24 times Saturday afternoon and evening, becoming more frantic with each call. In a fit of desperation, he called another friend, Eddie, and the two of them went to Cliff's house around 11pm that night, after the parade.

They found the front door to Cliff's house slightly ajar. That didn't seem like Cliff. Neither was the mild mess left about the home: drinks still on the table, a pack Benson & Hedges cigarettes left scattered nearby, along with an opened package of crackers. Cliff didn't smoke Benson & Hedges and he never left his place messy, unless… Cody and Eddie decided Cliff must've found a date and went somewhere special with another friend. They quietly left, leaving the front door like they'd found it.

*   *   *

Sunday morning, December 7, 2008, Cliff's neighbor from across the street, Mr. Lemmerick noticed Cliff's gate was open. Although he really didn't know his neighbor well, he did know that Cliff was rather persnickety about neatness and security. Mr. Lemmerick walked inside Cliff's yard and went to the front door, which was still ajar, and yelled for Cliff. Not hearing anything and thinking about Cliff's age, Mr. Lemmerick called 911 in case Cliff had had a medical emergency inside.

Palm Springs 911 dispatch is located within the Palm Springs Police Station. Two officers, Bergman and Crampton, were assigned as the first responders to what was designated 'Suspicious Circumstances.' They arrived on the scene at 10:17am and found the front door locked but not pulled tight enough for the lock to catch. They entered the home and did a cursory check of the premises, noticing that a Rolls Royce was parked in the garage and the house was in relatively good condition. There were no immediate signs of a robbery or foul play. They exited back out the front door, locking it behind them.

At 11:59am Palm Springs Police were notified that Cliff Lambert was thought to be "Missing" by his friend Eddie Milliken. Eddie filed a missing persons report with Officer Sawyer at PSPD. Eddie said he and his friend Cody had called Cliff several times in the past day and a half and Cliff was not responding. Officer Sawyer took a thorough report and tried to call Cliff himself via his cell phone. There was no answer. He also wrote down the make and model of Cliff's Mercedes and ran a DMV check for the license plate number. After Eddie left, Officer Sawyer contacted Officer Bergman who confirmed that he had already been to Cliff's residence that morning on a 'Suspicious Circumstance' call but, he hadn't seen anything to justify further investigation.

* * *

Also on December 7, 2008, Danny Garcia was arrested for drunk driving and placed in Sacramento County Jail. He'd been with his boyfriend, Matthew, and decided to drive the two of them home after a night of drinking. It was his second DUI in two months, which could mean a felony if convicted. He also had a pending trial concerning an assault on a police officer while attending a Gay Day festivity, earlier in the year. Danny had been at his hotel, near California's Great American Theme Park in Santa Clara, CA, at the time of the incident and enhanced his story by claiming the police had wrongfully beat the crap out of him during the arrest at the hotel, then beat him again while in jail, and finally tossed him in a cell in San Jose with a bunch of Mexican gang bangers who'd raped him.

Nothing would ever come of Danny's accusations against the police.

* * *

Monday morning, December 8, 2008, Cody was still wondering what had happened to Cliff and called Cliff's handyman, Robert, asking if he'd connected with Cliff. Robert said he'd gone in to work today but, Cliff was not there. So, he left. Cody had already tried Cliff's phone number a couple times and not gotten an answer.

The week before, Cliff had given Cody attorney Sam Orin's phone number as a precaution just in case something happened which they weren't prepared for. Cody dug out that number now and gave it a call. The first few times it rang and rang with no answer. About the third or fourth time Cody called it, the number was disconnected.

*   *   *

That same morning, Dennis and Danny drove back to Palm Springs to assess the home and its contents. Danny's job was to fence the goods found inside the home. They arrived at the residence as the sun was setting and parked in front of the home. Danny had a key and opened the front door. Inside, he rummaged around in the cabinets, hutches, closets, drawers, dressers, everywhere and anywhere Cliff might have hidden his valuables. He stacked on the dining room table what he thought to be the most valuable or easiest to sell. There was more than he and Dennis could easily fit in the car. Danny separated the stuff he thought he wanted most. Dennis declined to take anything for himself. Then the two of them loaded what Danny wanted into the car.

Danny noticed the silver Mercedes was not in the garage. Kaushal had never come out plainly and stated that Cliff was dead to Danny. Danny still thought it likely Cliff was somewhere in a Mexican jail, just like Thomas White, or being held captive by some of Kaushal's friends.

He didn't know for sure and didn't want to ask.

*   *   *

Several more days passed and Cliff did not contact any of his friends or staff.

Cody and Eddie decided to do a second check of the home. When they entered, the drink, cigarettes and crackers were off the table. Several pieces of art and silver knick-knacks were missing from the home. Other valuable items were stacked neatly on the dining room table. Some doors were open or closed that were not the same way as the last time they'd been here. Cliff's bed was made as if he hadn't been sleeping in it.

They left, unsure what to make of how they'd found the home.

*   *   *

Wednesday, December 10, 2008. Russell Manning went to the Pacific Western bank near downtown Palm Springs to pick up the Power of Attorney forms needed to authorize a controlling interest in Cliff Lambert's bank accounts.

The bank had just locked its doors. However, the ladies inside were friendly and allowed Russell to come in as their last customer of the day. They gave Russell the documents he needed and the next day, he Fed Ex'd the documents via overnight express up to David Replogle's law office in San Francisco.

*   *   *

On Friday, December 12, 2008, detective Browning of the PSPD did a drive by of Cliff's residence and found no signs of anyone being home. The mailbox was full of mail and the Christmas lights were on. It was daytime.

*   *   *

Also on December 12, 2008, Kaushal Niroula and attorney David Replogle continued their financial prying into Cliff Lambert's estate. They'd received the Fed Ex documents Russell Manning had mailed and Replogle had created a Power of Attorney and other documents necessary to promulgate the sale of Cliff's home. They thought it worth upwards of $1 million and nothing was going to stop them from accessing that kind of money.

They contacted a mobile notary to witness signatures, Replogle pretended to be Cliff via a fake driver's license. Upon request, he placed a thumbprint into the notary book. All the documents were signed, witnessed, verified and notarized.

Kaushal immediately hopped onto a place for Palm Springs and by 1pm that afternoon he walked into the Palm Springs Pacific Western bank branch with Russell Manning and the notarized forms. The two raided Cliff Lambert's accounts. Kaushal had the teller draft a cashier's check for $185,000 and instructed her to wire the money to Lambert Studio Corporation in San Francisco. Kaushal had recently created the Lambert Studio Corporation as a ploy to make the tellers comfortable about transferring the money. Kaushal was the sole owner and share holder in the dummy corporation.

Kaushal told Russell to write out a check for $5,000 for his services, which the bank immediately cashed.

*   *   *

The afternoon of December 12, 2008, was the pay day for Miguel, for his role in the murder of Cliff Lambert. To make the transferring of money easier, Miguel had opened a checking account at Wells Fargo, the same bank where Cliff Lambert kept a number of his accounts.

Kaushal had flown back to San Francisco and was now with Miguel. Together, they withdrew several amounts from Cliff's checking and savings accounts, using a checkbook of Cliff's Kaushal had written a check for $30,000 made out to Miguel. The check cleared immediately.

In the next few days, Kaushal would cash numerous checks from $9,000 to $14,000. One was made directly to the Law Offices of David Replogle for $5,000. Money transfers were also made to Guatemala and withdrawals from New York City, where Miguel had gone travelling.

Miguel was also given Cliff's silver Mercedes, which he left parked in his garage.

Before he left for New York City, Miguel paid Craig $5,000 for his help in Cliff's murder.

* * *

Monday, December 15, 2008. Danny and Kaushal returned to Palm Springs and booked a room at the Hyatt downtown.

They went to Cliff's house and emptied out the mailbox and cleaned up the newspapers that had collected on the front entry. Using Danny's key, they entered the home and together collected more items of value including: a favorite Tiffany clock of Cliff's and some computer hardware. Then they went back to their hotel room feeling like kids in a candy store.

Over the next month, Danny and Kaushal made several trips to Palm Springs to pillage Cliff's home. Here's a list of some of their ill-gained loot: furniture, electronic toys, a tanning bed, clothes, including underwear, three laptops, silver tea sets, trays, silverware, a crystal statue, Louis Vuitton luggage and a $3,000 chandelier.

Danny kept a ledger of the items he old. Miscellaneous silver knick-knacks totaled over $80,000 themselves.

Strings Unraveling

Since grabbing Cliff Lambert's money clip out of Craig's hands at the murder scene a week and a half ago, Kaushal had passed Cliff's American Express card over to Danny, who used it like a bottomless ATM, purchasing items on the internet.

Within a few days of the murder, he had a virtually endless stream of packages being delivered to his apartment. It seemed as if every delivery company on the planet was stopping by his place. His neighbors even jokingly mentioned something in the hallway about Danny being fencing stolen goods. His face went white. Luckily,

Dennis laughed at the joke and the ice was broken. Inside Danny's apartment Dennis viciously gave Danny an 'I told you so,' verbal thrashing and told him to stop spending so much.

* * *

Meanwhile, Kaushal was trying to get Cliff Lambert's home sold. Back in November, he'd contacted a married couple, Mark Evans and Sharon LaFountain, to assist in the real estate transaction. Mark was a licensed California Palm Springs Realtor and Sharon was a senior escrow officer for Chicago Title. Kaushal knew them as friends from a few years back. They had no hard feelings towards Kaushal, though they thought his story of being a rousted Nepalese Prince was a big line of bullshit.

Of course, they would help him sell a Palm Springs property. Yet, as Kaushal described the situation of a home being under the control of a Power of Attorney, Mark and Sharon grew cautious and wanted to review the documentation. Kaushal felt confident David Replogle's paperwork would be correct and obligingly agreed. It was, although over the course of discussing the transaction with Mark and Sharon, Kaushal's description of the situation changed several times. Evans and LaFountain also noted that Kaushal seemed to have an exorbitant amount of different cell phones he was answering and though the home should easily fetch just above $1 million, Kaushal wanted to list it for $800,000. They grew suspicious.

A meeting was set up at the Realtors's home to review all documents pertaining to the sale and to sign the listing agreement. Kaushal brought along his attorney, David Replogle, who made the agents much more comfortable; especially after they Googled David's name and confirmed he was an actual lawyer.

* * *

On December 18, 2008 David Replogle realized he'd made a griev-ous error. When getting the Power of Attorney notarized he'd imper-sonated Cliff Lambert with a fake driver's license and then placed his own thumbprint in the notary book. That thumbprint would even-tually become evidence which could easily incriminate David in the fraud scheme to steal Cliff Lambert's finances. Furthermore, it would implicate him in Cliff's murder. He had to get that notary book.

* * *

Also on December 18, 2008, Kaushal was still attempting to get Cliff's home sold. He called Mark Evans and Sharon LaFountain and asked if they could talk. They were going to Christmas party. But, it would be alright if Kaushal and his driver, Sami, drove them. They could discuss it on the way.

Mark noticed the titling and Power of Attorney situation was changing again. Now, Kaushal was getting the property as part of a settlement to him but, it was coming to Kaushal via a Power of At-torney. Then, the Power of Attorney was going to a gentleman named Russell Manning. Then another change, the Power of Attorney had already been handed over to Russell by Cliff directly.

To legally protect himself and Sharon, Mark suggested they do a new Power of Attorney with witnesses and a notary at the title company after Christmas.

* * *

Four days later, on December 22, 2008, a woman named Lisa called Mobile Notary for an appointment at 53 Woodward Street, a rough section of San Francisco. Gary answered the call. When Mo-bile Notary asked the woman to spell her name she spelled it by "L" as in "Liar." Usually people say "L" as in "Larry." She also urged the notary to hurry.

Gary went to the address and had to squeeze his car into the only available space behind a silver Mercedes with two people inside lying back in their seats, apparently relaxing. He grabbed his backpack and went to the appointed door. Rang the bell. The lady inside said there was no Lisa that lived there.

While scratching his head out front on the sidewalk, trying to figure out what to do next, a black man came up to him and asked the time. Gary told him and the man remained. The man demanded Gary's backpack. Gary told him to, "Fuck Off!" The man grabbed the bag and started yanking it, knocking Gary off his feet. In trying to get the bag away from Gary the man dragged Gary down the street by the straps. Gary yelled for help, the police, 911, anything and everything for assistance. There were people nearby on the sidewalk and they did nothing to assist. When Gary struck a telephone pole with his head, he anchored himself to it with his arms and hands. The fight for the bag proved too much for the man and he ran away.

Gary sarcastically thanked the crowd of do nothings and wished the same would happen to them. Then, he stalked back to his car, which was no longer blocked in by the silver Mercedes. It had left during the struggle.

Unbeknownst to David, Mobile Notary had two notaries named Gary and even if the black man had stolen the backpack and gotten the notary book, they would have gotten the wrong one.

*   *   *

December 29, 2008. Kaushal called Chicago Title in Palm Springs and spoke to Sharon La Fountain. He told her the Power of Attorney had already been signed and offered to fax it to her. She gave him her fax number but, when she received it, Sharon noticed the fax was on attorney David Replogle's letterhead, yet it was sent from Kinko's; not of David's office. Sharon was tired of all the changes in the deed and Power of Attorney. It was her job to make sure homes had what is called a 'Clear Title' in real estate transactions so buyers wouldn't purchase a home that wasn't legally allowed to change hands or left the purchaser with a bunch of debts against a property. To satisfy her suspicions, she ran an internet search on Cliff Lambert and discovered the authorities listed him as a missing person. She immediately called Mark and he then called the police.

*   *   *

One day later, on December 30, 2008, Mark Evans and Sharon LaFountain met with Kaushal and Russell at Mark's office while Sharon sat in the next room on the phone with Detective Browning of the Palm Springs Police Department. Browning asked if the car they were driving was a silver Mercedes. It wasn't.

Mark and The Boiz signed a listing agreement and then Mark made copies of all documents, including the Power of Attorney and Russell's driver's license. Kaushal asked for a title transfer right then and there.

Detective Browning asked Sharon to stall. Sharon told Kaushal those documents would have to be drawn up and she would need an hour or so to complete them. She suggested Kaushal and Russell and Mark go to lunch while she prepared the new documents.

When they returned, Sharon informed Kaushal she needed assistance to draft the correct documents and had reached out to a friend at Fidelity National Title. The Power of Attorney did not necessitate a traditional deed and would therefore require an Accommodation Deed, which would facilitate Kaushal getting the money once the home sold.

Kaushal was in a rush, he always was. He and Sharon worked it out so he could sign the necessary papers in a Fidelity National office in Santa Clara, near San Jose, and then the papers would be overnighted back to Sharon. Kaushal agreed and left.

In contrast to what Kaushal thought was going to happen,

Sharon worked with Detective Browning and Cliff Lambert's real attorney to prevent any changing of the deed to Cliff's home. An Emergency Order and a Petition for Conservator was filed that same day with the Riverside County Probate Court. There would be no other transfers of title in regards to Cliff's property. Therefore, Sharon could draw Kaushal and Russell into a trap, filling out papers and having them sign them, without causing any real effect on the true ownership of Cliff's Palm Springs home.

* * *

Detective Min had been brought onto Cliff Lambert's missing person case by Detective Browning just before Christmas to help in the financial and real estate aspects. Min started the financial investigation with Cliff's local Pacific Western bank and was surprised to find out that Russell Manning had presented a Power of Attorney to access Cliff's bank acounts. Min also came across a Mutual Release of Goods document which was notarized and signed by Kaushal Niroula. The document included a San Francisco address and a copy of a driver's license.

Picking up the phone is half of any detective's work. Detective Min called SFPD and found Investigator Ovanessian on duty. The SFPD was very familiar with Kaushal Niroula. Investigator Ovanessian shared background information on Kaushal with Detective Min. Kaushal had been in and out of jails several times. He had multiple open fraud cases. He was presently out on bail awaiting trial for his immigration status. David Replogle was Kaushal's attorney of record. Min mentioned the notarized documents he had in his possession and asked Ovanessian if he would contact the notary and get his signature book. By December 31, 2008, Detective Min had the book and ran the fingerprint next to Cliff Lambert's signature. It came back as a match for attorney David Replogle.

PALM SPRINGS TRUE CRIME

*   *   *

The New Year dawned brightly for the Boiz, or so they thought. As far as they knew, things were proceeding nicely. They had made a lot of money selling Cliff's personal items of decoration, his art and ravaged his financial accounts with great abandon. The sale of the home was proceeding and in the very near future they would score over $700,000 when the home found a buyer. Life was good.

On January 3, 2009, Sharon pretended to record documents showing Russell had transferred the home to Kaushal via a Grant Deed.

For the next week or so, Russell Manning and Kaushal Niroula flew back and forth from San Francisco to Palm Springs conducting real estate business they thought would lead to the sale of the home and the eventual delivery of hundreds of thousands of dollars.

Arrested

January 6, 2009. Miguel had spent his $30,000 and needed more. Kaushal gave Miguel the keys to Cliff's house, agreeing to let Miguel go back to Palm Springs and remove the last of Cliff's personal belongings so Miguel could get another infusion of cash.

Miguel got to Palm Springs about 11am, checked into the Motel 6, hired some Mexican day laborers, giving one of them Cliff's house key and telling them to hop the fence and go inside and start packing. Miguel then went off to rent a U-Haul truck, saying he'd be there tomorrow to pick everything up.

The next day, Miguel showed up as expected and parked the truck in front of the house. Two neighbors, Allen and Bob, were sitting on their porch when he did and they thought it strange. They knew Cliff was listed as a missing person since a month ago. They didn't recognize the man who'd gotten out of the truck and was rattling the front gate as if he didn't have a key. Allen walked over and asked the Hispanic man at the gate if he needed help? The man said he'd been hired by a couple of Chinese guys to clean out the house.

Allen grew suspicious and said he should call Mr. Lambert' attorney, who'd recently asked some of the neighbors to watch for anything out of the ordinary occurring at the home. This definitely qualified.

Bob came over and asked the Hispanic man if he wanted some ice tea. Bob and Allen wanted to keep this man here until the authorities arrived. Miguel came over for the tea and while Allen was calling Cliff's attorney and 911, he noticed the U-Haul drove away. Strange that the truck should leave, Allen thought, leaving behind Miguel.

While this was happening, a Maxwell Security car drove by. Bob flagged it down and asked the security officer if he'd hang out a moment until the police arrived. He did. Miguel was told to remain at Bob and Allen's home by the security officer.

Officer Fernandez, a female officer, of Palm Springs Police Department was the first on the scene. She asked Miguel what his intentions were at Cliff Lambert's home. Miguel replied that he'd been hired to do a moving job by a Chinese man who ran an ad on Craigslist. He told the officer he was staying in room 120 at Motel 6 and that he'd hired a crew of laborers to assist in the moving. While Miguel had nothing to hide, he informed Officer Fernandez that he'd told the laborers to leave and drop the truck off back at the hotel so they wouldn't get in trouble as most of them were probably illegal immigrants.

Fernandez asked Miguel if he had a key to the home. He said he did not. She then asked if she could search Miguel. He gave his permission. She found a small stainless steel surgical knife wrapped in foil, his money clip, a Home Depot receipt for a pair of bolt cutters and a key. Miguel changed his story to include picking up a friend in Salinas to come to Palm Springs with him, at which point, Officer Fernandez grew suspicious Miguel might have something to do with

Cliff Lambert's disappearance.

Officer Fernandez called the precinct and spoke with Detective Browning about her finding Miguel ready to steal from Cliff Lambert's home and informed him of Miguel's hotel room. Browning had already received a call from Martina, Cliff's attorney, and was on his way to the home when he received Fernandez's call. Fernandez then talked to dispatch and asked for back up. There might be more people in the home.

On his way to Lambert's home, Detective Browning saw the U-Haul truck leaving the neighborhood; he pulled it over and questioned the driver, who said his name was Marco. He didn't have a driver's license. The truck was empty. Detective Browning let Marco and truck go.

Detective Min, who'd been brought on the case as a real estate specialist, was part of the police backup who arrived at 317 Camino Norte to assist Officer Fernandez. Attorney Martina arrived soon also and gave the officers permission to enter the home. Since Cliff was still listed as missing and Miguel was at the home under suspicious circumstances, it was possible that Cliff could be held captive inside the home, possibly even injured. It was all the reason the police needed to enter.

The Detectives went room by room searching the house. Nearly all the remaining possessions were neatly stacked at precise vantage points. Artwork, luggage, the television and personal items were obviously prepared for easy removal.

A few blocks away, Detective Browning made it to the Motel 6 where he was met by two other detectives. They talked to the front desk and obtained a key to the room, still under the premise that Cliff Lambert might be being held captive, this time in the hotel. There was no Cliff but, they did see some items they felt belonged to Cliff.

Browning left to get a search warrant and one of the other detectives, Araiza, remained in the hotel room. Someone knocked on the door. It was the U-Haul driver. He had returned to confess that he'd been scared and given a false name to Detective Browning. His real name was Jose and he said Miguel and he were hired by an Egyptian guy up in San Francisco.

When Detective Browning returned to the hotel room with the search warrant, he did a thorough search and found more art, Louis Vuitton luggage matching the rest of the set back at Cliff's home, tiffany boxes, watches, figurines, sixteen pairs of loafers, and the paperwork transferring title to Cliff's 2004 silver Mercedes convertible into Miguel's name. Browning also found a copy of Cliff's Will, his personal checkbooks and the Grant Deed to Cliff's home. Browning called in Cliff's friend, Cody, to verify the items as belonging to Cliff; which Cody did.

Jose was arrested and brought to the station by Detective Araiza while Detective Browning went back to Cliff's home and asked Cliff's attorney, Martina, to press charges against Miguel for burglary and possession of stolen merchandise. She agreed. Miguel was read his rights and taken away in handcuffs. The home was finally declared a crime scene. Forensics technicians were called to process the property for evidence.

*   *   *

At the Palm Springs Police Station, Miguel asked to speak to Detective Browning without an attorney, saying he wanted to come clean and get his life back. Browning asked Detective Min to sit in on the interview, whereby Miguel confessed to being hired by Kaushal Niroula to clean out Cliff's home. Miguel admitted to having already completed one load; the items which the detectives found in his hotel room and then he willingly offered up his cell phone and password so the detectives could glean contact information on Kaushal. Furthermore, Miguel admitted to David Replogle hiring him to be the getaway driver in the silver Mercedes the day the San Francisco Notary was attacked and his backpack with his log book was attempted to be stolen. The attacker was a 'crack head' friend of Miguel's.

Detectives Min and Browning thanked Miguel for his testimony and left the room to ask a judge to increase his bail from $25,000 to $1 million under the pretense that Miguel had no ties to Palm Springs and an extensive criminal history of assaults, burglaries, and more.

By the time Miguel was completely processed at the station, it was well into the afternoon. Later that evening, around 10 pm, a man named Timothy Higgins called the precinct jail and asked who the detective was on the case and how much was Miguel's bail.

* * *

On January 7, 2009, Kaushal went to a new Title company and recorded another transfer, this time from himself to a man named Jay Shah. Kaushal had conspired with Shah to purchase Cliff's home for the ridiculously low price of $298,000. Kaushal enacted this second deed transfer, without Sharon LaFountain's knowledge, in an attempt to sidestep his own partner in crime, Russell Manning. The maneuver created a cloud on the title of Cliff's home which would remain in effect until September, 2010.

Also on January 7, Detective Min of PSPD called Daly City, CA, police, (near San Francisco) and informed them of Miguel's address, seeking help locating the silver Mercedes. Two days later, Daly City Police called back to inform Min the Mercedes had been found at Miguel's address. The car was impounded and photographed.

Detective Min thought it time to delve deeper into the financial records of Cliff Lambert. He contacted Charles Schwab and, with the help of a senior fraud investigator, made a complete list of Cliff's banking accounts. He was surprised to discover all of Cliff's accounts had withdrawals over the past month. Min contacted the banks and asked for video footage from their ATM's and inside the banks at the times the withdrawals were made, producing positive photographic identification of Russell Manning, Kaushal Niroula and Danny Garcia taking Cliff's money.

* * *

Miguel was afraid of being beaten up and raped in jail. He reached out to a Tank Boss, Arturo, for protection. A Tank Boss is a prisoner given leadership status by the other prisoners to work with the guards to sort out what cells everyone lives in as a way to promote the most hospitable conditions within a certain cell block. Miguel was grateful the Tank Boss in his block had taken him under his wing. Still, he was very scared.

Miguel's confided to Arturo that he knew where Cliff's body was. Arturo wanted a better deal for himself and he knew that Miguel was gay. Arturo could easily turn Miguel over to the men in prison and let them have their way with him. Instead, Arturo played with Miguel's mind, like he would a cat with a string; stretching his safety out in front of him and then pulling it back just as Miguel would reach for it, until Miguel had told him a lot of the details of Cliff Lambert's murder. Miguel even drew a map for Arturo to where Cliff's body was buried.

On January 29, 2009, Arturo spoke with Detectives Min and Browning and showed them the map. They determined the body was buried somewhere off the I-5 Freeway, in an area called The Grapevine, north of Los Angeles.

* * *

February 5, 2009. Detectives Min and Browning went to the area where they thought Cliff's body was located and drove from off-ramp to off-ramp searching for the exact location. When they found the place they thought matched the map, they contacted a local police department with access to a cadaver dog used to sniff out burial sites.

The dog sniffed and sniffed and then sat on a spot indicating where a body was buried but then, the dog got up and walked around some more and sniffed the area a second time. The fact the dog did not remain seated in the same spot was a bad omen.

The police dug for several hours. No body was found. Detectives Min and Browning went back to Palm Springs empty handed.

* * *

February was a bad month for the Boiz. Danny Garcia was picked up for his second DUI and had court appearances, many of them at the same time Kaushal was being scheduled to appear to handle his immigration case.

The Palm Springs home was still not sold. It seemed that one delay followed the next, even though Kaushal had brought forth the buyer, Jay Shah.

Palm Springs police contacted David Replogle concerning the thumbprint in the book and David was running out of excuses to avoid talking to them.

The police were also looking for Danny's cousin, Dennis. They'd nearly captured him once at Danny's parent's house; making Danny's mom and dad aware that something bad was going down.

Then a shocking thing happened to The Boiz. An anonymous tip was posted on a website called www.findthemissing.org, plainly stating that Danny Garcia and Kaushal Niroula were the likely culprits in Cliff Lambert's disappearance. Danny and Kaushal's computer hacker friend, Alec, quickly stepped in and made the website remove their names under threat of a major lawsuit. Still, the posting was noticed by the police and was one more clue alerting authorities to Danny and Kaushal.

Kaushal, always looking to the next mountain to climb, was already on to his next Grift: The Rincon scam. He had fraudulently

ERIC G. MEEKS

placed his name on the deeds of three condominiums worth about $2.5 million total in one of San Francisco's swankiest and tallest housing structures, called the Rincon Building. Kaushal was simultaneously excited and worried that this scam would net him millions or that it would lead to his eventual arrest. The rest of The Boiz were mad at Kaushal for not including them in this newest scam. They were tired of his lies and didn't want him in their group any longer.

* * *

March 2, 2009. Detectives Min and Browning made a trip to the San Francisco courthouse at a time when Kaushal had an appearance scheduled. The detectives were banking on the fact that David Replogle would be there also, representing Kaushal. They were right. Both Kaushal Niroula and David Replogle were put in handcuffs and taken back to lock-up in Palm Springs.

It didn't take long for each to turn on the other.

David Replogle first claimed Guatemalan terrorists were forcing him to act his part in the scheme. Then, he changed his story, saying Kaushal was the mastermind of the group and he had only been following orders for what he thought was a legitimate property settlement case. As far as he knew, Kaushal's had been infected with AIDS by Cliff. Replogle said he was unaware of a murder. Then, he changed his story again to say he was aware of the murder but, he'd taken no part in it. Finally, he asked if he could talk to the District Attorney and get a deal.

Kaushal was asked about his frequent comings and goings to and from Palm Springs; about the first time he met Cliff Lambert, and as to why he had access to Cliff's money and property. He claimed Lambert was Russell Manning's friend – after all that's why Russell had the Power of Attorney over Cliff's Estate – and that Russell had introduced him to Cliff in October, 2008. Since then, they had had dinner together and Cliff had welcomed Kaushal over to his

139

house a couple of times where they had had sex and Cliff had infected him. Kaushal told the police that Cliff settled with him for $1.5 million instead of going through a lengthy court battle and had given him the home as part of the settlement. The police told Kaushal his lies were all bullshit and they knew he did not receive the house from any settlement. They knew Kaushal had forged the documents and even posed as an attorney to gain Cliff's trust. Suddenly, Kaushal had no more lies to tell. He could see his world crumbling and his inevitable incarceration; after which he would be deported to live out his life in poverty back in Nepal; that is if he ever got of jail at all. He needed time to think. Kaushal no longer wanted to talk to the police. He invoked his right to an attorney.

Kaushal asked for a phone call while in jail. He telephoned Danny and asked him where he was. Danny replied he was in his apartment. Kaushal warned him the police had him and David and told Danny to run as fast and as far as he could. The police were coming for him.

Shortly after his phone call, Kaushal asked to speak to Detective Browning again. This time, Kaushal turned on David, placing the blame squarely on him, claiming David had orchestrated the whole thing with Danny's help and saying he thought they would kill him if he didn't play along. He wanted to know if he could get a deal with the District Attorney if he came clean.

* * *

March 3, 2009. An arrest warrant for Danny Garcia was issued by Palm Springs police in conjunction with the Riverside County District Attorney's office. Danny called Dennis and cried to him, asking him, and then begging Dennis to come pick Danny up. Dennis refused to be of any more help. Danny kept begging until, finally, Dennis hung up.

Without knowing what else to do, Danny kept a low profile

for a day and considered his options, then he called Investigator Ovanessian at the SFPD to proclaim his innocence. He fully placed the blame on Kaushal Niroula and David Replogle and informed the investigator that Russell Manning was being held in a Mexican jail. Less than a month prior, Russell had been framed as a drug dealer by Kaushal and David after they'd bribed the Federales to place cocaine inside Russell's suitcases.

Danny promised to turn himself in to Investigator Ovanessian in the next few days once he'd put together his own bail money.

* * *

A few days later, Danny and Dennis were driving around with their computer hacker friend, Alec, trying to fence some stolen jewelry as a means to raise bail money. Alec had helped extensively in the collecting of personal information on The Boiz victims via the internet, while simultaneously removing any online reporting of their crimes from victim's blog sites.

After a day of finding their jewelry not worth what they'd hoped for, Dennis parked the car around the corner from a private collector who'd been recommended by one of the jewelers to act as a fence for the stolen goods.

Danny got out of the car and walked around the corner to the appointed apartment. An hour passed and Danny didn't return. Dennis and Alec got nervous and Alec said he'd go check on Danny. This time Alec didn't return. Dennis tried calling Danny and the phone went straight to Danny's message center. Dennis was both angry and worried. Yet, instead of going and checking on Danny himself, Dennis left and it was smart he did. Both Danny and Alec had been caught in a bullet-proof locked-glass entry way used to screen customers before entry. The fence was a front or a SFPD sting operation to capture Danny and his accomplices.

* * *

Alec made bail within 24 hours. He was obviously part of the criminal ring of The Boiz although, he wasn't part of the murder.

Danny, however, was another story. He was one of the kingpins of the gang and the police knew it, regardless of Danny's portraying himself as Kaushal and David's patsy.

Danny decided to pull in a favor from one of his Sugar Daddies. He knew a man whom he and his friends referred to as "Leo the Lion." Leo was big in the Republican Party and had Homeland Security clearances. Leo always wanted very rough sex with Danny, which Danny didn't exactly like. Still, Leo would be better than prison sex. Danny made the call.

True to his word, Leo walked Danny out of jail, straight through the front doors and into his waiting V-12 Mercedes. Danny thought Leo was going to take care of everything but, that wasn't the case. Danny was sprung from jail but, not from court and other crime databases. He was listed as an escaped criminal and an all points bulletin was put out on him with a 'shoot to kill' order.

For the immediate weekend, Danny performed as Leo's sex slave in a high rise hotel room in Las Vegas. On Monday, Danny called Dennis to come pick him up and Dennis told Danny the police had been extensively searching for him. Danny had been screwed in more ways than one by Leo.

* * *

On the Saturday Danny was peforming as a boy toy in Las Vegas with Leo the Lion, a former victim of Danny's, Tyson Wrensch, who coincidentally lived in Las Vegas, read some of the other victim's blog sites about The Boiz and their legal troubles.

On March 6, 2009, Tyson decided to throw some gasoline on Danny and Kaushal's troublesome fires. Tyson called Detective

Browning in Palm Springs and told him Danny might be hiding at either his boyfriend, Matthew's, house or at Alec's apartment. Both locations were in the San Francisco/Central California area. When Detective Browning said he already had information leading him to believe Danny was in Sacramento, Tyson grew excited. Danny had to be at Alec's then. He spelled out Alec's last name for the detective, "S-h-a-b-a-z-i-a-n." He wasn't sure where Alec's residence was but, if Danny was with Alec then the two were doing everything they could to divert attention away from themselves while simultaneously collecting information on the in the internet. Alec was The Boiz computer hacker guru and if the police could find Alec they should be prepared to confiscate every computer at Alec's disposal. Tyson made sure Detective Browning understood there was a veritable wealth of criminal data on the gang to be found in Alec's possession.

* * *

Palm Springs Police finally got the break they'd been hoping for on Monday, March 9, 2009, when Detective Min received a phone call from Sergeant Rick Carter of the Sacramento Police Department, saying that had information leading them to the known whereabouts of Danny Garcia. He was staying at a friend's apartment and SPD were about to go serve a warrant for Danny's arrest.

When Sacramento police showed up and knocked on the door, Alec answered. 'No,' he said. 'Danny wasn't there.' The police were ready for this response and searched the home anyways. Danny was found scrunched down in a hot water heater closet at the back of the apartment. When the police asked him what he was doing in there, Danny replied 'I got better phone reception in here.'

Danny and Alec were both taken into custody.

Inside the apartment were multiple computers and some fifty miscellaneous hard drives. Many of the computers were set for automated searching of the internet to gather data on individuals so The

Boiz could steal identities. This would prove to be the evidence necessary to convict the entire gang and stop their perpetrating of crimes, permanently.

Danny and Alec were booked in San Francisco and transported to the Robert Presley Detention Center in Riverside, California. Danny would never again see the light of day as a free man.

In police custody, Danny portrayed himself as a pawn in Kaushal's and David's shenanigans. He claimed to have tried to protect Cliff from the two, especially Kaushal, because Kaushal would go after anyone who had money. Danny said he liked Cliff as a friend. When he'd heard about the art inheritance scam that Kaushal and David were playing on Cliff, he'd gotten mad because he knew that Cliff wasn't as rich as the little Nepalese thought him to be. Danny said he'd hoped the whole thing would just barely brush Cliff and then he'd be left alone. He never thought that Kaushal and David would take the crime to the extent they did. Danny went on to implicate David by confirming that David had both put his thumbprint in the notary book and that he'd used his attorney skills to produce fraudulent documents to trick Cliff, allowing Kaushal to steal his possessions while falsely claiming Cliff had given Kaushal AIDS. In all of these crimes, Danny said he was an outsider, never participating more than one would while overhearing gossip in a bar, and never actually a participant.

Danny kept spinning his own storied web to the police about everything: Cliff's death certificate, Russell's bribed arrest and subsequent imprisonment in Mexico, and how Kaushal had been at the home during the murder and let the actual killers (Craig and Miguel) in through a sliding glass door into the kitchen of Cliff's home. Danny thought he was telling the police new information which would eventually minimize his own involvement in the crime. He didn't realize he brought very little information to the police they didn't already have. He was just confirming his own conviction.

* * *

There was only one member of The Boiz still at large, Danny's cousin and part-time driver, Dennis Domine. He would never be found. The police made several attempts to pick him up at his places of residence, his marijuana farm, his parents home, and more. Dennis eluded arrest at every turn and junction. The last known attempt was made by authorities in 2011 when he was arrested in San Jose on a traffic warrant. Before SFPD or PSPD could act, he was released on his own recognizance, never to be seen again.

Most of the police involved in seeking Dennis believe he is currently living somewhere in Mexico.

* * *

On August 19, 2009, Craig McCarthy, who had never wanted to kill Cliff Lambert in the first place, who thought he was just being hired to move some stuff, asked to speak to the District Attorney. He wanted a deal. The D.A. agreed. In exchange for Craig turning states evidence and testifying against his other co-conspirators, he would receive a lighter sentence. He wasn't the only one of The Boiz who would receive such a deal.

* * *

Russell Manning was released from his Mexican jail under an extradition agreement reached between the United States and Mexico. He was placed on a non-stop flight to Los Angeles on August 20, 2009. When he got off the plane, Detective Browning of Palm Springs Police Department was there to greet him. Russell was escorted back to the desert in hand cuffs.

During the ride, Russell asked if Kaushal had set him up in Mexico? The police thought yes, and told him so, at which point,

Russell proceeded to confess every aspect of the murder and the fraud crimes against Cliff Lambert, placing the blame squarely on Kaushal. When they got to Palm Springs, the police told Russell that Kaushal had claimed Russell had been present at the scene of the murder, Russell said that was a lie. He had never met Cliff.

That would be for the District Attorney and the court to determine. Russell Manning was given a plea bargain in exchange for his testimony against Kaushal Niroula, Danny Garcia and David Replogle.

The Trials

September 10, 2010. Deputy District Attorney Lisa DiMaria was assigned to the case. She was a short, feisty and a deceptively pretty brunette in her early 40's who been practicing law for nineteen years and knew her way as a prosecutor around the court room. She easily accepted the judge's decision to separate the defendants into two groups. David and Miguel would be tried as one group. Danny and Kaushal would be tried on their own at a later date. After more than a year of legal wrangling the trials could finally begin.

David's and Miguel's trial lasted about three months. Russell Manning and Craig McCarthy took the stand against their former partners in crime. Arturo, the Tank Boss, had a change of heart and told D.D.A. DiMaria that he'd been informed Danny Garcia had put a hit on him in prison if he testified. He wouldn't risk his life for The Boiz incarceration. This redaction of testimony did not slow down the prosecution; D.D.A. DiMaria doggedly explained David's utilization of his attorney's skills and attributed Miguel's muscle in the murder of Cliff Lambert. The two men looked more and more guilty each day they went to court.

There was one minor twist near the end of the trial when David Replogle decided not to testify on his own behalf. He'd been on the witness list the entire trial and D.D.A. DiMaria was looking forward to interrogating him under oath. Perhaps, she might even get him to implicate himself in other crimes, like the false conviction and Mexican imprisonment of Thomas White on the trumped up child molestation charges. She would be denied that pleasure.

When it came down to the jury deciding David Replogle and Miguel Bustamante's fate, they were given a verdict of guilty on all charges. David and Miguel were convicted of murder in the first degree of Cliff Lambert. Their crimes were punishable by life in prison without the possibility of parole.

* * *

Danny's and Kaushal's trial would take approximately two years. During that time, they were allowed to prepare for their defense on their own terms, each actively becoming their own counsel. The judge even furnished them brand new laptops – with software of their choice but, no internet connections – to aid in the formation of their own defense. They were given legal assistance and investigators, all at the public expense.

The pre-trial motions were ridiculous and numerous, with Danny and Kaushal sometimes being on the same side of the argument and at other times viciously smearing each other's character. They made multiple erroneous motions and requests for mistrials, which were constantly denied, though most of their requests for extensions were granted. They were given access to technical advisors and experts to support their testimony, again at the expense of the public.

D.D.A. DiMaria was again seated at the prosecutors table. Just like she'd done with David Replogle and Miguel Bustamante, she would lead the charge in convicting these two Grifters of murder. Alongside her was Detective Min from PSPD who would be the PSPD's chief liaison. Riverside County Superior Court Judge David B. Downing would be presiding.

On June 25, 2012, near the end of pre-trial hearings, Danny

Garcia was discovered tape recording the proceedings on his laptop. He was also leaving the device recording when he was not in the court room as a way to eavesdrop on D.D.A. DiMaria while she prepared witnesses. Danny even successfully recorded Judge Downing in private conversations. The judge was furious and confiscated Danny's laptop, claiming to have locked it up in a private vault for safekeeping. He issued Danny a new laptop, this time with no recording software on it. Danny protested, saying the recordings proved judge had shown himself to be prejudiced in favor of convicting himself and Kaushal prior to hearing a shred of testimony. Danny demanded the judge to recuse himself. Judge Downing refused Danny's request and said he could take it up on appeal.

The trial began. Kaushal was prone to long meritless speeches and wild questioning of witnesses. He often did more damage to his case than he helped. Again, he and Danny would sometimes appear to be on the same side of an issue and then they would be at each other's throats as they tried to throw the blame off themselves.

D.D.A. DiMaria was methodical in her approach, lining up all the text messaging evidence between the defendants with flow charts and blow-ups of select statements. She produced every document, every forgery, every detail of the financial and real estate portion of the crime and walked the jury through the evening of the murder, moment by bloody moment. Every day of the trial she kept a poster-sized photograph of Cliff Lambert in the court room for the jury to see so they wouldn't forget who they were defending. Cliff Lambert was a loner, although in this courtroom, he was not alone. D.D.A. DiMaria kept Cliff very much in her thoughts, and in the jury's thoughts, as she doggedly prosecuted Danny and Kaushal.

The biggest obstacle in the prosecution's case was that Cliff's body, despite having a map, had never been found; nor was there any blood at the crime scene. The evidence easily supported a fraud case against Danny and Kaushal but, how could they be convicted of a murder that couldn't be prove? Danny and Kaushal recognized the weakness of the prosecution's case and made it the center piece of their defense.

At one point in the trial, a video was presented to the jury depicting a re-enactment of the murder with Kaushal and the other participants (Craig and Miguel) stabbing Cliff to death. At another point a Mercedes similar to Cliff's was used to show how a body could fit into the trunk only by breaking a bone or two of the deceased.

The climax of the trial happened near the end, when Kaushal Niroula took the stand in his own defense, against his legal counselor's advice. Kaushal bravely proclaimed in court, "The jury deserved the truth."

He turned his testimony into a two day long rambling free for all whereby he blamed Danny and David for tricking him into being a part of the crime. He blamed society and his poor upbringing in Nepal. He admitted to other nefarious crimes, like his Rincon scandal, his Hawaiian real estate swindle against the Japanese lady and Russell Manning's set up in Mexico. He even called himself a 'Gay Grifter.' Kaushal was a convoluted mess as a witness.

He went on and on and on.

On his second day on the stand, Kaushal's testimony rambled to its eventual conclusion. It was Danny's turn to question him. Kaushal refused to answer any of Danny's questions. At times he stuck his chin out in defiance. At times he hung his head low in shame. Always, Kaushal repeatedly stated that 'He respectfully declined to answer.' Danny tried a multitude of different ways to pry some shred of testimony out of Kaushal that would aid in Danny's defense. Kaushal refused to speak.

When it was D.D.A. DiMaria's turn, at first, Kaushal seemed willing to cooperate only to then turn against the prosecutor and used her time to start yelling at the jury. He claimed his cell was bugged and DiMaria had confidential recordings of his defense strategy sessions.

When he was calmed down, D.D.A. DiMaria began ask questions again only now all Kaushal would say was, 'He respectfully refused to answer questions.'

D.D.A. DiMaria suggested he remove the word 'Respectfully" from his statement. Regardless, Kaushal would say nothing else except that his attorneys had advised him not answer any questions and he was removed from the witness stand.

During closing arguments, Danny and Kaushal both continued their wild allegations of prosecutorial misconduct and the fact that there was no body, no real evidence of a murder having ever taken place. Neither The Boiz nor the authorities knew where Cliff Lambert was and it was entirely plausible Cliff had simply moved to another country. When a jury member made a grunt of rebuttal, Kaushal pointed at the jurist saying, "I heard that."

D.D.A. DiMaria was succinct and to the point. She effectively summarized her arguments against the defendants while simultaneously tearing apart their defense strategy. She spoke for less than an hour and ended with the directive that someone had to stand up for Cliff Lambert. She had moved Cliff's large portrait to a imposable position in the court room and pronounced it was the jury's duty as citizens to be Cliff's family while making their decision. Then, D.D.A. DiMaria rested her case.

* * *

On Wednesday, September 5, 2012, the jury went into deliberations. They would discuss the case for two days before rendering a verdict. It was a very strenuous time for both the defense and the prosecution. The defense, of course, didn't want to go to jail for life. The prosecution knew their case was weak on the one point the defendants had made clear in their defense: There was no body.

Though the prosecution and the police had searched extensively they could not find the body of Cliff Lambert. They had driven thousands of miles, split up and searched various areas, searched by helicopter from the air, been assisted by search dogs in multiple locations and then dug up supposed grave sites and yet, despite countless man hours and many, many frustrating weeks and months, they had not found the one piece of evidence which would make their case against The Boiz a slam dunk.

Kaushal and Danny knew this fact to be their greatest defense and made good use of the missing body. They'd been smart in at least one way in strategizing their defense. They had built upon this fragment of hope utilizing all the tools the judge would allow them. They had hired the experts, sent out the investigators, tried to make the police appear inept, and did their best to make the witnesses stumble in their testimony. All in all, the trial took nearly two years to transpire and during its course, the defendants spent some $300,000 of taxpayer's money representing themselves.

Though they had no evidence to support this theory, authorities believe at some point shortly after Cliff's murder, Kaushal went to Cliff Lambert's grave site, dug up the body and then moved it to another location, hiding it forever.

And now, Kaushal Niroula's fate and the fate of Danny Garcia were up to the jury.

* * *

Just before noon, on Friday, September 7, 2012, the Jury Foreman informed Judge Downing they had reached a verdict and all participants were called back into the courtroom. The gallery filled with spectators and news people.

The Judge asked the Foreman if the jury had reached a verdict.

"We have your Honor," the Foreman replied.

"Guilty."

Kaushal NIroula was found guilty on all ten charges against

him, including first-degree murder.

Then it was Danny's turn and again, he was found guilty on the same group of ten charges against him. Danny hung his head in defeat and mumbled 'no' to himself over and over, rocking slightly back and forth against the balls of his feet. His over the top character had been a charade, a bluster, he knew he was doomed to a life behind bars.

Danny Garcia and Kaushal Niroula would never again live life as free men. They were convicted of only a fragment of the crimes they had committed. Still, it was enough to ensure they would never hurt unsuspecting citizens again.

After the trial, when Deputy District Attorney Lisa DiMaria left the courtroom she was greeted by cheers from the spectators, the waiting jury and the news people.

* * *

October 5, 2012. Danny Garcia was in court for sentencing. He tried to get the judge to admit errors in not forcing Kaushal to testify. Danny made another motion for a mistrial and then accused the judge of prejudice, the evidence of which was on his confiscated laptop.

All motions were denied.

Danny Garcia was sentenced to life in prison without a chance for parole and he was to pay restitution in the amount of $215,000 to Cliff Lambert's estate.

* * *

December 17, 2012. Kaushal Niroula was sentenced to pay restitution to Cliff Lambert's estate in the amount of $300,000 and he also received life in prison without the possibility of parole.

* * *

If by some stroke of luck or some proven error of due process, any of The Boiz are capable of winning an appeal leading to their release from prison, three of them will be extradited to Mexico. Danny Garcia, David Replogle and Alec Shabazian have pending warrants for extradition, issued in March, 2013, by the Mexican State authorities for falsely filing a lawsuit which lead to the conviction of Thomas White, while conspiring with underage boys, whom they plied with drugs and alcohol, to accuse White of sexual crimes. Mexico would love to get their hands on The Boiz.

PALM SPRINGS TRUE CRIME

Sources:

Author unknown, KAUSHAL NIROULA SENTENCED IN CLIFF LAMBERT KILLING (CA), http://www.estateofdenial.com/2012/12/22/kaushal-niroula-sentenced-in-clifford-lambert-killing-ca/, December 22, 2012.

Author unknown, CLIFF LAMBERT, http://www.charleyproject.org/cases/l/lambert_cliff.html.

Demian Bulwa, 'I AM A PREDATOR' – RUIN FOLLWS HIM EVERYWHERE, SF Gate, http://www.sfgate.com/news/article/I-am-a-predator-ruin-follows-him-everywhere-3187513.php, May 23, 2010.

Sherrie Lueder and Tyson Wrensch, UNTIL SOMEONE GETS HURT: A TRUE STORY, Lueder Board Press, LLC, 2013.

Matt Smith, THE DARK PRINCE, SF Weekly, http://www.sfweekly.com/sanfrancisco/the-dark-prince/Content?oid=2171976, April 1, 2009.

Ryan Tedder, ART DEALER CLIFFORD LAMBERT'S MARINE VEETERAN KILLER CONFESSES TO SAVE HIS OWN SKIN, http://www.queerty.com/art-dealer-clifford-lamberts-marine-veteran-killer-confesses-to-save-his-own-skin-20100901, September 1, 2010.

ERIC G. MEEKS

NARCOTICS

Glen Stewart Godwin

Glen Stewart Godwin
FBI's Fifth Most Wanted Fugitive

Palm Springs, CA – Up until 1980, Glen Stewart Godwin, 22, appeared to be a non-criminal hard working young man, earning his money as a mechanic, a construction worker and a tool salesman. He did a little drugs, sure, but then who didn't in those days? Apparently hard work eventually lost its appeal for him; because one day, Godwin and his roommate, Frank Soto, Jr., decided to rob their drug dealer Kim Robert LeValley.

To commit the crime, Godwin and Soto invited LeValley back to their condo to make a drug sale. Once there, Soto held LeValley while Godwin punched, kicked and strangled the dealer into submission. When all these attempts failed and LeValley still wouldn't give up the cash, Godwin, in his frustration at the dealer's refusal, grabbed a butcher's knife and stabbed LeValley twenty-six times.

As soon as they'd killed LeValley, Godwin and Soto knew they'd screwed up. They had to dispose of the body. They decided to load LeValley into Godwin's pick-up truck and drive him out to the middle of the desert, where they tried to eliminate the body by strapping homemade explosives to it. 1-2-3, they detonated the charges. A few days later, some Eagle Mountain residents came across a blown up pick-up truck abandoned in the desert with a body inside it.

Police identified the truck as Godwin's; easy enough. Then they used phone records to tie Godwin and Soto to the crime. Soto cracked first and admitted his involvement and testified to the fact

154

that it was Godwin who actually did the killing but, he made a poor deal with the District Attorney and only received one less year sentence than Godwin who, In 1982, received 26 years to life for the crimes of robbery and murder. Soto got 25 to life.

They were both sent immediately to jail.

Five years later, Godwin was being held at Deuel Vocational Institute, a temporary placement facility in northern California, a facility known for violence amongst its nearly 4,000 inmates. The convicts at Deuel Vocational spend their time as laborers working a grain farm and a dairy with some 1,200 milk cows. Godwin was temporarily there awaiting transfer to wherever his more permanent housing location would be. Sometimes, in prison, temporary housing can last a long time. While there, Godwin grew impatient and tried to escape. He was caught and subsequently moved to the maximum-security prison at Folsom, California.

Once at Folsom, Godwin escaped for good. Authorities are convinced Godwin's former cellmate at Deuel, Lorenz Karlic, and Godwin's wife, Shelly Rose, helped plan and facilitate his escape. A hacksaw and other small tools were smuggled into Folsom and later found in his cell. On June 5, 1987, Godwin snipped his way through the wire fence surrounding the prison and slipped into a storm drain via a manhole cover, then he shimmied his way some 750 feet down a pipe through pitch black muck. (reminiscences of The Shawshank Redemption) The pipe emptied into the American River. Either Karlic, now released, or Rose left a small raft at the river and Godwin floated away.

In June of 1987, Lorenz Karlic was arrested and convicted of assisting in Godwin's escapee, while aiding and abetting, a known felon.

In January of 1988, Shelly Rose was classified as a fugitive for assisting in the escape and on February 7th, 1990, was caught in Dallas, Texas by the FBI.

Godwin would be free for only one more year than his accomplices. He escaped to Puerto Vallarta, Mexico and became a drug dealer himself until he was finally arrested in Guadalajara in 1991 by Mexican authorities. He was sentenced to 7 years and 6 months in Puente Grande prison.

American authorities wanted to extradite Godwin from Puente Grande, but Godwin killed another inmate – a member of the Mexican drug cartel – and his extradition was delayed. While waiting for processing and extradition, Godwin used the time to plan yet another escape, which he successfully executed in September, 1991.

Glen Stewart Godwin is still at large. The FBI has listed him as #5 on their Top Ten Most Wanted list and is offering a $100,000 reward for information leading directly to Godwin's arrest and capture. They say he is fluent in Spanish and may be traveling throughout Central and South America, or Mexico, working as a mechanic or a construction worker. They believe he is still involved in narcotics distribution. Godwin's known aliases include: Michael Carrera, Miguel Carrera, Michael Carmen, Glen Godwin, Glen S. Godwin, Dennis H. McWilliams and Dennis Harold McWilliams. He has black salt and pepper hair, green eyes, is white 6 foot tall male of about 200 pounds and is most likely armed and considered extremely dangerous.

Sources:

Various contributors, GLEN STEWART GODWIN, https://en.wikipedia.org/wiki/Glen_Stewart_Godwin, Wikipedia.org.

FBI website, FBI TEN MOST WANTED FUGITIVE: GLEN STEWART GODWIN, https://www.fbi.gov/wanted/topten/glen-stewart-godwin/view, December 1996, revised November 2009.

© PSPD Mugshot

Robert Downey, Jr.'s mugshot.

Robert Downey Jr.'s
Thanksgiving Cocaine Bust

November 27, 2000, two days after Thanksgiving, the Palm Springs Police Department received an anonymous 911 call about someone possessing drugs and guns at the luxurious Merv Griffin Resort and Givenchy Spa. (now called The Parker)

When PSPD Sergeant John Booth knocked on the door of the room in question, he found actor Robert Downey Jr., 35, of *Ironman* fame, who at the time was doing a remarkable job guest starring as Calista Flockhart's love interest on the hit TV show *Ally McBeal*. Downey was charged with possession of cocaine, valium and meth amphetamine and released early Sunday morning on $15,000 bail.

I remember at the time of Dwoney's bust, there were rumors of him having a prostitute with him, dressed in a female superman outfit but, upon doing research for this book, I discovered information on the website Cinema.com that indicated there was no woman in his room with him, although, records indicate there was a female Wonder Woman outfit hanging in his closet and his limousine driver is said to have been waiting outside the hotel to bring Downey and a female guest to dinner.

Even though, if convicted, Downey could face a prison sentence of nearly five years for the Thanksgiving weekend arrest, he was allowed to sign a contract with 20th Century Fox saying he would appear in eight more *Ally McBeal* episodes. Then, Downey went on to nearly violate his parole in April, 2001, when he was found wandering barefoot in Culver City, CA. He was arrested on suspicion of being under the influence of drugs. Luckily, he was released just a few hours later, even though tests confirmed cocaine was in his system.

Ally McBeal producer, David E. Kelly, determined Downey to be too much of a liability, even though Downey had been nominated for an Outstanding Supporting Actor in a Comedy Series Emmy Award. His character came to an abrupt end on the show and while Downey had several projects completed at this point in his career, "in the can" so to speak, other projects were suddenly yanked out of his life. Mel Gibson had to cancel a movie production of *Hamlet* in which Downey was to play the lead. Woody Allen had to find another actor play the lead role alongside Wynona Ryder in *Melinda and Melinda*. Years later, Downey would tell a reporter that this period had been the lowest point in his life.

Robert Downey, Jr., was 36 years old and had a long rap sheet of drug and alcohol related arrests.

Downey had only been out of jail three months at the time, after serving a year's sentence in Corcoran State Prison for a 1999 drug conviction charge. California Judge Lawrence Mira had sentenced him to three. Downey was given many breaks by the judicial system due to his popularity and notoriety as an acclaimed actor. The actor had been released early for good behavior. After his Culver City arrest though, Judge Mira had had enough and chastised Downey in court, calling him "manipulative" and saying he had, "…exhausted the court's options." It was in Mira's courtroom where Downey made an incomprehensible plea to the judge stating, "It's like I got a shotgun in my mouth with my finger on the trigger and I like the taste of gun metal." He went to say he'd been addicted to drugs since the age of eight.

Prior to his being in front of Judge Mira, Downey had been arrested in April, 1996, on another drug charge, and possession of a loaded .357 Magnum pistol, while speeding in his pick-up truck down Sunset Boulevard in Hollywood. He had been placed on probation and then two weeks later was arrested again, after mistakenly stumbling into a neighbors Malibu home and passing out on their bed while under the influence. Both incidents were combined into a single judgment which put him on probation for three years with mandatory drug testing.

The Palm Springs, November, 2000, arrest of Downey seemingly ended his downward spiral. Downey had fallen greatly since his Best Actor Oscar nomination performance of Charlie Chaplin in 1992s *Chaplin* at only the age of 27.

Two years later, Downey's career began to rebound after doing a lip-synching video for Elton John's single "I Want Love" and then shot up again when actor/director Mel Gibson, who had been a close friend to Downey since co-starring with him in *Air America*, 1990, used Downey in the lead role of Dan Dark in *The Singing Detective*, 2003, which then led to producer Joel Silver casting Downey as the crazed psychiatrist alongside Halle Berry in the psychotic supernatural thriller *Gothika*. Silver held back 40 per cent of Downey's salary as insurance forcing the actor to complete his role without incident, which Downey did with exceptional acting chops and style. The movie was a big hit in the summer of 2003. That year Robert Downey, Jr. had two hits in theaters and his career was back on top.

In 2004, Downey was talking Oprah Winfrey about himself going into rehab in the third person, "Well, you're a wreck. You've lost your job and your wife left you. Uh. You might want to give it a shot." He went on to say, "It's not that difficult to overcome these seemingly ghastly problems. What's hard is to decide to do it."

In 2007, Robert Downey, Jr. released a comedy-buddy-action film *Tropic Thunder* alongside Ben Stiller and Jack Black, while simultaneously playing Tony Stark, the lead in the film *Ironman*. Downey was catapulted to mega-stardom.

Sources:

Josh Meyer, ROBERT DOWNEY JR. ARRESTED AGAIN ON DRUG CHARGES, Los Angeles Times (.com), November 27, 2000.

Tribune News Services, ACTOR ROBERT DOWNEY JR. ARRESTED ON DRUG POSSESSION CHARGES, Chicago Tribune, November 27, 2000.

Unknown author, MUG SHOTS-HOLLYWOOD: ROBERT DOWNEY, JR., http://www.thesmokinggun.com/mugshots/celebrity/hollywood/robert-downey-jr, April 1, 1999.

Various contributors, ROBERT DOWNEY, JR., https://en.wikipedia.org/wiki/Robert_Downey,_Jr., Wikipedia.org.

Wenn, ROBERT DOWNEY JR. WAS STAYING IN HOTEL WITH MYSTERY WOMAN, http://cinema.com/news/item/1744/robert-downey-jr-was-staying-in-hotel-with-mystery-woman.phtml, November 25, 2000.

ERIC G. MEEKS

Operation Falling Sun

Desert Hot Springs.

Early Friday morning, May 22, 2009, well before the sun was even casting a glow in the eastern sky; a coalition of local, state and Federal authorities played a game of "Knock Knock" on some of Riverside Counties' worst criminals, displaying an unprecedented show of force on the most notorious drug and criminal enterprises in the Coachella Valley.

In a well-orchestrated plan of attack, nearly 700 officers did their utmost to protect the law abiding citizens of the desert by serving search and arrest warrants on dozens of drug dens, "safe" houses, and known hideouts on the drug dealers, thugs and other criminals who had been preying on the good nature of society for far too long. The warrants were executed based on months of surveillance information duly obtained first-hand by officers and confidential informants.

38 arrest warrants were served, along with 54 search warrants. 100 parole searches and 185 probation searches were conducted. Simultaneously, 70 undocumented immigrants were targeted by Immigration officials for deportation.

The results were dramatic. An illegal meth amphetamine lab was discovered. A total of 400 grams (over 14 pounds) of meth was confiscated. 3,000 grams (over 100 pounds) of marijuana was discovered. 50 unlawful firearms were found and confiscated. 120 arrests were made.

The agencies involved included: Desert Hot Springs Police,

165

the FBI, the U.S. Department of Immigration, Customs Enforcement, the Coachella Valley Gang Task Force, Riverside County Sheriff's deputies, the Department of Homeland Security, the Department of Correction Parole Officers, and regional police authorities.

It was the single biggest day of drug busts and criminal arrests in the Coachella Valley's history.

VICE

Jimmy Swaggart

ERIC G. MEEKS

Jimmy Swaggart's Prostitute

On October 11, 1991, televangelist Jimmy Swaggart fell from grace when in the wee hours of the morning, well before daylight, he was issued three traffic tickets simultaneously: Driving on the wrong side of the road, driving an unregistered vehicle and not wearing a seatbelt. At the time, he had a passenger in the car, Rosemary Garcia of Coachella. She admitted to being a prostitute.

The area in Indio where Swaggart was stopped was a well-known 10-block area where local police target Vice, Prostitution and Narcotics operations. The police officer who pulled Swaggart over knew Garcia by sight as a street walker.

When asked by local TV News KMIR about why she was with him, Garcia responded, "For Sex, I mean that's why he stopped me, that's what I do, I'm a prostitute. He asked for sex." She went on to explain how Swaggart had seen the police behind his 1989 Jaguar and became upset. He started swerving as he hid pornographic magazines under his seat. The police pulled him over.

When Swaggart finally got back in front of his congregation at the Family Worship Center, he boldly told them, "The Lord has told me that it's none of your business." Then his son, Donnie, went before the shocked church members and announced that his father would be stepping down temporarily as head of the Jimmy Swaggart Ministries for a time of "healing and counseling."

Jimmy Lee Swaggart, born March 15, 1935 in Ferriday, Louisiana, was 56 at the time of the Indio incident. He is the cousin of rock 'n' roll star Jerry Lee Lewis and country music star Mickey

169

PALM SPRINGS TRUE CRIME

Gilley.

This was the second such incident for the famed preacher. The first happened in New Orleans in 1988 after a fellow preacher, Marvin Gorman, from the Assemblies of God church released photographs of Swaggart with another prostitute. The photographs had been obtained by Gorman's son Randy and son-in-law, Garland Bilbo, as retaliation for Swaggart having defrocked Gorman in 1986 by revealing several affairs, Marvin Gorman, a married preacher had. As retribution, Randy and Garland staked out a Travel Inn in New Orleans with a telephoto lens camera and captured shots of Swaggart and a prostitute outside their room. Upon trying to leave, Swaggart discovered he had a flat tire. The two young men had purposefully deflated Swaggart's tires to create the incident and then called Marvin Gorman to confront Swaggart.

Gorman attempted to use the photographs to force Swaggart to publicly denounce Gorman's illicit affairs as a lie, therefore helping reinstate Gorman to the ministry. Swaggart delayed and delayed, till a year later. Gorman let Swaggart know his time was up and Gorman was ready to go public with Swaggart's digressions.

On February 21, 1988, After some wrangling within the church's executive board, Swaggart went live on television and declared, "I have sinned," tearfully speaking to this church goers, who unexpectedly forgave their flamboyant preacher and he became more popular than ever.

In 1991, after the second incident in Indio, the congregation was not as forgiving and Jimmy Swaggart's career as an honored preacher was over.

Jimmy Swaggart is still alive. He is now 80 at the time of this publishing; married to the same woman since 1952, Frances Swaggart. Their son, Donnie, preaches on tour at various churches throughout the United States and abroad while running the Family Worship Center, television programs and websites.

Sources:

Associated Press, WOMAN RIDING IN SWAGGART CAR SAYS SHE'S A PROSTITUTE, Los Angeles Times (.com), October 12, 1991.

Joanne Kaufman, THE FALL OF JIMMY SWAGGART, http://www.people.com/people/archive/article/0,20098413,00.html, People (.com), March 7, 1988.

Unknown author, SWAGGART PLANS TO STEP DOWN, News Brief, New York Times (.com) October 15, 1991.

Various contributors, JIMMY SWAGGART, https://en.wikipedia.org/wiki/Jimmy_Swaggart, Wikipedia.org.

The Death of Shauna Grant

Her real name was Colleen Marie Applegate. She was a beautiful 18 year old girl who left her small town of Farmington, Minnesota, where she had lived since her parents moved there from Bellflower, CA, in 1973. Colleen left Farmington to return to southern California, this time bound for Hollywood and hopefully fulfill her dreams of becoming a star or at the very least a working actress.

Before she left Minnesota, in December, 1981, she had a nervous breakdown that lead to a pill popping attempt at suicide. It was really only a handful of sinus pills, hardly deadly. Her parents thought she was simply seeking attention. They tried counseling and found that no one wanted to open up to the shrink. Everyone in the family talked at least once to the doc. No results were forthcoming, so they stopped.

When she finally packed her bags, Colleen left her high school cheerleader skirt and a cashier job behind and, along with her high school boyfriend, Mike Marcell, headed for the bright lights of Hollywood in March, 1982, leaving behind her parents, a brother and three sisters.

They made it to Los Angeles, found an apartment and then started applying for jobs. Nothing was working out. Bills were coming due and money was dwindling fast. Colleen saw an ad for young attractive women to do "Figure Modeling" with The World Modeling Agency in Van Nuys, CA. She called them up: "Yes, they were looking for women like her.' She went down to their offices for an interview. Marcell went with her and together they met the agency's owner, Jim South. He immediately set up a photo session for Colleen with soft-core pornography photographer J. Stephen Hicks, who set up a mock camping theme. The photos were good enough that they were bought by the men's magazine Club.

Money changed hands and Colleen's and Mike's bills were paid. More photography shoots were discussed. Colleen's wholesome American mid-west blonde looks were in great demand. Everyone she met told her how beautiful she was. For a lot more money than just photography modeling, say, if she were willing to do some adult films, she could make a lot more money.

How much? Enough that Colleen was soon making hardcore pornographic films. Her income jumped from what she made in nearly a month as a clerk back home in Farmington, to the same amount in a day.

The money was well and good, or so she thought yet, her boyfriend was not interested in watching from the set sidelines as other men bedded Colleen no matter how much the money. Nor, was he interested in staying with her in Los Angeles if this was the life she was going to lead. She had wanted to be an actress. Instead she became a Porn Queen. He packed his bags after only two month in southern California and went back home to Minnesota to join the Army. Before shipping off he informed Colleen's parents and other residents of their small community exactly what it was that Colleen was doing in California. Her parents were embarrassed and ashamed of what their daughter had become and they told her so. A friend from back home, Brenda, came out to Los Angeles to try and talk her into ending her film career. She said she'd help her get a respectable job.

Colleen wasn't about to stop. As far as she was concerned, she was surrounded by people who cared about her and were going to help her become a star through the back door to Hollywood. After all, Sylvester Stallone started his acting in the porno film The Italian Stallion and even Norma Jean posed nude for a calendar before becoming Marilyn Monroe. If they could do it, so could she.

She was rechristened with the stage name of Shauna Grant by veteran hardcore porn producer Bobby Hollander because the name was more "classy" and launched a significantly more substantial career into the world of real porn.

In that world, her star rose fast. She made the movies Virginia, Suzie Superstar and Flesh and Laces I and II. Her pay climbed to $100,000 a year. She was told she was getting the best scripts available, ones with plots. Yeah, okay. In Suzie Superstar she portrayed the leader of a rock band. Before she knew it, she'd made more than a dozen films and her life had changed dramatically.

As Shauna Grant, she was invited to the best parties. She travelled around in limousines. Cocaine was everywhere. It was the early 1980s. She was young, beautiful and important to a lot of people. Doors opened for her, usually into a bedroom set where she screwed men in front of cameras for money. Her make-up artist became her best friend. After all, she and 27-year-old Laurie Smith had already enjoyed each other on camera in Suzie Superstar, The Young Like it Hot and Bad Girls IV, so why not be friends off camera too? Besides it gave her someone to trust while she was snorting up all that cocaine.

By the time a year was up, Colleen Applegate, aka Shauna Grant, was used meat. The cocaine addiction had earned her the industry nickname of "Applecoke." In her first year she contracted Herpes and had an abortion. On the up side, she was nominated for several awards at the 8th Annual Adult Film Association Awards at the Coconut Grove Ambassador Hotel. Francis Ford Coppola even sat at her table. But, no standard movie roles came her way. She was also a presenter at the gala. The highlight of her career was handing an award to someone else. Her star was already fading. On film, she'd had sex with 37 men, in just over 30 films and now lacked enthusiasm for performing the act on camera. Off camera who can say how many she slept with; first to land the roles, then as the superstar taking lovers, and finally as her star ascended and she had to beg to get roles – all in less than two years.

The night of the Adult Film Awards she accepted another porno role for what would be called Teen Idol and shooting would begin in San Francisco in ten days. Then, Grant decided not to make the film. Instead she asked Kelly Nichols, a friend of hers, to play the role. Grant was weighing the option of returning home to Minnesota. Her parents had offered to pay her college expenses if she would come home. Former boyfriend Mike Marcell even flew out to Palm Springs to meet Shauna Grant (Colleen Applegate). But, instead of meeting him at the airport, Grant got wasted with her girlfriend Laurie Smith and lost track of time. Days had slipped by since the Film Awards and the two ladies had plummeted into a drug riddled haze. Grant forgot entirely to meet Marcell and he went back to Minnesota without seeing her.

Shauna Grant found a new boyfriend. Jake Ehrlich owned a respectable downtown Palm Springs business called Pelle's Leather Goods. Grant adored Jake and followed him from room to room. This annoyed him and he suggested she go see a psychiatrist. As far as we know, she never did.

Things didn't shake out so well in Palm Springs. By February, 1984, Jake (44) had been sentenced to prison for drug trafficking and he told her the relationship was over. He called her from his jail cell and told her to move out. Her response was to tell him that she was thinking of killing herself because her life was so shitty. He either didn't believe her or didn't care.

On March 23, 1984, Colleen Applegate, stage name Shauna Grant, committed suicide using Ehrlich's .22 long rifle in his Palm Springs home at 352 West Dominguez Road a few blocks away from The Racquet Club. Just after 7pm that night, she lay down in bed and placed the barrel of the rifle against her temple and squeezed the trigger, causing star shaped holes in her head as the bullet passed through. Who called the police or paramedics is unclear. They arrived shortly thereafter and rushed her to Desert Hospital. The damage was too great. She was brain dead. After two days, all life support was removed and she died. Her body was returned to Minnesota for her funeral.

Colleen Applegate's parents, and others, believe a conspiracy exists here and that Grant did not kill herself, but was instead murdered; as the long rifle was too long for her to stretch her arms easily, aim and pull the trigger.

Sources:

Wikipedia, SHAUNA GRANT, https://en.wikipedia.org/wiki/Shauna_Grant, multiple contributors.

Los Angeles Times (.com), 'DEATH OF A PORN QUEEN': STUNNING STORYTELLING, http://articles.latimes.com/1987-06-09/entertainment/ca-6084_1_palm-springs, by Howard Rosenberg, June 9, 1987.

https://jl10ll.wordpress.com/2012/04/22/life-and-death-of-a-porn-star-when-innocence-meets-hollywood/, LIFE AND DEATH OF A PORN STAR AND HER ALTER EGO: WHEN COLLEEN APPLEGATE MET SHAUNA GRANT, posted by helthnut, April 22, 2012.

MISSING PERSONS

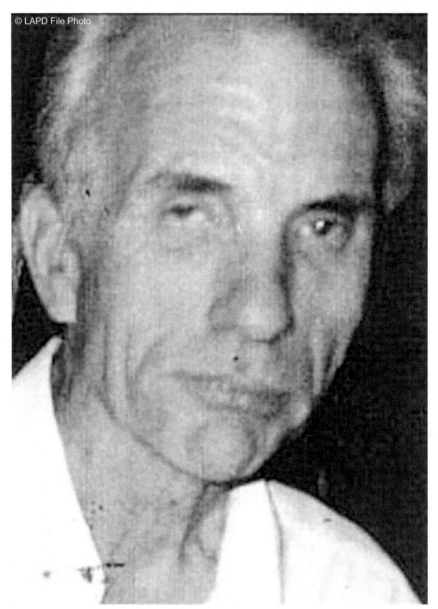

© LAPD File Photo

**Jeremy Crocker
Missing since 1996**

The Disappearance of Jeremy Crocker

On December 9, 1996, Jeremy Crocker, 62, son of Francis Crocker, who co-built the Palm Springs Aerial Tramway, disappeared from everyone who knew and loved him, never to be seen again.

Description: White male, 5'11", 160-170lbs, gray hair, blue/green eyes, in slim healthy condition, last seen wearing a short sleeved shirt with large pastel colored squares, black Dockers pants, tan shoes and a wedding band.

Jeremy Crocker was an educated man. He had a Bachelor's degree in Mechanical Engineering and a Master's degree in Medical Science from the California Institute of technology. He was a clear talker and a sound thinker who could decipher complex problems and deduce them to a logical end. During the early to mid-1990s, he was a frequent shopper at my store, CelebrityBooks.com, often buying the Wall Street Journal, the New York Times or Barron's magazine. We would get into conversations about city politics or state and national issues and I always respected his opinion. He was married, had adult children, did not appear to have a job of any regular sort and yet, he never seemed to lack for money. I later found out he worked as an engineer. He always paid cash and did not appear to lack for any personal necessities even though he was not ostentatious, his clothes were sometimes rumpled and his hair was not always brushed. For all purposes, he seemed to be an old money person from a family of long standing in the community, which he was.

He was also a gadfly at Palm Springs City Council chambers at the same as my dad and I, speaking out during public comments on whatever issue he felt needed greater clarification than what city staffers were providing. It was largely due to this commonality that he became a customer at my store and a friend of my dad's and I. Jeremy and my dad were of roughly the same age and this helped them to discuss things that a youngster, like myself (then about 32), might not fully comprehend the long term ramifications thereof.

I did not know any of Jeremy's family: his present wife, his sons, his sister, or to what extent his family's structure of siblings and children and other relatives extended into the community. I still don't. I did know Jeremy's first wife: Sally McManus. She ran the Palm Springs Historical Society; was a very nice older woman and anytime Jeremy's name was mentioned there seemed to be a certain respectful silence that indicated her love for Jeremy had never quite come to the end she had wished for. I liked Sally. I still do. Jeremy would be 81 if he were still alive in 2016. I liked Jeremy too.

Then, one day, Jeremy simply stopped coming to the store for his daily papers.

According to Police reports and data available from the Center for Missing Adults, Jeremy was last seen at the Los Angeles Public Central Library during the afternoon of December 9, 1996. He had departed his home at 1PM that same day, taking the Greyhound bus from Palm Springs to Los Angeles and then a subway to the library. He was researching the controversial July 1996 plane crash of Trans World America Flight 800. Jeremy never returned home that day nor was he ever seen again. Based on ATM withdrawal records, he had up to $200 on his person at the time he went missing.

I always thought there might be some connection of Jeremy's disappearance with his most recent City Hall crusade to stop a developer named Solomon from building a condominium complex in South Palm Springs. Jeremy often spoke out about the effects the development would have on local wildlife. He even filed a lawsuit to prevent construction from beginning due to the mishandling or non-creation of an Environmental Impact Report. Solomon would sometimes speak out at city council meetings too. He was a big guy, barrel-chested and thick armed, fifty-ish, with a full head of shiny shoulder-length black hair, sporting a pinky ring and designer suits covering expensive shirts and he had a gorgeous chestnut-haired slim and curvy wife almost half his age who was hard to not stare at from the safety of my chair in the midst of the crowded hall. Solomon spoke with an east coast accent. Perhaps he was from New Jersey? Solomon, to me, seemed the perfect candidate to make Jeremy disappear.

Other rumors abounded. One was that Jeremy was disgruntled and separating from his present wife, who was a reformed Jehovah's Witness and that their marriage was heading towards dissolution. Followers of this belief claimed that Jeremy simply wanted to leave the marriage and that it was not illegal – immoral maybe, but not illegal – for a man to simply walk away from his marriage.

One Palm Springs Police Sergeant even told my dad that Jeremy had been found at the Los Angeles bus station and he simply had told Los Angeles investigators that he did not want to go home and that they couldn't make him. This didn't seem right. So, my dad called the Los Angeles Police Department, in my presence, and asked for the lead investigator on the case. I don't remember the officer's name. But, my dad got him on the phone and he told us the PS Sergeant was misspeaking. Jeremy had not been found. The police believe Jeremy, who at the time was living alone in Hollywood, with frequent visitations to Palm Springs, was struck by unfortunate health issues like a stroke or an aneurism and that he was probably a John Doe laying in some hospital somewhere. The LAPD detective took some notes as to my dad's statement and we never heard from him again.

The Desert Sun wrote articles on Jeremy's disappearance; as did the Press Enterprise and even the Los Angeles Times. Some time slipped by. Follow-up articles were written and then the news of Jeremy being gone became old and he slipped away from the news stream. Years went by and nobody ever heard from him again.

Almost twenty years later, in 2014, I was selling books on a Thursday night at the street fair, called Villagefest, downtown Palm Springs – Palm Springs is too hoity-toity to have a regular old street fair. So, they call it Villagefest – and an attractive older lady hands me a credit card to pay for her purchase. I notice the last name on the card is Crocker and ask if she's related to Jeremy. She says she's Jeremy's sister. (Later, another friend tells me she was Jeremy's former wife. Why she doesn't tell me this I don't know.) I ask her if anything was ever found out about her brother. She tells me no. He was never found and I quickly tell her my own theory about Solomon. She politely demurs, saying my idea is not the likely source of her brother gone missing, nor is the source to be the claims against his wife for religious reasons. She and her family firmly believe that Jeremy went missing because of his public claims about TWA Flight 800.

In 1996, TV's Hard Copy aired a segment based on the disappearance of Jeremy Crocker and his connection to the conspiracies surrounding the downing of TWA Flight 800. Jeremy's son, Jonathan, said his father was, "Somewhat of a crusader. Jeremy had wanted people to be accountable and honest and he felt that wasn't happening. He was willing to dig for evidence that might point fingers."

Five days before his disappearance on December 9, 1996, Jeremy Crocker spoke fervently as an invited guest on a Los Angeles based nightly radio talk show about his beliefs that TWA Flight 800 had not had an engine or structural failure shortly after its take off from John F. Kennedy airport in New York, as experts claimed, and consequently crashed in one of the United States worst plane disasters at the time; instead, Jeremy professed, as the Boeing 747-100 headed towards Europe, increasing in altitude over the Atlantic; it and the 230 passengers and crew aboard had been shot down by a missile.

Here are Jeremy's own words from the Peter Ford Show, **KIEV Radio, on December 4, 1996:**

JEREMY CROCKER: I contribute to KIEV my presence here because it was questions on the Ray Bream show and others and particularly his guests such as Captain Richard Russell who brought out the questions that I've spent several months trying to answer.

PETER FORD reads from Ron Lewis's Air Forces Monthly report, citing the terrorist fax.

JEREMY CROCKER: I think I could add something on that. The London Telegraph covered some of that activity in the Middle East particularly because some terrorist camps had been established around Tehran and were seen from U.S. satellites, and it looked like the U.S. was going to have a pretext there for an attack on Iran at that time. I would guess that they did not have the evidence to show that Iran was at the root of the TWA crash is the reason for not doing it.

PETER FORD speaks about Nov 18 report of streaks of light seen by Pakistani pilots off Long Island.

JEREMY CROCKER: Yes, on that one Peter keep in mind on the Ray Bream Show earlier in the week had an expert in the field, Captain Richard Russell. And I have been privy to something that came by another airline captain, a flight going from FLL, which is probably a Florida origin, to BOS, which is Boston, was headed for Providence at 33,000 feet and was crossing over the course of the Pakistani airliner at the time it made that report, so you have two credible sources.

CALLER says he thinks TWA 800 investigation is a cover-up, citing FBI and NTSB relations.

JEREMY CROCKER: Well I think particularly the 23 of the month, I forgot which month, maybe it was August, quite an analysis by Joe Sexton in the New York Times in which he analyzed the interior of the investigation and it supports your conclusion that there's something fishy there with the way the organization is constructed.

PETER FORD speaks about the shows plan.

JEREMY CROCKER: Could I speak to that and sort of sketch out the picture which we have and also the places where there are holes and invite listeners to fill those holes? First we'll talk about the things that did not bring down the airliner, contrary to what you may have heard from the frequent press conferences at Calverton Long Island. It wasn't a bomb. It wasn't a bomb for several reasons. Not only were there no appreciable amounts of explosives recovered, and you heard from Rodney [Stich] that it takes a couple hundred pounds to take the nose off a plane that has a 20 foot diameter fuselage and has to fly at Mach .86 and all the forces that that requires, so that we can throw out. Then secondly it wasn't the fuel tank, which had no fuel in it, it never has fuel when crossing the Atlantic, it has a center fuel tank for trans-Pacific flights only. So, then we come down to a missile. It wasn't a small missile because small missiles go right through planes. And there's an Aviation Week study which shows some 25 airliners have been hit by missiles over a period between 1978 I think through '94, so we need to have people who have contacts in military, in aviation, and particularly, as we'll talk about a little later, in foreign countries; there's been some interesting things that have happened in the way of cover-ups in Italy and Korea indirectly.

SEVERAL CALLERS call in, mostly off-topic talk.

JEREMY CROCKER: We wonder why governments fail to have proper investigations and I think we can help to understand that if we look at some cases in history. One that we were talking about, the first one, was one in 1980 when an Italian airliner on its way from the mainland to the city of Palermo in Sicily fell into the ocean and 81 people died. At the time there was some supposition that maybe a bomb then a little later they thought maybe a missile from Libya had hit it. And it stayed like that. There was an organization of survivors of those related to the victims, and I've spoken to someone who knew of that. I also talked to some Italian visitors. And finally in 1995 Agency France Press, which writes about events all over the world, had an intriguing little story, which you can find by archiving, that indicated that amongst the various things Italian prosecutors were looking into in items of corruption was the unexplained crash of that airliner.Then again a year later the English Guardian came out with quite a story based on papers discovered in the secret, in the archives actually, of one of the Internal Security, which is a nice name for their version of the FBI, in which it laid the whole thing out, that Italy in cooperation with other NATO members had attempted to kill Qadhafi in route from Libya to somewhere. But they brought their forces to bear and discovered that Qadhafi was escorted by MIGs, and in the ensuing fire fight knocked down some of their planes and unfortunately caught an airliner that was passing by, which was the one we spoke of, a DC-9.

PETER FORD talks about the Italian crash.

JEREMY CROCKER: I have had some personal anecdotes on that. You mentioned Palm Springs, I spent some time toward the end of the week at a library which also functions as a visitor center, and I keep listening and I hear Italian accents and I ask questions. A young man said yes, when they brought the airliner up it has a piece of French jet in it.

PETER FORD talks more about the crash and asks Jeremy
 if a US Navy P-3 was involved in the Italian incident.

JEREMY CROCKER: Well P-3 comes up with the TWA crash, which is an interesting point. But in any case let's be kind of easy with the Italians. They had what seemed like a good idea at the time. Qadhafi was very unpopular. If most of our listeners remember being in line for fuel in 1979 because of the second oil shock, which Qadhafi had arranged. So had it worked, it would have removed Qadhafi, an irritant to NATO, and been popular, even though they probably wouldn't have admitted it. But when it failed and knocked down an airliner they were really in difficulties. And the article goes on to explain what they did about it, which is to clamp down and they've kept it clamped down ever since.

PETER FORD asks if the commercial airliner that was caught in the fire fight went out of business.

JEREMY CROCKER: It was called Itavia, a domestic airline, and then the New York Times index shows it to have gone out of business by the end of the year.

PETER FORD goes into KAL 007. Jeremy Crocker expressed belief that the U.S. Government used KAL 007 to penetrate Soviet airspace, but that KAL may not have penetrated.

PETER FORD reads a Jerusalem Post report on French Intelligence sources who say it must have been a U.S. military missile and the U.S. will never admit it.

JEREMY CROCKER: If I could interject something, you mentioned the French, and the French have been quite helpful on this, because they have quite a few people that have been victims of the TWA crash. The quote that you gave us from the Jerusalem Post originated with French sources, and we can look overseas for perhaps an investigation that is not clouded by U.S. interests.

PETER FORD talks. Presents closing question: Is there any hope to sleuthing this thing out, or where is this all this going?

JEREMY CROCKER: I have great faith in thinking Americans and in thinking people of Europe in particular because these are people I've heard from [words I can't decipher], and people also in Britain who do understand these things probably with a subtlety we don't, that governments lie and people have to figure it out despite their lies.

End show.

Five days later, Jeremy mailed to Peter Ford a last packet of information containing his findings as to the plane crash and then he vanished.

(From Wikipedia) Trans World Airlines Flight 800 (TWA 800) was a Boeing 747-100 which exploded and crashed into the Atlantic Ocean near East Moriches, New York, on July 17, 1996, at about 8:31 PM EDT, 12 minutes after takeoff from John F. Kennedy

International Airport on a scheduled international passenger flight to Rome, with a scheduled stopover in Paris. All 230 people on board were killed in the third-deadliest aviation accident in U.S. territory. (End Wikipedia)

The government's analysis of the crash was two-fold and extensive. The National Transportation Safety Board (NTSB) conducted a review of the plane as to the cause of the crash and the Federal Bureau of investigation investigated the possibility of criminal activity or a terrorist attack due to the witnesses claims of seeing a bright flash just before the plane exploded.

Initial witnesses were other airplane pilots in the air around JFK airport. The captain of a nearby Eastwind Airlines Boeing 737 circling above Boston reported to his Air Traffic Control Tower that he, "Just saw an explosion out here about 16,000 feet or something like that, it just went down in the water." Many air traffic control towers in the New York and Long Island areas received calls from other pilots in the area.

Some of the witnesses were even more definite in their statements. Over 244 witnesses altogether were interviews by the FBI. Individuals from all walks of life gave testimony. Some of them were very well respected individuals.

A Mr. Roland Penney and his group of eight were along the coastline that morning and saw a "missile-like object rise up from the haze of the sea, leaving a thin gray smoke trail." They then describe a bright white flash "Like a flashbulb" just before the streaking object struck Flight TWA 800.

Another witness, Mr. Jim Naples, who was out on his boat with his wife and two daughters, said, "I looked up and my immediate response was, I never saw an alert flare go up like that. It was projecting upward with a stream of smoke behind it."

More than fifty other witnesses sighted similar distinctions in their description. One person was very noteworthy, Senator Orrin Hatch, R-Utah, chairman of the Judiciary Committee, was interviewed by CNN within 48 hours of the disaster. He stated, "I won't go so far as to say it was terrorism, but there was sabotage here. We're looking at a criminal act. We're looking at somebody who either put a bomb on it or shot a missile, a surface-to-air missile. The National Transportation Safety Board should run turn the investigation over to the FBI because the crash was not related to an aviation problem. It's very…almost 100 percent unlikely that this was a mechanical failure. It looked pretty darn conclusive that it was an explosion caused either internally or externally by a criminal act."

Initially, a New York Air National Guard HH-60 helicopter was just eight miles away and arrived at the crash site so quickly that debris was still raining down as they searched the area for survivors. There were none. A wide net of local, state, and national government response teams came onsite to help rescue efforts and every feasible attempt was made to collect all possible data and materials. Remote operated vehicles (ROVs) were deployed, side-scan sonar was utilized and laser line scanning equipment used to collect every item of significance. Three areas of wreckage were designated: a yellow zone for the front of the plane, a red zone for the mid-section and a green zone for the tail section. All pieces of the aircraft were transported back to a leased hangar at the Grumman Aircraft facility in Calverton, New York and both the FBI and the NTSB provided personnel to preserve the chain of evidence of each piece of debris.

Victim's corpses were recovered and transported to the Suffolk County Coroner's Office in Hauppauge, New York, for identification and forensic study. Some claim that the Coroner's office spent too much time on identification of the bodies and not enough on forensics due to victims family members wanting immediate identification of all body parts of their loved, an understandable desire. Ultimately, the remains of all passengers and crew were discovered and identified, though some were found months after the crash.

A week after the initial crash, U.S. Navy divers found the cockpit recorders referred to as Black Boxes and as the weeks rolled on, the FBI and the NTSB each continued their investigations. For their part, the NTSB made it very clear that they did not investigate criminal acts but, would support the FBI in their investigations. For their part, the FBI said they would take the lead in determining if foul play was involved in the crash. Yet, representatives from the International Association of Machinists and Aerospace Workers Union, who were brought in by the NTSB to help identify pane wreckage parts, complained about the FBI's repeated undocumented removal of salvaged plane parts from the hangar and the NTSB spokespeople were told to not discuss any possibility of the plane being the source of a criminal act.

Over the course of their investigations, the government agencies spent more than $40 million dollars of taxpayer money. It was the most extensive investigation ever into the most horrific air disaster in America.

18 months later, the FBI, now joined by the CIA, released its investigative findings on Flight TWA 800. They'd interviewed 244 witnesses in all. There were many more that had not been interviewed. The crash was not an obscure event. It had been seen by a large number of individuals over a widely-visible high-population area.

"There is no way a missile brought down this plane," CIA spokeswoman Carolyn Osborn said. "Based on analysis from 244 eyewitness reports, radar data, infrared data, and cockpit recorder information, CIA analysts have determined that the eyewitnesses' sightings thought to be that of a missile actually took place after the first of several explosions on the aircraft. What these eyewitnesses saw was, in fact, the burning 747 in various stages of crippled flight, not a missile."

Skeptics abound.

Those first responders in the Air National Guard helicopter included pilot Major Frederick C. Meyer and co-pilot Chris Bauer. Meyer was an attorney from New York when not active in the Guard.

Quotes from Meyer were placed on a conspiracy theory website called WINDS (World Internet News Distributary Source) and on a subsidiary of APFN.com (American Patriot Friends Network).

Meyer recalled his seeing the event while practicing helicopter landing techniques nearby, "I leaned forward in the seat to look up and look forward and began to scan the sky more intently than I would normally," because a small plane had also been cleared for landing on the same runway. "At that moment, I saw a streak of light moving to my left. It was very curious because it looked like the streak that you would see from a shooting star at night, except that it was broad daylight and the streak was orange-red in color. It lasted three to five seconds. There was an interval in which I saw nothing and then on the same trajectory, further to the left, I saw a high velocity explosion which to me looked like ordnance, a war head exploding. Whether it was a naval rifle, or a missile, or a bomb, I couldn't distinguish. Then a second high velocity explosion took place, it was brilliant white light. The third event was the fuel explosion."

Meyer tried not to form any conclusions and informed the NTSB of his unique position to view and decipher his sighting that day. "I stayed away from it because I really believe that I had a unique view and that it was my responsibility to be as precise and as accurate and to make no assumptions. I really believed that the NTSB would probably do video tapes of an interview and be very interested in having a very accurate, very carefully explained, but not analyzed eyewitness report to help determine the cause. I was wrong...That is what leads me to suspect, not to know, but to suspect that they knew before they asked the first question, what brought that aircraft down, because they did not seem to be interested in anything they heard."

A public hearing on the crash was conducted by the NTSB in December 1997 in Baltimore, Maryland. The day before the hearing was to commence the NTSB cancelled any comments from the

ERIC G. MEEKS

public during the hearings, claiming the FBI had requested the report not be influenced by the discussion of eyewitness accounts and explosive residue at the five-day hearing into cause of the crash and requesting that the NTSB avoid issues touching on the possibility that a missile or bomb brought down TWA Flight 800. The FBI was concerned that the hearing could create new controversy. The NTSB agreed with the FBI, stating, "Although it would normally be a part of NTSB practice to evaluate eyewitness observations of a particular accident, (we) have agreed not to do so." At the weeklong public event, little tolerance was made for those who wanted to include alternative causes of the tragedy. A reporter from Worker's World implicated the Navy as a possible source for the missile theory and called for an independent investigation and was quickly removed from the hearing. During his ejection, he shouted, "We have to know the truth!"

The FBI did release to the NTSB, their own accumulation of eyewitness accounts and resulting conclusions, which the NTSB assigned a subcommittee and research team to review.

The NTSB took four years to compile its findings and on August 23, 2000, released its own report which determined that the accident of TWA Flight 800 was the result of:

"[An] explosion of the center wing fuel tank (CWT), resulting from ignition of the flammable fuel/air mixture in the tank. The source of the ignition energy for the explosion could not be determined with certainty, but, of the sources evaluated by the investigation, the most likely was a short circuit outside of the CWT that allowed excessive voltage to enter it through electrical wiring associated with the fuel quantity indication system."

Sources:

Google groups, https://groups.com/forum/#topic/misc.activism.militia/63Ts_Llf Vpk, JEREMY CROCKERS LAST WORDS –.

LAPD Missing Persons Unit, MISSING PERSON PROFILE: JEREMY CROCKER, http://www.lapdonline.org/lapd_adult_missing_persons_unit/missing_person_view/470.

Unknown author, JEREMY FREEMAN CROCKER, The Charley Project, http://www.charleyproject.org/cases/c/crcoker_jeremy.html.

Unknown author, WITNESSES ALLEGE NTSB COVERING EVIDENCE OF MISSILE ATTACK: NTSB CLAIMS WITNESSES DIDN'T SEE WHAT THEY SAW http://www.apfn.org/thewinds/arc_features/government/flight_800_coverup12-97.html, December 15, 1997.

Various contributors, TWA FLIGHT 800, https://en.wikipedia.org/wiki/TWA_Flight_800, Wikipedia.org.

The memory of Eric G. Meeks.

POLITICS

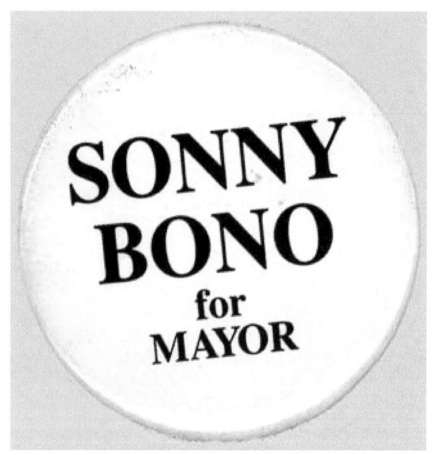

Campaign button

How Sonny Bono Killed Spring Break

The end started in 1986. That year there was a full-scale riot after a group of girls started baring their breasts at the beckoning of the boys. Hormones exploded. Fights ensued. Property damage resulted. I remember an ambulance being tipped over. Cement city trash cans were cracked like Humpty Dumpty. The police were called to squash the hundreds of thousands of teenage and twenty somethings who had made downtown Palm Springs their bastion. The Bacchanalia was soon to be over.

I remember being on a second floor balcony of what was then called Chillers Nightclub (now a steakhouse) overlooking Palm Canyon Drive as hundreds of police officers arrived in force, donning helmets, standing shoulder to shoulder with clear hard plastic shields in a double row phalanx formation and brandishing Billy clubs. A senior officer stood behind the solid blue line with a bull horn in his hands. He raised it to his mouth and blared, "You will leave the downtown area immediately. In five minute we will begin arrests." The officer saw me and a group of others on the second floor and re-peated his mantra directly at us. I went down to him and showed him my press badge from the local community college. At the time, I was the managing Editor of College of the Desert's student newspaper The Chapparal. I had a camera and clip board for note taking. He told me to stay behind him and to stay close.

As the clock wound down to the final few seconds before the PSPD were to march, the tension dripped from the air thick as mo-lasses. Youngsters couldn't believe that the police would actually arrest, let alone strike them with clubs. It seemed to be something from a 1960s anti-war protest come back to life. College aged kids were just having fun right? They were dressed in bathing suits and T-shirts, eating candy and drinking soda and whooping it up as they cheered each other on in an Easter week tradition that had gone on for decades. The police wouldn't actually strike them and mow them down in a show of force would they?

They did.

The bull horn blasted, "We will start arresting now. Vacate the area immediately. Please leave in an orderly fashion." The officer with the shields and clubs were told to advance. Girls were grabbed and struck with clubs. Boys who resisted were subdued violently. As the officers struck person after person, the injured were passed to the rows of officers behind the shielded front line to be treated by paramedics. As the police proceeded through downtown Palm Springs block by block the crowds soon realized that this was no laughing matter. Resistance was futile. Those who could run away did. Pandemonium ensued and the crowd struck up a terrified scream. Behind the police line was left a catastrophe of bleeding heads, drunken revelers sitting on curbs, cradling their injuries, rounded up by police men and women who brandished handcuffs, their captives placed in good old fashioned Paddy wagons awaiting transport back to the city jail. In the wake of the police and the newly departed, only mounds of trash, littering of cups and papers and other debris lined the streets, a reminder that only a few minutes ago throngs of people were there. City cleanup crews would sweep away the debris by morning. Spring Break, Easter Week as we knew it, was over.

Though it would continue on for five more years, it would never again be the fun frolicking youthfest revelry of college kids blowing off steam before returning to their dorms and higher education. The world had changed from the Technicolor days of Robert Wagner and Connie Francis in that memorable 1950s movie Palm Springs Weekend into something more sinister. The shadows were now walking amongst us, mixing in with the good kids, no longer hiding in silent numbers. They had come out to play and they were mean.

The townspeople had had enough. At the next available City Council meeting city elders were loud and outspoken in their dissatisfaction of the Spring Breakers. Merchants cried theft. Their expensive merchandise was stolen as the crowd shoved into the stores and only paid for dollar items. Hoteliers shouted that their rooms were destroyed and that the better clientele stayed away from the Palm Springs and its onslaught of raucous party-goers. The more affluent and genteel tourists sought safer vacations for themselves and their daughters. Restaurant owners struck a discord over the fact that their tables were left empty as the young crowd dined on cheap hot dogs, soda and those who could – and many who shouldn't – guzzled beer in the parking lots.

City tax dollars were down. Police, paramedics and cleanup costs were up. The benefits of the annual event were gone. The city had to do something.

The town went back and forth on the issue for the five years following the 1986 riots. The population was nearly evenly split between those who tried to cast Spring Break as a positive thing and those who were vehemently against the revelers. The next four Easter Weeks did not see a recurrence of the riot of 1986 but, the crowds did seem to get nastier. Women wore less and less. Thong bikinis became the norm; especially if the girl could ride on the back of a motorcycle called a crotch-rocket. Mixed in with the youths were gang members from Los Angeles and Riverside and other big cities; drug mules and gun toting gangsters who had no business hanging out with college kids. The mix was like a roofy. Overdoses were fairly common with such large crowds and a ready supply of dope. The daily paper would inevitably tell a tale of a girl who had her top ripped off, or who'd gotten raped. Fistfights exploded like dynamite within the crowd. It didn't erupt like the riot yet, the hedonistic detonations were enough to remind the town of the bad influences in the crowd. The Nay-Sayers of Spring Break took each incident as vindication that the annual event should go away and those who supported it saw their numbers dwindle.

I remember two of those years.

My brother and sister and I were cruising downtown – separately of course, in cars of other friends – and we'd hear rumors of a party at The Travelodge. By the time we got there, close to 10 pm, there were thousands of kids around the pool, loud music blasting, hotel room doors open, a keg of beer here, and a keg of beer there. Anyone with a cup could get a drink. It didn't take long for the police to show up in more than a dozen cars and start wading into the crowd with bullhorns, clubs and handcuffs. We ran. So did everyone else.

The following year, the same thing happened at the Riviera hotel. I recall hundreds of people lining the hallways, drinks in hand. Seeing inside one room and there five or six people sitting on the floor in a drunken stupor. There was a haze of marijuana smoke in the air. I never did make it to the pool that year. The police came. I left.

In 1990, a committee was formed to study the event and write proposals on what to do. The group met for nearly a year and in February, 1991, little more than a month away from the next Spring Break, the City Council and then Mayor Sonny Bono took action. Laws were passed.

No baring of breasts or buttocks would be permitted even on private property if it was visible from a public location. Thong bikinis were specifically outlawed.

Fines were increased for public intoxication and speeding.

Poolside drinking was prohibited after 11pm at any hotel.

Even brandishing a squirt gun was made a punishable offense.

Then the big killer: Palm Canyon Drive would be barricaded, eliminating the possibility of cruising.

And, it was publically posted, with press releases to college campuses via the City's Public Relations department to college campus newspapers statewide that Palm Springs was closed to anyone who wanted to come to town and create a ruckus.

The word got out. A lot fewer teens and twenty something's came to town. Those who did saw a massive police presence and if they got even an inch out of line they were arrested. The jails filled up quickly and each arrestee shared his bad experience with friends and family back home.

By 1992, almost none of the youths from earlier days descended upon Palm Springs for Easter Week. They found places like Cancun, if they had money and could fly, and Newport Beach, if they only had a car. They tried Tijuana but, most understood that Mexico wasn't a safe place to go get drunk on a large scale and it soon died off as a Spring Break site. For a few years there was no specific place to go for the young. There still isn't, at least not on the scale of the days of Palm Springs being the hot spot.

The city was left with a vacuum of empty space for what should be the end of season blow out of business. Instead, downtown was an empty hole. You'd think tumbleweeds should be blowing across.

Merchants developed a new mantra: We need business! We need business!

The city tried. They created a new Easter Week event called The Harvest and Wildflower Festival. Vendors were brought in to give the city an air of festivity. There were no wildflowers. There was no harvest. It was weak and drew no crowds. Villagefest grew on Thursday nights. At least that was a success. Even though the college kids only spent money on dollar items, soda and beer, their spending was missed somewhat. Hoteliers didn't miss their hotels being treated like hostels but, they didn't like empty rooms either.

For a few years, stores struggled to keep their doors open. Many closed. Downtown vacancies escalated. Windows that once show cased sparkling merchandise became dusty, dirty and empty. Citizens complained that not enough was being done to support business. Most of the citizens shopped elsewhere too. Palm Desert grew strong as a place for middle and upscale desert residents to buy appliances, clothing, books and music. Normal life's staples of living were commonplace down valley. The only stores that seemed to survive in Palm Springs sold cheap T-Shirt and tourist novelties. How many Vacation Palm Springs shot glasses does one need?

Somewhere during the 1990s, a formerly small time event grew in popularity to fill the void left by city fathers over the Easter Week vacancy: The White Party. The annual gay event had been quietly going on since 1988. Now it was the only game in town for the newly vacated city and it began hosting bigger and bigger events and moving closer to downtown rather than just poolside at a single secluded resort. It rented the convention center and brought in big name bands. It grew to a weeklong event rather than just a weekend. Multiple venues were added. And the gay men responded in droves, coming to Palm Springs to party.

The town was again divided on how to accept this newfound wealth of business. It was still a group of raucous alcohol drinking barely clad party goers. But, they were all adults and every one of them had rights that a partially 18 and under college crowd couldn't defend. Besides, it was becoming more and more politically correct to welcome the gay community into your own city and here was a group of mostly men wanting to fill hotel rooms, eat at restaurants, shop some at stores, and drink up life.

I remember one early morning in the mid-1990s, driving to my book store downtown Palm Springs before breakfast and seeing a bare legged man standing at the corner of Arenas and Indian Canyon Drive wearing a small biker's hat, a leather vest and a string black leather sheath that did nothing to hide to his buttocks and only accentuated his penis. I thought, "My how the world has changed."

Sources:
Shawn Hubler, PALM SPRINGS VOTES TO TONE DOWN EASTER BREAK, http://articles.latimes.com/1991-02-08/news/mn-641_1_spring-break, Los Angeles Times, February 8, 1991.
Kevin O'Brien, WHITE PARTY 2015: JEFFREY SANGER'S LONGTIME LOVE AFFAIR WITH THE DESERT CONTINUES, http://www.sdgln.com/news/2015/04/06/white-party-2015-jeffrey-sanker-longtime-love-affair-desert#sthash.Qu1fDnYl.dpbs, San Diego Gay and Lesbian News, April 6, 2015.
Carrolyn Patten, THE PARTY THAT NEVER ENDS, THE PARTY THAT NEVER ENDS, http://www.palm-springslife.com/Palm-Springs-Life/August-2013/The-Party-Never-Ends/, Palm Springs Life, August 2013.
The Memory of Eric G. Meeks.

Darrell Meeks, Richard Sroda
and the "T" Runs

In about 1994, the City of Palm Springs decided to outlaw the selling of books at Villagefest, rubber stamping the proposals of the Village-fest committee who in their infinite wisdom claimed used books brought the wrong type of people downtown. It sounds crazy right? It was. My Dad (Darrell Meeks) and I were the only used book sellers at Villagefest at the time. We took it personal.

It was a long and stupid fight. After about a year, we finally won and then only due to threatening a lawsuit against the city which would read negatively in the press towards the council and the Mayor. After all, the question was, "Which of the City Council wants to be known as the Councilmember who decided to ban books?" You'd think this should be a simple easy discussion handled in one meeting. It was anything but. My Dad and I spoke out in 30-40 City Council public comments, went to subcommittee meetings, prepared arguments, counter-arguments, documentation, etc., etc.

We did finally win though. Thing was, once we won, it was hard to not keep fighting for other causes and to speak out when other idiotic decisions were made. It became a sort of hobby for my Dad and me. We also collected a few really great friends during what became known as our 'Gadfly' days. One of those friends was Richard Sroda and he and my Dad became best-friend co-conspirators in gathering evidence from within the walls of City Hall, revealing the corruptness and stupidity of high level city administrators and elected officials. Richard and my Dad got very good at this.

There were whistle blowers within city staff and appointed officials who would privately contact my Dad, Richard or me. Generally, they would seek out my Dad at the weekly street fairs where he ran booths selling books or reading glasses and once with him, would whisper confidential information on something they thought was wrong. My Dad was a great talker. He would talk to anyone about anything and he just had a way of breaking down people's walls until they were comfortable he was just the right guy they could talk to. We built a sort of localized Underground Railroad of information. People in the community started noticing what we were saying.

We never had enough support to become popular by a majority of citizens. My Dad and I both ran for City Council in those years and lost. But, a significant plurality of Palm Springs citizens saw us as our own sort of Freedom Fighters who would wage war against City Hall for the little guy.

We got the California State Fair Political Practices Committee to rule that the Mayor couldn't vote on Airport issues and thereby won efforts for homeowners to get subsidized home improvements due to the extension of the Palm Springs Airport's runway. My Dad and Richard fought valiantly against the spending of a couple of million dollars for a train depot out at the end of Indian Avenue – something which still hasn't proven profitable or brought in even one extra tourist in over twenty years. We lost against a Utility Tax which was promised to be a short term budget fix and is still in effect twenty years later, and tried to support taxi drivers not being overly regulated by SunBus Corporation: their competition. We won a few and lost many more. But, regardless of the outcomes, lots of people respected our ability to gather information and embarrass the Council and city staff over and over again.

We built a following of silent citizens who would tune in biweekly just for our ranting and ravings because every Council meeting, and therefore every Public Comment, was televised on Public

Access TV and in a way, on a local level, we were a precursor to the reality TV stars who are so popular today.

And, while the outpouring of secret information from connected citizens, commissioners and city staff was significant, there was a particular endeavor taken on by my Dad and Richard that leveraged our already steady flow of information into something substantially more.

The following is an excerpt from a 2015 email of Richard Sroda's detailing my Dad's and his personal covert-ops they ran on City Hall in the mid-1990s:

The T run came about when Palm Springs City Hall went to a brand new computer system. They were supposed to convert everything on paper to electronic. One night we were sitting in my house in PS and I said to your Father, "I can't believe they are shredding all that stuff. It is too much work. Maybe they are just throwing it in the basket. We should check the waste bins." Your Dad loved the idea so the night before the scheduled collection date, I think it was Sunday night, (I believe trash was picked up on Monday), we took my old Toyota pickup and went to city hall to load the bags in the truck and then back to my house.

We would sit on the floor in the living room and go thru all the paper. There was a lot of stuff you didn't want to go through; half cans of soda, half eaten lunches, some of it was pretty messy. I told your Dad they should pass an ordinance that you could only put paper in the trash containers. We found a lot of good things to read at council meetings, like private memos. Your Dad loved doing it. There were some things we didn't even want to see. Some policeman had gone on medical leave and the staff threw away all his medical history and doctors notes instead of shredding them. I remember your Mom going through the stuff with us at least once.

When we were done we re-bagged everything and took it back to City Hall and dumped it in their dumpsters. After all, it was their trash.

City Hall had no idea how we were getting the information and to this day most of them do not know. They assumed we hacked their new computer system so the city hired an expensive outfit to go through everything. When I heard that I couldn't believe it.

Richard and my Dad would read these heretofore detailed private emails aloud in public comments and people were amazed at how much information we had about the goings on in private chambers at City Hall. In truth, the mid-1990s were times just slightly ahead of the days when shredding machines became common use and my Dad and Richard were simply data mining the trash. The effect upon City Hall top administrators of having emails and interoffice memos they thought would never reach public ears read aloud on television was profound.

More from Richard:

They even had someone call me directly and asked if we broke into their new system. I gave the guy a resounding "No", which was correct but also implied that they had a "snitch". That was even better for us but not too good for the grilling the employees must have had to put up with. The only time I spoke publicly about this was when I made the comments at your Father's funeral service in Yucca Valley.

Our online newsletter "Palm Springs News" was a follow-up to the T runs. Your Dad was excellent at getting information. He loved the swap meets. Everyone talked to him and he talked to everyone and they would tell him things that no one else knew. When he got some information he would call me and tell me who he talked to and what they told him. I would go to my computer and update "Palm Springs News." I know lots of people read it. One council man wanted to read it but didn't know how to use a computer. He went to city staff who showed him how to get to our newsletter. Several Desert Sun reporters read our newsletter to get story ideas to write about. They never credited us, of course. We even had a column called "WatchDog" with a picture of an actual dog. The dog belonged to a Desert Sun reporter I knew, but shall remain anonymous. No one knew who was writing the column, but everyone was guessing. The Chief of Police at the time told me that the first thing he did every morning was turn on his computer and go to Palm Springs News "to see if there was anything he needed to know." That made our whole effort worthwhile. I think we had the newsletter about two to three years. After that your Dad moved out of town and I moved out of town and it became too hard to get the stories.

Dad's dead now. It's been more than 20 years since the sun set on most of our politically active days. Yet, there's still a former Palm Springs Mayor out there in the world who hates me enough to uninvite me to lunch and a former Council woman who seems to paste her false smile on just a little too thick when we encounter each other around town. I've been black balled from the Rotary Club, snubbed by the Chamber of Commerce and lied about by the Downtown Development Director. But then there's also retired police, staff and other officials, both appointed and elected, and a nice mixture of aging Palm Springs residents who greet me warmly out at Villagefest on a weekly basis where I still sell books to this day.

Fun times.

Sources:
   The memories of Eric G. Meeks and Richard Sroda.

ERIC G. MEEKS

Tribal Casino Origins, The Octopus
and
Indian Head Nichols

Foreword
To all my readers, the police authorities, friends and family...
Sometimes these stories I am writing about in this book scare me.
People are still alive whose crimes I've detailed or their kids are alive
or maybe just someone who is a fan of the criminal mindset; lunatics
abound, at times. If there were a single story I've written that scares
me the most – this is it. Should anything malevolent befall me or my
loved ones after this book is written, I would ask that police start
with this story first as a source of the crime.

The Beginning
One man's vision: to create an economic empire that would sustain
generations of his family ad infinitum. On the path to achieving his
dream, he would assist a small group of Native Americans gain sovereignty and control their own land...under his leadership, of course.
The funny thing was he wasn't an Indian.

In 1978, a self-proclaimed expert in applying for government
grants swept into the Coachella Valley, promising to help the Indians
lift themselves out of poverty. His name was Dr. John Philip Nichols
and he brought along an eleven page resume of his capabilities. He
professed an expert on "socio-health and economic-development
planning" with more than 25 years' experience working for a com-

Fantasy Springs Casino in 2016

pany called Pro-Plan International, operating in both the United States and South America. He further claimed to have been a union labor organizer, a former manager of a South American Coca-Cola operation, that he was an ordained minister and that he had a Ph.D. He even claimed to have a Master Brewers Certificate. Nichols also came loaded with letters of recommendations from U.S. Senators, doctors, the U.S. Ambassador to Poland, and a Chilean priest.

His employers however did not have the capability to verify his claims. They were poor, dirt poor. They were the Morongo Band of Mission Indians in Cabazon. At the time, the approximately 500 member tribe was living on their own reservation with little or no money beyond the U.S. government subsistence that tribes across the country were being given as retributory hand-outs. Most of the tribe lived in small cinder-block or run down wooden homes. The roads were literally dirt, and the members lacked for everything that most American families considered necessities, let alone an education.

It was a different world in 1978, and the Indians needed a savior. The grandfatherly John Nichols seemed to be exactly what they were looking for, almost as if he was custom-made to deliver unto them a salvation of income generating business and growth and help them out of the century or more of depravity that the American Indian had been living in since the days of Custer.

He was immediately hired and put in charge of the tribe's health insurance fund. For reasons unknown, his employment with the Morongo Indians didn't last long and he was quickly let go. The tribe claimed he hadn't delivered services as promised. However, he did make quite the impression on another man in another tribe.

Joseph Benitez was the leader of the tiny Cabazon Band of Mission Indians in Indio. I know it gets a bit confusing. But trust me: the Morongo Indians live in Cabazon and the Cabazon Indians live in Indio on 1,700 acres of nearly uninhabitable raw desert, spread over three large parcels of land. It's just this sort of confusion mapped out by the U.S. government as they set up Indian reservations in the 1800s which spawned the cracked foundation leading to generations of crumbling decline in both Indian habitats and lifestyles. They created the perfect environment for a man like Nichols to step into a respected position by a people who were eager to accept any help they could get.

Once John Nichols was hired to help the Cabazon Band in Indio, help he did. At the time, neither the tribe's poorly educated leader, Joseph Benitez, nor did any of the small tribe of 24 Indians have full-disclosure of Nichols shadowy past, eventually uncovered by other reporters. My investigation indicates that more than one of those reporters may have been killed for his research. Within a dozen years of Nichols getting in bed with the tribe there would be a bloody trail of bodies left in his wake but before he was through, Nichols would open the floodgates on a revenue stream unparalleled on reservations nationwide. From the humble beginnings of unpaved roads and broken down trailers, he would rock the foundations of the United States in their highest court and win victories worthy of calling his efforts an empire. But first the groundwork had to be laid. Familial and emotional relationships had to be strengthened, pockets needed to be lined, emotional roads built and authoritative infrastructure inlaid. Almost immediately after Nichols was hired, he and his family became embroiled in the Cabazon Indians tribal affairs and the Indians either didn't care or couldn't get rid of their "savior."

According to SPY magazine, April 1992, John Philip Nichols did not have a minister's degree from the Philathea Theological Seminary which he listed as his Alma Mater. They can neither confirm nor deny his earning one. Nor does Nichols have a Ph.D. in any study and his claims to have been a union organizer failed to mention that he was jailed in Milwaukee for mishandling Teamster funds.

His resume also forgot to mention that he was arrested as a fugitive in Washington, D.C. in 1964. Nichols told Spy magazine that he, "…took the fall for Hoffa and his friends." In Nichols defense, the charges were eventually dismissed. He also denied that he was ever arrested a second time. This is where his shadowy past really starts to slip to the dark side. SPY's researchers discovered that Nichols criminal history was expunged from United States National Crime Information Center records, as if they never even happened. However, if someone goes abroad internationally and checks Interpol records they will find data on his second arrest. This leads to the belief that either Nichols was extremely lucky and clerical errors have covered his path or that he was very well connected and someone did him a favor.

Back to the tribe: initially, Benitez and other tribal members, including Art Welmas, who was vice-chairman of the tribe, were impressed and Nichols was hired. Since the tribe had no money to speak of, the Bureau of Indian Affairs (BIA) was convinced to grant $10,000 to Nichols to develop tribal-management skills. The Cabazon's were astounded that Nichols had convinced the BIA to grant the money and they quickly ignored Nichols most recent troubles with the Morongo tribe. Here was a man who could get things done. Nichols negotiated a 10-year contract which allowed him to be a partner in the tribe's proposed financial ventures, earning 50% of the profits from any future enterprises he brought to the reservation. Nichols was confident that he would be able to control this small tribe to do his bidding.

The Indians quickly placed Nichols in a leadership position and deferred all important decisions to him. He could not officially run the tribe, only an Indian of one-quarter verifiable bloodline or more could do that. So, instead, Nichols became its administrator and from this position he was able to control all aspects of tribal life: its money, its legalities, and its land. According to the Indian Reorganization Act of 1934, Indian reservations were sovereign nations and could enact their own laws and run their own territories outside of United States laws. However, until Nichols was hired by the Cabazon Band of Indians no one had tested the concept of Indian sovereignty to the extent that Nichols could foresee. In a way, he was a visionary and tribes all across the nation would benefit from his foresight.

The grandiose secret, and some would say devious, plans of Nichols needed funding in order to be implemented. His goal was to build an empire and if not directly challenge U.S. authority, he definitely didn't want to have to adhere to its binding agreements unless it suited his purposes.

The first steps Nichols took to build his economic and political empire were simple, yet they clearly showed the path he was choosing. He decided to sell tax-free cigarettes via mail order from a second-hand trailer on the reservation based on the legal reasoning that the Indians were not subject to taxes by the State or Federal governments. Untaxed cartons of cigarettes were sold for as little $8 and the business was an instant success. He had about 10 employees and they would all sit in the un-air conditioned trailer stuffing envelopes with cigarettes, working shifts that lasted all day – the Indians couldn't have been more thrilled. For the first time in their life money was rolling into their tribe.

Nichols paid tribal members about $100 a week. The enterprise was generating about $10,000 a week in gross sales, according to Nichols eldest son, John Paul Nichols, who left a job in Florida and come work for his father in 1979.

Two years later, they started selling untaxed alcohol too. But, the state of California sued the tribe for unpaid taxes and won. Somehow though, the state never received a check and the tribe was never pursued by collectors.

As John Nichols became more comfortable in his position as Tribal Administrator, he would talk to his new friends and brag about his connections. He claimed to have friends in high places and to have worked for the CIA and even been involved in an assassination attempts on Fidel Castro of Cuba and on Salvador Allende of Chile. Later, researchers and reporters would uncover connections of

Nichols that would also implicate him in drug running and arms supplying to Nicaraguan rebels. However, if pressed hard on any subject about which he did not want to disclose any specific facts, he would defer to calling himself nothing but a social worker doing the good work of helping out a tribe in need.

Not all the tribe members were comfortable with what Nichols was doing. Fred Alvarez, who was a tribal leader and former chairman, became suspicious. He noticed all the non-Indians that John Nichols was bringing onto the reservation and he began to quietly collect evidence of Nichols business dealings.

Wackenhut
From the very beginning, Nichols had tried to get the tribe involved in several deals that a mere social worker would've had little ability to negotiate. To help his endeavors, he proposed joint ventures with the then $600 million a year Wackenhut Corporation, which was based out of Coral Gables, Florida. Wackenhut corp. is a who's who of former espionage experts including CIA, NSA, Secret Service and FBI directors, ex-military personnel, former Joints Chief of Staff, and more. Wackenhut's legal counsel at the time was Edwin Meese III, who coincidentally was Ronald Reagan's Presidential Advisor and would in 1985 become the country's Attorney General. Wackenhut was the sort of company that select politicians and government officials could, and still can, go to and get things done when obtrusive things like laws and ethics prohibit direct official action.

It's very hard to prove anything in regards to what happened or all that happened between the Cabazon's, Nichols and Wackenhut, but, here's a chunk of what has been uncovered.

In 1979, John Philip Nichols and the husband of the Mayor of Indio, Peter Zokosky, created what appears to have been the first joint venture of Wackenhut and the Cabazons. Zokosky was the former President of Armtech, an ammunitions manufacturer, and Nichols sought Zokosky's help in attempting to create what would become known as Cabazon Arms, a weapons manufacturing plant on tribal land that could operate without concern for U.S. law with the ability to supply arms to rebels worldwide, regardless of whether or not Congress had passed a law forbidding such arms sales by a U.S. company. Their first customer was to be the Contra guerillas of Nicaragua.

Nichols and Zokosky even went as far as to bring a Contra leader to the Coachella Valley to participate in a field demonstration of night vision goggles from a lot of 300 they had purchased from a New Jersey company. The test was performed at Lake Cahuilla police firing range on the night of September 10, 1981, along with high-tech guru Michael Riconosciuto and Nichols' ever present bodyguard, Jimmy Hughes, an ex-Army Ranger Vietnam veteran. For two hours, the goggles were demonstrated for three Contras, one of whom was Eden Pastora, known as Commander Zero and another was Raul Arana, one of three rebel leaders within the Contras.

According to SPY magazine, in a letter dated August 1, 1980, the president of Wackenhut's international subsidiary, Robert Kirk, agreed to conduct an exploratory survey of Crown Prince Fahd's palace in Tiaf, Saudi Arabia, with the intention of creating a complete security system. However, a letter Kirk wrote to Nichols indicates that the Cabazon's were already engaged in soliciting for the private security contract for the Saudi palace and the letter recognized that the Cabazon's supplied the plans for the Tiaf palace. The Saudi government was interested enough in the idea that they conducted a background check on the Cabazons. Mohammed Jameel Hashem, consul of the Royal Embassy of Saudi Arabia in Washington D.C. wrote a letter to former South Dakota Senator James Abourezk at his offices in Washington D.C. seeking a referral regarding for the security proposal. Abourezk's response stated, "According to our black list for companies, the Cabazon Band of Mission Indians/Cabazon Trading Company and Wackenhut International are not included." The inference the Senator was not writing down was that neither the

ERIC G. MEEKS

Indians nor Wackenhut were Jewish owned or managed companies.
. When Nichols was asked by SPY's reporters how he could
get such a contract with the Saudi's he replied, "I know a lot of people."

Michael Riconosciuto was one of those people Nichols knew.
Riconosciuto was supplied to the Cabazon tribe by Wackenhut as a
computer programmer in 1980 and was described by Nichols as an
"Important asset" to the tribe. Unbeknownst to the Indians, Riconosciuto had a history of drug dealing and other shadowy schemes.
He had been arrested in October of 1972 for breaking and entering
into the home of his drug suppliers, only a month after being arrested
for manufacturing PCP and LSD himself. Both of these drugs require
an above average knowledge of chemistry to create. Strangely,
records show he was convicted of Grand Larceny the same day as
his arrest. He was given a 15-year sentence, but the very next day
his sentence was suspended. Most times, when these types of events
occur it indicates that a deal has been made with prosecutors for the
defendant to turn informant; though one has to wonder if perhaps Riconosciuto might have similar friends as Nichols, who also had his
records mysteriously cleared. A decade later, while in a Seattle prison
again on drug charges, he would claim involvement in what had become known as "The October Surprise" when it was theorized a conspiracy existed between Iran and Ronal Reagan for the hostages to
be held until Reagan was elected president. This allowed the political
backlash over Jimmy Carter's inability to free the Americans held in
their own embassy and the embarrassment which caused his defeat
at reelection.

It was also Former South Dakota Senator James Abourezk,
now a high priced and well connected Washington D.C. attorney,
who represented the Cabazon Indians in their partnership agreement
with Wackenhut Corporation to form a production facility called
Cabazon Arms. It became official on April 1, 1981, and was to be
located on the largely uninhabited desert wasteland of the Cabazon

reservation in Indio.

Working under the direction of the Special Projects Division of Wackenhut and in conjunction with the Cabazon tribe partnership, Michael Riconosciuto, who was dubbed Director of Research for Wackenhut, and Robert Booth Nichols, representing the tribe became business associates on the reservation in 1981.

I have to take a break here and explain something, because Robert Booth Nichols is still a bit of a mystery to me.

My research thus far – and I may have gone to print without full knowledge of who Robert Booth Nichols is – leaves me unsure about how Robert Booth fits into the Nichols family. Cheri Seymour, in her book The Last Circle: Danny Casolaro's Investigation into the Octopus and the PROMIS Software Scandal claims Robert Booth Nichols is of no relation to John Philip Nichols and that Robert was the son of a prominent Los Angeles doctor. This may be true. However, in later readings, which I now have trouble unearthing from the voluminous sheaf of papers and books I have researched to write this story, I remember a Jim Nichols saying, while attending law school at the time and talking to another reporter, that he had a brother who had been disowned by the Nichol's family due to the bad paths he had decided to travel. I'm now certain I will never know for sure. Perhaps their names are merely a strange coincidence. John Philips Nichols was born in 1925. Robert Booth Nichols was born in 1943. Robert could either be a much younger brother than John or Robert is the son of a very young John, who would have been only 18 at the time of Robert's birth. Still, another reporter stated that Robert Booth Nichols and John Philip Nichols are not related at all. Any scenario is possible, but I cannot verify this fact. If I had to guess, I would suggest that Robert Booth Nichols is the oldest son of John Philip Nichols. I also think that Robert Booth Nichols is the strongest connection the Nichols family had to international crime syndicates and world-wide espionage agencies.

So, Robert Booth Nichols and Michael Riconosciuto teamed

up together in 1981 in to help Wackenhut Corporation and John Nichols/Cabazon Indians create the first military weapons venture on the Cabazon Band of Mission Indians reservation. They operated under the business name of Meridian Arms, a subsidiary of Meridian International Logistics, owned by Robert Booth Nichols. Riconosciuto was the technical assistant for Wackenhut on the proposal because his past drug conviction would not allow him to get the necessary U.S. security clearance to be fully involved in the transaction. However, a letter obtained by reporter Danny Casolaro (who will be discussed later), shows that Patrick Cannan, Director of Relations for Wackenhut was able to push Riconosciuto's clearance through government channels after a meeting with Wackenhut's Indio Vice-President Robert Frye and Dr. Harry Fair, chief of propulsion technology at the U.S. Army installation in Dover, New Jersey. They had what's called a blackboard exercise on a railgun for the Army and Riconosciuto proved he completely understood the physics of how the gun worked and even made suggestions for the weapons improvement. It was a highly technical and theoretical exercise and Riconosciuto was a very smart man who proved he fully understood not only the theoretical physics of it, but the manufacturing realities of how to produce it and the military applications of the gun. After the meeting, Dr. Fair commented that it would be a shame if Michael Riconosciuto couldn't be used for military/research projects. Dr. Fair even went so far as to call Riconosciuto a "potential national resource." From the descriptions of the projects that Riconosciuto worked on for Wackenhut and John Booth Nichols/Cabazon Indians, it seems that Riconosciuto did get his security clearance. This sort of thing is difficult to prove since it is definitely into the area of "black ops" and "military research."

Riconosciuto brought the first incident of murder to the table when, In January, 1982, Paul Morasca was found hog-tied and fatally strangled by Riconosciuto in his San Francisco apartment. Morasca had been brought in by Riconosciuto to work with John Philip

Nichols on the Cabazon Arms transaction and Morasca had access to secret off-shore bank accounts with millions of dollars in them supposedly made from illegal drug sales; money that would now be used to start up a Military-industrial enterprise on the reservation. Three days after Morasca's murder, the aunt of another Riconosciuto workmate was murdered in what at first appeared to be a vicious mugging, but would later be found out to have a connection with Morasca's off-shore money-laundering.

The story gets far more complicated here and we'll delve a little deeper into the details later when we discuss the 1991 murder-suicide of reporter Danny Casolaro and The Octopus Murders. For now, let's witness a worried Riconosciuto making it back onto the Cabazon reservation to disclose his entanglements with the police and the murders and how he sought John Philip Nichols advice on the matter. Nichols listened to Riconosciuto's tale and basically told him not to worry about it. Nichols picked up his phone and told Riconosciuto that he was contacting his Los Angeles Attorney, to whom he gave a quick sketch of the gory details. After Nichols hung up, he told Riconosciuto the problem was fixed and for nearly a decade, Nichols statement held true.

Nichols, Wackenhut, and his tribe's desire for arms manufacturing knew no end. In 1983, the Cabazon Band of Mission Indians was given government clearance to manufacture weapons by the U.S. Department of Defense. Nichols began talks with Stormont Laboratories, a genetic engineering company in Woodlawn, California, about producing a biological weapons detector on the reservation while also promoting the Cabazon's ability to manufacture a 9mm submachine gun at a cost of $75 per gun. He claimed in a letter to Dr. Harry Fair, a leading propulsion technology expert, the weapons, "…meets the needs of a small, poor democracy."

On May 12, 1983, John Philip NIchols wrote a letter to La France Specialties of San Diego, another weapons maker, to discuss a cooperative venture on the reservation. They sought assistance in making and marketing armaments of various types. They all involved new technology not yet on the market, including: a 9mm machine pistol, an assault rifle with laser sighting, a long-distance sniper rifle with a one-mile plus range, a portable rocket system, a night-vision scope and a battlefield communication system that was undetectable by counter-technology of the day. There appeared to be some urgency to Nichols request of La France because he asked for a response in 90-days or less. The most likely answer to Nichols haste is that the Nicaraguan rebellion had heated up to a boiling point and Congress was set to enact the Boland Amendment, which would effectively prohibit all government agencies, the White House, Oliver North, the NSA, CIA and FBI included, from helping the Contras in any way. At the stroke of a pen, this would create a lucrative open market for Wackenhut and Nichols and the Cabazons to take advantage of.

It has been surmised that one reason for Wackenhut to see value in partnering with Nichols tribe of Indians is that, as a minority owned business, they would receive priority consideration for government contracts. Couple that with the new national recognition of Indian rights and the implied non-government intrusion upon tribal lands and there was a ready-made formula for a partnership able to conceal any activity desired. This was a match made in legal heaven. It allowed for a sovereign nation operating within the borders of the United States to do things that the United States itself could not do and yet simultaneously the government could distance itself from any knowledge of the corporation's activities.

From Weapons to Gambling

At the same time Nichols was leading the tribe into weapons manufacturing, the tribe diversified into their first profitable on-site reservation gambling venture: a Bingo Parlor, which they started in 1980 in a converted run down warehouse on the reservation. They expanded, thanks to a $90,000 grant Nichols was able to secure from the Department of Housing and Urban Development under the premises of building a museum of desert Indian history and culture. Instead of a monument to their heritage, the tribe erected a huge white tent and invited the locals in for a chance to turn in their cards for a quick return of cash. The parlor was a huge success, immediately filling night after night to the point of bursting the tent at the seams. The city of Indio and the County of Riverside however, were not thrilled with the Casino operating in their jurisdictions. Two weeks after the parlor opened it was raided by Indio Police and County Sheriffs. Employees, managers and customers were arrested on the grounds of participating in illegal gambling activity. Evidence and money were seized. Despite the raid, day after day the Indians opened the doors to the Bingo parlor and card room and every day more and more people came to try their luck. The raids continued. The casinos kept reopening after each one. And the people kept coming.

According to an ABC News 20/20 TV story in 1985, bingo was not enough to satisfy Nichols hunger for bigger operations in the early 1980s, nor would it meet the needs of the expanding of his commercial Mecca. He sought the assistance of three mob connected businessmen: Irving "Slick" Shapiro, Rocco Zangari and Tommy Marson of the Gambino crime family. Nichols wanted a card club attached to his Bingo Parlor. Marson was the money man and supposedly gave Nichols $50,000 to assist in starting an actual casino. This would become the genesis of their gambling empire in the Coachella Valley. A 30,000 square foot casino was added soon thereafter.

Prior to his Cabazon involvement, in the early 1970s, Irving Shapiro, a Jewish mobster known never to make a "hit" on Shabbat, Yom Kippur, or similar holy days due to his religious beliefs, started the Alfa Chemical Company. He was been accused of strong-arming Nevada hotels, forcing them to use his products. In 1960, Shapiro opened the Aku-Aku club in the Town House Motel in Toledo, Ohio.

In the mid-1960s, Shapiro obtained gambling licenses for Anthony Zerilli and Michael "Big Mike" Polizzi. All the names mentioned in this paragraph have east coast mob connections. Shapiro and his men were believed by authorities to have killed some 500 people over their lifetimes.

Rocco Zangari was a member of the Los Angeles based Caci family, under mob boss Peter Milano. He started off as a bookie in Palm Springs, where his brothers owned a restaurant and a gift shop.

Shapiro and Zangari ran the day to day operations of the Card Club and Bingo Parlor that, at the time was simply called Cabazon Indian Casino. It would eventually grow to be the Fantasy Springs Resort and Casino.

Zangari's involvement in the Casino operations would be short lived however. He was hired on a contract under the management firm of P.N. Associates, Inc., on September 25, 1980, and was discharged only 3 months later on November 5, 1981. Zangari filed a lawsuit to reclaim the money owed him for the uncompleted contractual amount of his services. Zangari lost the suit on the legal basis of a Federal statute called (United States Code) 25 U.S.C. 81, which basically states that a normal citizen of the United States can't sue an Indian except in very limited instances. However, the case against Zangari did reveal to Nichols and the tribe that they had a flaw in their executive structure. The flaw was that Nichols had placed himself in an ownership position of the Casino and he wasn't an Indian. He had his son, John Paul Nichols, signing contracts for the Indians and his signature left him arguably responsible for unpaid debts by the tribe or at the very least open to possible litigation should the tribe have a lawsuit thrown against them.

Zangari saw the flaw too and on January 28, 1982, appealed the lower court's decision to the United States Bankruptcy Appellate Panels Ninth Circuit Court. On December 25, 1983, the Appellate Court ruled in favor of Zangari on the basis that the tribe cannot claim sovereign immunity against a contract when they have entered into the contract as a partnership whereby some of their partners are non-Indians. The Appeals Court reversed the lower court's ruling, thereby making the Cabazon tribe and Nichols responsible to pay Zangari's, and other plaintiff's debts. Whether or not Zangari or others owed money by the Cabazon/Nichols operations were ever paid is uncertain. One thing that is true is that the Cabazon/Nichols venture could not have this kind of legal exposure if the full potential of the operation was to reach its maturity.

Even before Zangari actually won his case, the Indians and Nichols saw the writing on the walls and to prevent this flaw from becoming more prominent as the enterprise grew, the Casino filed for bankruptcy protection and reformed the partnership into a corporation under ownership of the tribe. Nichols rewrote his management contract and profit sharing plan to benefit the new legal entity and the tribe rubber stamped it. They were, after all, making more money than any other tribe in the country now with their new gambling enterprises.

What could possibly go wrong?

The Alvarez Murders
Almost every member of the tribe was willing to keep quiet and cash their monthly paychecks, no one else had ever been able to help them acquire. Still, not everyone on the tribe was willing to turn a blind eye.

Former Cabazon Tribal Chairman Fred Alvarez disagreed with current Chairman Joseph Benitez and Tribal Elder Art Welmas granting Nichols extended powers of control over tribal affairs. He suspected Nichols was mismanaging the tribe's money and that most of the profits were going into Nichols own pockets. Something was to be said for this as Alvarez found that his own share seemed to forever be small and Nichols appeared to have an endless pocket of cash from the first day he came to work for the Cabazon Band. Even though Alvarez was afraid of Nichols and rightfully so, he spoke out critically and publicly about the tribe's savior.

In 1980, Fred Alvarez wrote a letter to President Ronald Reagan, detailing the criminal enterprises of John Philip Nichols and seeking help in righting the wrongs being perpetrated on the tribe's reservation. Five copies of the letter were made and placed into Alvarez's personal files concerning what he considered mismanagement of the tribe's affairs.

In June of 1981, Alvarez spoke with the Indio Daily News saying that there were people on his own reservation who wanted to kill him because he saw he elaborate lengths Nichols and his group of immorally driven compatriots were willing to undertake. He spoke to an Indio Daily News newspaper reporter, telling him that Nichols was part of a larger enterprise wanting to "ramrod" Indian gaming through so they could then sponsor casinos across the country on reservations. He confessed that he was scared for his life because there were people working with Nichols who would "kill you," backing him. As Alvarez became more outspoken, the tribal council voted to send him away on trips.

The spark that ignited Alvarez's desire to speak with the Indio Daily News was probably lit in early June, 1981, when he returned from a conference in Denver, Colorado. While in Denver he was approached by a man who offered him a large sum of money if he would carry drugs back with him on the plane to California. Alvarez refused the request but, when he stepped off the plane onto the tarmac, the police were ready and waiting. They grabbed Alvarez and threw him up against a car. Apparently word had not made it back to the desert that Alvarez did not have the drugs on him. Police searched him viciously before letting him go.

Alvarez was sure of Nichols was mishandling the tribes finances for his own personal gain. He even told his sister, Linda Streeter that the non-Indians running the tribe were skimming gambling profits and that they wanted him dead. At the time, she didn't think he was serious but, Alvarez was sure Nichols wanted him gone.

Less than a month later, on July 1, 1981, Alvarez decided to meet with attorney Steve Rios in San Juan Capistrano and the current tribal chairman, Joseph Benitez, to discuss his accusations against Nichols. When Benitez arrived at Alvarez's Rancho Mirage home to pick him up for the meeting, no one came to the door. Upon inspection, Benitez found Alvarez, 32, in a chair in his back yard, shot in the head execution style, along with his girlfriend, Patricia Castro, 44, and his best friend, Ralph Boger, 42. All were similarly shot. The police estimated that the bodies had been dead for about two days. The crime remains unsolved to this day.

Sources claim the police did a poor job of investigated the Alvarez murders. Boxes of evidence, supporting Alvarez's claims that Nichols and Wackenhut were conspiring to skim casino profits and build weapons for the CIA to sell to foreign governments and Contra rebels were removed from Alvarez's home by investigators. But nothing ever came of the evidence. It's been said the detective who landed the case was friendly with Nichols. It is true that the detective took a vacation two days immediately after being assigned the murders, allowing the case to grow cold from the outset. What followed was the most cursory of inquiries and over the next three years the investigation drifted further and further into the department's bottom drawer files.

During the course of the investigation, all of the papers notes; the complete files, which Fred Alvarez supposedly kept at his home as evidence and supporting documents to verify his claims of illegal activities going on at the reservation, disappeared. The police would later say it wasn't at the home when they arrived; though earlier reports indicated different. The Indio Daily News wrote that Indio City Manager Philip Hawes confirmed that Los Angeles attorney William Cole was working on connecting the Alvarez murders to the Cabazon Casino and that the Sheriff's department had confiscated papers from the Alvarez home that he expected to be turned over soon. However, the Sheriff's department claimed no knowledge of such papers. Even the copies of the letter Alvarez had written to Ronald Reagan had disappeared, though; a response from Reagan on White House stationary somehow survived the lost paper trail. Reagan's response stated that Alvarez's claims against Nichols and Wackenhut were "very interesting."

The investigation eventually stalled due to "lack of evidence" and though it remained open, it became a cold case file and wasn't worked.

Finally, in 1984, Nichols's former bodyguard, Jimmy Hughes, 27, had an epiphany of conscience and informed police that John Philip Nichols and his two sons, John Paul Nichols and Mark Nichols, had given him $25,000 in cash and told him to deliver the bag money to two men in Idyllwild, a mountain town nearly an hour away from Indio, as final payment for the murders of Fred Alvarez and his unfortunate friends.

Peter Zokosky, husband to the mayor of Indio and a business partner of John Philip Nichols, joined Hughes in asking Indio Police to re-open the investigation into the Alvarez murders. The Indio police contacted the FBI and the Department of Justice who came out and asked Hughes to repeat his story. Consequently, he was offered participation in the witness protection program, which he turned down. Instead, he left town on his own. Instinctually, he didn't trust the authorities to be able to hide him from the far reaching tentacles of Nichols connections within the bureau. Hughes was right to be concerned about being held in protective custody away from anyone who knew him. Nichols might have been able to get him. Others would not be so smart about pulling at the threads of Nichols life as they investigated him and his empire. The thought of being whacked while behind bars, or snuffed out while being hidden by a few choice agents in some small town, did not appeal to Hughes. He made a wise choice and hid out on his own, relying on no one else, until a deal was worked out for total immunity in exchange for his testimony.

Hughes testimony was videotaped and filed away. The investigation stalled again and two months later he grew impatient and hosted a private press conference, where he stated, "Nichols admitted to me the ordering of the Alvarez murder. He stated there was a U.S. government covert action." Including, "...pressures from unknown Washington, DC, government agencies which have caused a possible shutdown of the case."

Hughes also openly admitted he was suspicious of authorities and that was why he refused the FBI's offer of witness protection. "Nichols has made a deal with the FBI through the Wackenhut Corporation. Possibly, he himself (Nichols) has been protected by the FBI." He went on to say that Nichols plan had been to manufacture weapons for use in Central America and Alvarez was going to interfere with the plans. Furthermore, he thought Wackenhut and the U.S. governments were jointly involved but, he couldn't speak to this without risking other people's lives. He did talk about a deal Nichols had had made to send arms to Contra leader Raul Arana for use in his planned invasion of Nicaragua. Hughes went on to say Fred Alvarez was "interfering" with covert operations and that the investigation into his murder was being blocked by "an agency out of Washington."

According to SPY magazine, the Riverside County District Attorney's office appeared to pursue Hughes claims. The case was assigned to investigator Patrick Kenneally but surprisingly he was ordered to stop his investigations. He wanted to continue, so he pursued it privately; until a death threat stopped him in his tracks. Decades later he would tell a reporter that two men in suits showed up at his home and menacingly showed him pictures of his children getting off the school bus. Soon thereafter, he quit his job and moved back to the Midwest.

Press reports confirm that at the time of the murders, John Philip Nichols, Peter Zokosky and Wackenhut vice-President Robert Frye were on an exploratory trip to Quebec, Canada, determining if they could jointly purchase Valleyfield Chemicals Products Corporation, a weapons propellant manufacturer, for $18million. The trio then flew to New Jersey, Indian and Washington, D.C. Along the way they'd put together deals to purchase weapons cartridges and 300 pairs of night-vision goggles. According to an exposed Wackenhut memo, the goggles were supposedly for sale to the government of Guatemala, which was legal. Later, in his questioning by the D.A., Zokosky refuted this claim, stating that they were for the Nicaraguans.

Peter Zokosky also explained how Nichols appeared to know that Alvarez was dead, even though Nichols had been out of town at the time. Zokosky claimed that it was he who told Nichols about the murders. Upon hearing the news, Nichols picked up a phone, punched in some numbers and said, "Alvarez is dead." He paused as someone else spoke on the other end of the line. Then Nichols said, "Okay, so long" and hung up. Zokosky was surprised at how little emotion Nichols showed.

Nothing was ever done by Federal officials about the arms sales and nothing was ever done by County officials about the murders.

In 1992, when SPY magazine was conducting interviews in the decade old case, they asked a Riverside County law enforcement official about the videotape of Hughes testimony and if it the D.A. was planning to pursue the allegations. "I was meaning to get around to that," was his answer. He never did get around to it and Jimmy Hughes, the former Nichols bodyguard who had been willing to testify, whereabouts were now unknown. The only reference to his location was 'somewhere in South America.' Peter Zokosky had moved out of the area too and was rumored to be living somewhere in the Los Angeles area. Neither was contacted.

Attempted Murder

In 1984, John Philip Nichols wife died. He was then 60 years old and he replaced her with a 27 year old heroin addict. Nichols liked the woman but not the drugs; he sought out a local hit man to take care of his problem. It turned out the hit man was an undercover cop and Nichols was recorded on police tapes stating, "I'll pay 500 and 500" – $500 for each murder. He wanted the dealers who were supplying his girlfriend to disappear, forever. Nichols even offered the undercover agent future work in South America, saying, "I do a lot of business down there," and suggested the hit man move to Las Vegas where opportunities for this kind of work came easier, even suggesting he might find himself with a guaranteed long term income.

In January, 1985, John Philip Nichols was arrested for the solicitation for hire of the murder of five people. Indio Police Captain Carl Kennedy told reporters at the time that the investigation stemmed from confidential informant who came to police on their own and agreed to wear a wiretap to capture Nichols request for a contract killer on tape. Captain Kennedy did declare the department was unable to connect the murder for hire of the drug dealers plot with the Alvarez Murders from four years ago.

Strangely, the case never went to trial even though the taped evidence was completely damning to Nichols defense. On February 22, 1985, Riverside County D.A.s, in a deal approved by Judge Noah Jed Jamin, instead allowed John Philip Nichols, 60, to plead no contest to two crimes and he received a four year sentence, plus a $5,000 fine. He then served 18 months and was released. The agreement did end Nichols administration of the Cabazon Indians and for the remainder of his life he only worked as a mental-health counselor for the tribe. California law precludes allowing anyone convicted of a felony to own or operate a casino.

District Attorney Bob Dunn told reporters that during an interview with probation officers, Nichols said he was "assisting law enforcement in stamping out local drug trafficking." Dunn denied there was any truth to Nichols comments.

During his imprisonment, the chief administrative position fell to Nichols eldest son, John Paul Nichols, who was 30 at the time and had been working in management positions for the tribe since 1979. The younger Nichols had an M.B.A. from Claremont College, his tuition paid via a loan by the tribe. Under John Paul's leadership a $150 million deal with the Colmac Corporation was secured to have a power plant erected on the reservation. It took another seven years to complete construction – but, in 1992 the plant began generating power and is still doing so. Initially, none of the plants 60 jobs were filled by Indians.

California vs. Cabazon Band of Mission Indians
In 1986, the state of California decided to shut down tribal casinos, which had proliferated to multiple reservations in California and the government chose the Cabazon Band of Mission Indians in Indio (and co-defendants the Morongo Band of Mission Indians in Cabazon) to be their battleground case. Since there were multiple incidents in the tribes past where the city of Indio and Riverside County Sheriff's had attempted to shut down the tribe's gambling operations unsuccessfully, the state felt they had ample evidence to support their claim of prohibiting gambling on Indian land.

Since the claimants were a state and federally recognized Indian tribe, the case fell under the jurisdiction of the United States Supreme Court. California and 19 other states would join together as plaintiffs against the tiny tribe from Indio.

The state of California argued they had never approved of the tribes Bingo and card room operations, verified by the fact that police had raided the illegal casinos repeatedly; that these venues violated state laws against gambling and they requested the court recognize their authority in governing reservations within their boundaries and by their subsequent Counties and City ordinances. Furthermore, California presented as evidence that six states; Alaska, California, Minnesota, Nebraska, Oregon and Wisconsin had been granted criminal jurisdiction over reservation lands by the U.S. Congress in its passage of Public Law 280 in 1953, which shifted legal authority from the Federal government to States in the enforcement of their own criminal justice system in relation to "Indian Country."

The Cabazon Band lawyers argued before the high court that California laws on gambling were more regulatory than criminal and therefore not enforceable on reservation lands since the laws did not expressly prohibit gambling in totality and therefore the state had no authority to try and oppose Indian tribes from establishing their own laws in regards to casinos. They supported their case by offering evidence of existing legal non-Indian card rooms throughout the state and the fact that the state of California sponsored its own lottery.

On February 25, 1987, the Supreme Court ruled in favor of the Indian's in what would become known as the "Cabazon Decision, going beyond the simple ruling of whether the tribes could establish a casino; but addressing "Indian Sovereignty" and granting a destiny of self-determination to tribal governments throughout the United States. The ruling made a lasting impact upon the tribes and the United States of America. Indian tribes could now legally say they were their own country. Sovereignty was addressed and established in the ruling.

The work of the Tribes and their casino managers was not done though. While the High Court had ruled in their favor, States still had wiggle room to attempt some legislating of their gambling operations, such as: the types of games and the amount of taxation. Congress was finally very quick to act. In 1988, the California legislature passed the Indian Gaming Regulatory Act (IGRA) which detailed which types of games the Indians could offer on their reservations and also established the first solid framework for regulating the fast growing Indian Gaming industry. It seemed that even with the legalization of their casinos, the government saw the

Supreme Court ruling as justification for intervening more on their lands. Indian casinos would grow at an alarming rate; from a dozen in the country in 1988 to almost 300 ten years later. On a Federal government level, the National Indian Gaming Commission was formed within the Department of the Interior, with its chairman appointed by the President, for the purpose of enforcing the goals of the Indian Gaming Regulatory Act, including: promoting tribal economic development, creating self-sufficient and strong tribal governments, maintaining the integrity of the Indian gaming industry and ensuring that the tribes are the main beneficiaries of their gaming activities.

Instead of the Supreme Court ruling giving the Nichols family and the Cabazon Band of Mission Indians greater freedom in their tribal activities and Casino operations, it instead had established a clear gateway for government intrusion into their economic revenue streams.

It was time for the Nichols family to double down.

Nichols to More Nichols

In 1990, John Paul Nichols was succeeded by his younger brother Mark Nichols as the chief administrator of the tribe. Funny thing though, SPY magazine claims that Mark Nichols has a 1978 drug conviction from Florida for the sale and possession of LSD for which he served a 6-month sentence in jail. Perhaps it's not a felony charge or perhaps state authorities simply didn't care. Mark is a step-Indian of sorts too. In 1985, he married Cabazon tribe member Virginia Welmas who is apparently not related to the earlier mentioned Art Welmas. Strange for people with the same uncommon last names in such a small tribe to not be related but, that is how the story goes. In 1988, Mark Nichols had proven his leadership prowess by helping the tribe open a pari-mutual off-track betting parlor attached to their existing card club. He also saved the tribe money by getting a $400,000 grant from the Department of Housing and Urban Development to pay for the 30,000 square foot remodel to accommodate the card room and of-track-betting center. The tribe now had a full-fledged official casino and business was good.

Although the money flowed, not all tribe members believed they were getting a fair shake from the Nichols family. Some still believe that money was skimmed and there was mismanagement of tribal funds.

There was a challenge to the Nichols's authority over the tribe in June of 1991 when former leader Art Welmas and tribal member, Linda Streeter, sister of deceased leader Fred Alvarez, openly attempted to attend a tribal meeting to oppose the continued leadership of Mark Nichols and his family. Nichols marriage to Virginia had helped anchor his relationship with the Cabazon's and to further cement his position. In addition, his daughter, Alexis Nichols, had been elected Treasurer of the tribe.

To get rid of Nichols they were going to have to get rid of current Tribal President John James. Only weeks before, Art Welmas and Linda Streeter had tried to vote out James in a Tribal Council session and failed by one vote. Now, instead of being allowed to enter the Cabazon Bingo Palace where the Council meeting was being held, as was their right, armed guards obstructed their path, preventing them from entering and inside the tribal members accused them of damaging the "dignity and integrity" of the Cabazon's by speaking about private tribal business to the press, – a serious "no no." They were also accused of taking actions that were to "the detriment of the band" by holding a meeting of a majority of its 19 member council win their earlier attempt to oust James.

The Tribal Council accused Welmas and Streeter of stealing tribal food: Fried Zucchini. Most of the meeting, which was more of a hearing, was used to read aloud into the minutes news articles to prove that the intentions of Welmas and Streeter was to get rid of not only James but of the Nichols'. Welmas and Streeter countered with the argument that James was only their stooge and that the Nichols family wanted to get all Indians out of the tribe so they could run the reservation as their own private enterprise.

Mark Nichols chaired the hearing against the rebellion and it was effectively crushed. Welmas was expelled from the tribe for ten years; Streeter for 10. Each was fined $50,000. Streeter went into hiding, moving outside of California and Welmas returned to his home threatening to shoot anyone who came to his house trying to evict him. He publicly defied the Nichols and his fellow tribe members, saying, "This is my land. This is Indian land."

In defending his commitment to bettering the tribe, Mark Nichols spoke with SPY magazine in 1992 and made it evident that every tribe member received $35,000 as an annual salary that year. What he didn't mention, and the magazine's reporter found out was that the payment was a onetime installment due to the sale of a chunk of reservation land to the state of California. Up until that time, the official profit sharing to the tribal members had only grown to $150 apiece a year.

Danny Casolaro and The Octopus
On August 10, 1991, a freelance journalist named Danny Casolaro was found dead by a maid in a Sheraton hotel room in Martinsburg, West Virginia. Casolaro's wrists were slashed and the bath water he lay in was tinged red from his own blood. The authorities filed it as a suicide. However, many theorists claim his death was the direct result of his conversations with Robert Booth Nichols about details involving the Inslaw Computer Scandal, which then segued into the Cabazon Indian tribes' casino, Michael Riconosciuto and the Wackenhut connections.

Casolaro's investigation seemed to branch out to such a wide net, connected to so many other conspiracies: The October Surprise, the Iran-Contra scandal, drug trafficking, pirated espionage software, money laundering by the Bank of Commerce and Credit International, and more. The conspiracy was so vast, so far-reaching and involved so many high level government officials and their legions of secret organizations, agencies and syndicates that Danny Casolaro dubbed the working title of his research "The Octopus."

Danny was born June 16, 1947 to a prominent McLean, Virginia, obstetrician. His parents were wealthy but, they had their own share of grief. Danny was one of six siblings and one child was born with a heart defect and died quickly after birth and an older sister died from a drug overdose when Danny was still a child. In his early twenties, Danny dropped out of college, went exploring for Incan treasure in South American and came back home to fall in love with a married woman who eventually divorced her husband and married Danny. They had a son together.

Thirteen years later they would divorce. In the interim, Danny became a stringer for the National Enquirer tabloid magazine and then a reporter for a new technology magazine called Computer Age. He had lots of friends, was well liked and had the habitual characteristics of many young men in the 1970s: he smoked too much though he was physically fit, drank sometimes to excess, and was considered good looking. He was popular with the ladies after his divorce and was known to have a handful of women who he slept with on a regular basis. Some would call him "Peter Pannish" saying he was like a boy who wouldn't grow up. His boyish charms ended though when he was at work, where he was quite obsessive. He worked his leads at Computer Age with ferocity and was the magazines number one reporter during the 1980s, a very exciting time for computer development.

In 1989, Danny took a second mortgage on his home and bought Computer Age. Then, in 1990, he got a lead on a story that would become his life's work and ultimately lead to his early death. It was a lead on the decade old Inslaw computer lawsuit Nancy and William Hamilton filed against the Federal government over their claims that an executive level conspiracy within the U.S. Justice department conspired to steal their software program PROMIS, which was originally created to keep track of complex legal investigations and high-security clearance national & international espionage operations. PROMIS stands for Prosecuting Management Information Software.

During the course of the Hamilton's lawsuit, in March, 1991, Michael Riconosciuto, now 44, sent the Hamilton's an affidavit saying he had installed a "back door" to the PROMIS software allowing the United States to access other countries versions of the software and in effect electronically eavesdrop upon their NATO partners who had purchase and installed the software as the latest in computer operations management technology. Specifically: Canada, England and Middle Eastern countries were being watched, although any country, and there were many, who utilized the software and were in danger of pre-programmed hacking access by the U.S. government.

Here is a copy of the affidavit:

I Michael J. Risonosciuto, being duly sworn, do hereby state as follows:

(1)During the early 1980's, I served as Director of Research and Development for a joint venture between the Wackenhut Corporation of coral Gables, Florida, and the Cabazon Band of Indians of Indio, California. The joint venture was located on the Cabazon reservation.

(2)The Wackenhut-Cabazon joint venture sought to develop and/or manufacture certain materials that are used in military and national security operations, including night vision goggles, machine guns, fuel-air explosives, and biological and chemical warfare weapons.

(3)The Cabazon Band of Indians are a sovereign nation. The sovereign immunity that is accorded the Cabazons as a consequence of this fact made it feasible to pursue on the reservation the development and/or manufacture of material whose development or manufacture would be subject stringent controls off the reservation. As a

minority group, the Cabazon Indians also provided the Wackenhut Corporation with an enhanced ability to obtain federal contracts through the 8A Set Aside Program, and in connection with Government owned contractor-operated (GOCO) facilities.

(4)The Wackenhut-Cabazon joint venture was intended to serve the needs of a number of foreign government and forces, including forces and governments in Central America and the Middle East. He Contras in Nicaragua represented one of the most important priorities for the joint venture.

(5)The Wackenhut-Cabazon joint venture maintained close liaison with certain elements of the United States Government, including representatives of the intelligence, military and law enforcement agencies.

(6)Among the frequent visitors to the Wackenhut-Cabazon joint venture were Peter Videnieks of the U.S. Department of Justice in Washington, D.C., and a close associate of Videnieks by the name of Earl W. Brian. Brian is a private businessman who lives in Maryland and who has maintained close ties to the U.S. intelligence community for many years.

(7)In connection with my work for Wackenhut, I engaged in some software development and modification work in 1983 and 1984 on the proprietary PROMIS computer software product. The copy of PROMIS on which I worked came to the U.S. Justice Department of Justice. Earl W. Brian made it available to me through Wackenhut after acquiring it from Peter Videnieks, who was then a Department of Justice contracting official with responsibility for the PROMIS software. I performed the modification to PROMIS in Indio, California; Silver Spring, Maryland; and Miami, Florida.

(8)The purpose of the PROMIS software modification that I made in 1983 and 1984 was to support a plan for the implementation of PRMOIS in law enforcement and intelligence agencies worldwide. Earl W. Brian was spearheading the plan for this worldwide use of the PROMIS computer software.

(9)Some of the modifications that I made were specifically designed to facilitate the implementation of PROMIS within two agencies of the Government of Canada; the Royal Canadian Mounted Police (RCMP) and the Canadian Security and Intelligence Service (CSIS). Earl W. Brian would check with me from time to time to make certain that the work would be completed in time to satisfy the schedule for the RCMP and CSIS implementations of PROMIS.

(10)The proprietary version of PRMOIS, as modeled by me, was, in fact, implemented in both the RCMP and the CSIS in Canada. It was my understanding that Earl W. Brian had sold this version of PROMIS to the Government of Canada.

(11)In February 1991, I had a telephone conversation with Peter Videnieks, then still employed by the U.S. Department of Justice. Videnieks attempted during this telephone conversation to persuade me not to cooperate with an independent investigation of the government's piracy of Inslaw's proprietary PROMIS software being conducted by the Committee on the Judiciary of the U.S. House of Representatives.

(12) Videnieks stated that I would be rewarded for a decision not to cooperate with the House Judiciary Committee investigation. Videnieks forecasted an immediate and favorable resolution of a protracted child custody dispute being prosecuted against my wife by her former husband, if I were to decide not to cooperate with the House Judiciary Committee investigation.

(13) Videnieks also outlines specific punishments that I could expect to receive from the U.S. Department of Justice if I cooperate with the House Judiciary Committee's investigation.

(14) One punishment that Videnieks outlines was the future inclusion of my father and me in a criminal prosecution of certain business associates of mine in Orange County, California, in connection with the operation of a savings and loan institution in Orange County. By way of underscoring his power to influence such decisions at the U.S. Department of Justice, Videnieks informed me of

the indictment of these business associates prior to the time what that indictment was unsealed and made public.

(15)Another punishment that Videnieks threatened against me if I cooperate with the House Judiciary Committee is prosecution by the U.S. Department of Justice for perjury. Videnieks warned me that credible witnesses would come forward to contradict any damaging claims that I made in testimony before the House Judiciary Committee, and that the U.S. Department of Justice would subsequently prosecute me for perjury for my testimony before the House Judiciary Committee.

One week after Michael Riconosciuto delivered the affidavit to the Hamilton's he was arrested for solicitation and manufacturing methamphetamines and confined to a federal prison in Tacoma, Washington. While in prison, Riconosciuto originally tried to turn states evidence and join the Witness Protection Program, using his knowledge of Wackenhut and illegal drug and weapons trades in the 1980s as a bargaining chip. Federal prosecutors weren't interested.

With his trial headed towards an inevitable conviction and no help forthcoming from the Justice Department or other government agencies, Michael Risconsosciuto sought advice and help from the only sympathetic ear to his cause, Bill Hamilton, the original owner of the PROMIS software. Hamilton put Riconosciuto in touch with reporter Danny Casolaro and Riconosciuto finally found a friendly ear willing to help the framed drug dealer and technical expert go public with his cries of concern. Riconosciuto was ready to go public with all his knowledge about Robert Booth Nichols acting as a U.S. operative involved in illegal drugs for weapons pipelines and the U.S.'s covert management of the entire affair via the NSA, CIA and FBI through Wackenhut. The Octopus reached as high as the Reagan and Bush presidencies and their tentacles reached all over the world, even connecting Colombian cartels with the drug riddled streets of many of the United States biggest cities; and, for his part, Casolaro was eager to add another tentacle to The Octopus.

As the Hamilton's Inslaw/PROMIS lawsuit was proceeding through its own highway of road blocks via lawyer's offices and private judge's chambers, Michael Riconosciuto found himself embroiled in a Tacoma, Washington, trial that was not going well for him and would ultimately lead to a lengthy prison sentence.

Despite his extensive evidence submissions and testimonials by himself and other key witnesses, the prosecution had an equally substantial arsenal of evidence and witnesses to contradict him. Michael's claim boiled down to this: He was being set up as a drug trafficker by the very people who were actually doing the drug trafficking on a much larger scale. As proof of the conspiracy, prior to his arrest, he had personally been responsible for gold transfers, money laundering, "virtual dead drops," altered Automated Clearing House daily financial reconciliations, and other transactions for various nefarious men, including Robert Booth Nichols, and others involved in National Security.

Riconosciuto continued to ask for insertion to the Witness Protection Program, which was repeatedly denied or simply not responded to. He also sought help from the Financial Crimes Enforcement Network (FINCEN), a division of the U.S. Treasury, to substantiate his claims of Wackenhut's and corrupt Justice Department officials involvement in money laundering and drugs for arms sales stemming from a Northern California group he referred to as The Company.

Again, despite substantial evidence that his claims were valid and verifiable, no help was forthcoming. Riconosciuto was even able to pinpoint a $50,000 cash payment Robert Booth Nichols made to Mike Abbell, who was a former U.S. government prosecution attorney, now handling the defense of Colombian Cali drug Cartel leaders Gilbert and Miguel Rodriguez and Jose Londono, who at the time controlled 80% of the international cocaine trade. The money was to be used to influence court officials, witnesses and/or jury members, by either bribes or terrorism, to decide in favor of the defense.

Up until now, Danny Casolaro had been using Robert Booth Nichols as a second source to verify many of Risconsciuto's claims. Often times he would call Nichols immediately after talking to Riconosciuto in jail or call Riconosciuto directly after talking to Nichols. Over time, Danny came to rely heavily on Nichols, eventually trusting him while his faith in Riconosciuto eroded. Phone calls to Nichols stepped up and Danny and Nichols often found themselves in deep cross-country conversations that would go on for hours in the wee times of 11pm to 2pm.

It was on August 5, 1991, five days before Danny's death, when the paths of Casolaro and Riconosciuto converged on Colombia drug kingpin attorney Mike Abbell and intelligence operative/weapons entrepreneur Robert Booth Nichols. A virtual hornets' nest of trouble was about to swarm out of its secret hidey-hole.

Riconosciuto, in his efforts to cough up some testimony worthy of plea bargaining away his inevitable trial conviction, was revealing to Danny that Abbell had used illegal techniques, like bribing witnesses and conspiring with investigators and judges and other foul methods to get the drug kingpins safely out of the country. Danny, being a good reporter started checking facts with people who could verify them. He called Robert Booth Nichols and challenged him about his connections with Mike Abbell and the Colombian Cartel. Nichols was furious and told Danny he should end this investigation or he might "end up dead." Casolaro also called a Texas oilman billionaire, Bob Bickel, and others. Danny felt he was nearing the head of The Octopus and he could foresee more than a year's worth of work coming to its final fruition. He was determined to go to Martinsburg, West Virginia, so he could get close to the source. Casolaro called ahead, bought a plane ticket, and set up appointments with the people he most wanted to see. He brought along a large penda flex of information containing detailed notes about the various arms of The Octopus he had uncovered so far. He typed for two days on his manuscript for the book wherein he would reveal all the secrets he had unearthed. On August 7, 1991, he left for West Virginia.

In the final three days before his death, while in Martinsburg, Danny Casolaro supposedly met with several tentacles of his Octopus: Bill Turner, a whistle-blower from Hughes aircraft; two FBI agents who were to give interviews and evidentiary documents relating to the Iran-Contra scandal and Ronald Reagan's October Surprise (a meeting which they later denied ever occurred); and a retired police officer who would reveal another tentacle concerning Laotian drug lord Kuhn Sa's proposed Golden Triangle.

Also, in those final days, Casolaro spoke over the phone with FBI agent Thomas Gates as a confirmation source on many of the arms of The Octopus and to Robert Booth Nichols who was willing to cooperate with information regarding drug sales, money laundering and weapons distributions throughout the world.

Nichols was livid at Danny for wanting to investigate in the direction of Mike Abbell and the Colombians. Nichols would later claim to both the police and to reporters that from August 5th on, the day he first learned Danny was researching the Cali Cartel, he'd tried to warn Casolaro off that investigation.

Nichols, Riconosciuto and other friends also knew that after West Virginia, Danny Casolaro would still have one tentacle of The Octopus to work on. That tentacle would be completing his investigations into the Cabazon Band of Mission Indians in Indio, Wackenhut and the Nichols family.

Danny Casolaro never got to make that trip out to the desert to research the final tentacle of the Octopus. On August 10, 1991, he was found dead in his Martinsburg, West Virginia Sheraton hotel room by a maid.

When the police arrived at the hotel, minutes after getting the 911 call, they found Danny in a bath tub full of pink water, tinged with his own blood, his wrists slashed deeply numerous times. The investigation would quickly be dubbed a suicide. The body was rushed over to the mortuary, before a coroner's exam even occurred and the body was embalmed, virtually ruining any solid conclusions which could be obtained from forensics. Only after he was embalmed would his family be notified of Danny's death.

Danny's family and friend cried foul right from the start. There was no way, in their minds, that he would've committed suicide. Danny had even recently paid his homeowners insurance. Would a guy do that right before he killed himself? Numerous discrepancies in the investigation, or lack thereof provided a clue that Danny Casolaro was murdered. What happened to his Penda flex full of notes and the manuscript for his book? Both were gone from his room, never to be seen again. The police would hear none of it and closed the case.

There is so much information about Danny Casolaro and The Octopus that it could easily fill a book and indeed, it has. Numerous books have been written on the subject. My favorite one was called The last Circle: Danny Casolaro's Investigation into The Octopus and the PROMIS Software Scandal by Cheri Seymour. Take the time to Google Danny Casolaro and The Octopus and you will lose days in reading one of the most riveting stories I unearthed in writing this book. Thankfully, shortly before his life ended, Danny Casolaro uploaded a very complete record of his notes and manuscript to a Boston University group discussion room website under the title The Octopus.

Campaign Contributions

Throughout the 1990s the Cabazon Band of Mission Indians became one of the country's biggest contributors to political campaigns. Just about every politician from the local dogcatcher to the U.S. Presidential candidates had their hand out and the tribe was donating money like they were printing their own; which they basically were – in the form of casino chips.

The tribe had grown to be a substantial force since the early days of selling tax-free cigarettes and firewater to the white man. They'd successfully battled the local police, the County Sheriffs, even the State Attorney General against the Supreme Court. Now, they needed backing for continued success and to deepen their hold on the entities that could turn against them at any time. The Indians realized they had to become reliable economic political partners with the very civic leaders who at one time couldn't lift a finger to help them. It was the same motivations and actions which had created American enterprises like the railroads or the modern day military-industrial complex, only now it was to be the civic minded Indians complex.

Perception was the key to guiding influence. Photo opportunities were available. Stand alongside the community, state and national leaders in a handshake pose, broad smiles gleaming and the mention of a check or a donation or a contribution to a worthy cause. Fire trucks were bought and donated to cities. Computers were provided for schools and Hospital equipment. All sorts of charity stemmed from the ever growing casinos. The marketing approach worked and most desert residents saw the Indians as good neighbors. Critics grumbled that it would be nice if everyone could be selective in what their taxes paid for but critics were few and their grumbles were hushed under the thunderous applause of acceptance.

Civic leaders lined up for the chance to be included in the photo opportunities of special gifts to the benefit of their respective constituents, organizations and districts. Behind the scenes, less publicized, an envelope handshake would pass from Tribal leaders to the politicos who always needed to be re-elected in exchange for support, if the tribe should ever need it.

But, getting involved in politics can, at times, get messy.

The United States Supreme Court may have considered Indian sovereignty a weighty issue in 1987 but, seven years later on June 21, 1994, they decided that sovereignty did not extend to the Indians being able to implement video-slot machines at their new and improved casino facilities without first getting permission from the state.

The justices were not willing to hear an appeal from eight joint plaintiffs of tribes, three from California – including the Cabazon's – in which they claimed they should not have to negotiate a compact with their respective states. The word "Compact" became the new word for "Contract" or "Treaty," which no state wanted to enter into with an Indian tribe again; lest they have to modify or break it in the future. Many of the Indians had already installed the machines, some as many 1,000 machines in their casinos, without adherence to state laws which expressly forbid such gambling. Card rooms and bingo were OK; but, full blown Las Vegas style slot machines were another thing entirely.

To segue briefly, let me say, during this time in the desert history, I was sleeping in the back of my bookstore in downtown Palm Springs, going through a divorce not of my choosing and not wanting to make a decision which might force me further down a path I wanted to go. My store was a half block away from the tented Bingo and Card room Casino of another tribe: The Agua Caliente Indians. Late one night or very early on a still darkened morning, I was woken by the air brakes of several 18-wheeled delivery trucks. This was strange because most deliveries were done between 6 and 8 in the morning when dock workers and hotel staff were on shift. I thought nothing about it and went back to sleep. Once the sun was up, the local news was rampant with stories about hundreds of video-slot machines being now available at the Spa Casino across the street from me. Apparently, as told to me by a friendly News Director at a local radio station, the Indians had brought in the machines on produce trucks to hide them from the state.

There are ways to get around the law. On the reservation, authorities had little legal muscle to raid the now legal casinos but, had they been able to stop the slot machines in-transit, on California soil, it would have been a different matter entirely. The machines made it safely to the hotel casino in the luxuriant company of heads of lettuce, juicy tomatoes and radishes – relish the thought.

Slot machines installed, the tribes welcomed the new infusion to tribal profits. Something about pulling the handle of the machines is addictive for the gambler and the longer people will sit there drinking the free alcohol, able to smoke freely in an ever-growing smoke free world and occasionally seeing the lights sparkle in front of them to declare another random ticketed payout, the more the Indians made. However, the Supreme Court was saying that the tribe had to negotiate a compact, which meant paying some type of taxes and limiting what sort of growth the tribes could anticipate.

Even though the Supreme Court would not listen to their appeal, the tribes still had a case pending in the 9th District Court of Appeals where they pinned their hopes. The tribes were arguing that the video-slots were not unlike the states own lottery machines. Indian slots paid out in tickets that were redeemed at cashier windows. Their casinos were eerily quiet, unlike Las Vegas where coins fall into a silver metal tray beneath the slot machines. It was this standard that created the similarity to California Lottery machines.

Both the Supreme Court and the Appeals Courts ruled in favor of state regulation via a compact with the tribes. The tribes complained bitterly that the rulings could cost them hundreds of millions of dollars in revenue. No sympathy was to be publicly found. Behind closed doors though, negotiations began.

In 1994, newspapers began running articles on Indian tribes contributing heavily to Democratic candidates coffers. Republicans, like California Governor Pete Wilson, were not so willing to accept the tribe's money. However, at the state level; Gubernatorial candidate Kathleen Brown, Attorney General Candidate Tim Umberg, and many other from state Assemblymen to County Supervisors, to City Council candidates were all willing to accept check or other denominations to forward their cause to get elected. Money poured out from many tribes throughout the state and the Cabazon's were not shy in their in their generosity. Mark Nichols was repeatedly shown to be alongside a known politico as they professed their accolades and support for each other's Mutual Beneficiary Societies. Often the reasons given publicly for the politicians to be seen with Nichols and tribe members was the candidates support for Indian sovereignty and to prevent another broken treaty. The tribes were not shy in stating that they were doing what was necessary to foster the elections of leaders who were supportive of their cause. By October of 1994, more than $500,000 had floated from Indian casino tables to candidates and shortly after Nichols met with Brown he publicly pledged to personally raise another $1.1million for Brown and another $550,000 for Umberg.

The tribes were particularly displeased with Governor Wilson's refusal to negotiate on a satisfactory timeline to legalize the machines. Wilson publicly despised the devices and had a persistent strategy to delay compact negotiations as long as possible, leaving the fate of the tribes and the machines in a constant state of limbo; all the while pursuing legal channels to end the placement of the slot machines.

In November, 1994, Californians re-elected Pete Wilson. Both Kathleen Brown and Tom Umberg were defeated in their respective bids for political office.

In other legal-political affairs, the Cabazon Band was not so generous. A neighboring tribe of theirs that had not been so fortuitous in the new gambling era, the Torrezs-Martinez tribe of the Salton Sea vicinity, wanted Federal permission to vacate their claim to many thousands of acres that had literally gone underwater back at the beginning of the twentieth century when a Colorado River calamity had created a waterway spill forming the Salton Sea over the top of their reservation. The Torres-Martinez tribe sought legislative relief from the United States Congress that would permit them the opportunity to buy land in Indian Wells and Rancho Mirage and then construct a casino on it. Even Lee Iacocca, an Indian Wells homeowner, was willing to partner with the tribe.

But, the Cabazon Band saw this effort as infringing on their market place and in a way that could be devastating to their own financial interests. So, the Cabazon Band used their newfound connections to squash the deal. Congress did not pass favorable bills that would allow the Torres-Martine tribe the ability to lift themselves from the poverty that the Cabazon's had so recently experienced. The Cabazon's convinced Democratic Senator Diane Feinstein to pull her support for the measure and it died in committee.

In the Cabazon's defense, Mark Nichols wrote a letter to the Editor of the Los Angeles Times stating his disagreement with the Times reporting on the issue and claiming that the Torres-Martinez tribe had been offered three different "options of compromise" to address their needs. According to Nichols all were rejected by the Torres-Martinez tribe. The Torres-Martinez now owns a casino close to the Salton Sea, far from a large and lucrative population and in no way comparable to the Fantasy Springs Resort and Casino, and in no way competitive.

Legal and political tension was mounting in the state as the tribes continued to keep the slot machines in their casinos, claiming that they were on Indian sovereign land. Some Californian's thought that while the Indians had elevated themselves, they had simultaneously reduced the rest of the population to second class citizens, since only a tribal member could own a casino within the state. In the spring of 1997, the U.S. Attorney General declared that due to the lack of a compact between the state of California and some Indian tribe's, soon Federal Marshal's, which is the only government agency with exclusive authority over the reservations, were going to have to raid and confiscate the slot machines and other illegal gambling devices from reservation casinos. By this time, many tribes in California had signed a compact allowing for a small measure of taxing casino profits in return for a limited amount of slot machines and other controversial types of gambling. Under California law, any gambling where the bet is made against the house was illegal, including blackjack. It's classified as Class 3 gambling. Nine tribes throughout the state had still refused to sign the compact which would severely limit this type of gambling. Five of them were in the Coachella Valley: The Cabazon Band of Mission Indians, The Caliente Band of Cahuilla Indians, The Cahuilla Band of Mission Indians, and the Morongo Band of Mission Indians, and The Twenty-nine Palms Band of Mission Indians.

Richard Milanovich, tribal chairman for the Agua Caliente Band in Palm Springs, told the L.A. Times that two-thirds of their profits come from class 3 gambling and that they use the money to provide health insurance and educational scholarships for tribal members.

U.S. Attorney Nora Manella responded that the fact that a criminal enterprise is profitable is no defense. If it were, then drug dealing would be legalized. She said that there were 12,000 illegal slot machines in the state of California and it was her job to enforce the law. No exact timeframe was given for her ultimatum to remove the machines and she said the Marshal's would act according to the law when the government was ready.

Some citizen's cried out in the Indians defense and a rally of some 3,000 individuals, mostly casino employees and Indians, gathered in downtown Los Angeles, vowing to fight the government crack-down. The protesters stood on the steps of the Federal Courthouse and shouted at the building that they would defy all orders and that the Indians were once again being sold a trail of broken dreams and promises. Tribal spokespeople said that more than 15,000 jobs were created statewide by tribal casinos which infused some $450million into state tax coffers and employee wages.

It was a largely peaceful demonstration. No arrests were mentioned in the papers and at the end of the day the protesters went to a picnic in a nearby park. To continue their campaign for slot machines, blackjack and Indian sovereignty, California tribes went on a media blitz, utilizing television, radio, newspaper and billboard advertisements to promote their cause. Action movie star Steven Segal was hired to be their TV spokesman.

On Thursday, June 18, 1998, a Federal Grand Jury indicted Cabazon CEO Mark Nichols, along with Public Affairs Director Greg Cervantes, for the laundering of hundreds of thousands of dollars in illegal campaign contributions. U.S. Attorney Nora Manella said there was no proof that any of the candidates, nor their staffs, who accepted the money were aware that the money was illegal. The candidates would get off Scott-Free.

Nichols would not be so lucky and claimed that the indictments were politically motivated and perhaps he was right. None the less, he was served. The indictment said that Nichols had recruited employees, sometimes coercing them, to make $1000 contributions (California's legal per person contribution limit) to candidates of Nichols choosing. Nichols would give the employee the $1000 either from his own pocket or from casino bank accounts, the employee would make the necessary legal disclosures and the money would go to the candidate. Nichols and Cervantes claimed that the money evidenced as flowing from the casino to its employees were bonuses that just happened to match the exact amounts which the employees had given candidates.

Nichols was charged with seven counts of using conduit donors to funnel thousands of dollars in illegal donations. Cervantes was charged with two accounts of laundering money and making false statements to the Federal Elections Commission.

In November, 1998, the Indians won another huge victory in the legal arena when multi-tribe sponsored statewide initiative, Proposition 5, was approved by 62.4% of California voters. The initiative had been opposed and financially backed by many Las Vegas casino corporations and this us vs. them dictum helped fueled Californians response at the ballot box. The proposition, among other thing, forced the Governor to sign a compact with the tribe, permitted

249

gambling devices and lotteries. It finally legalized slot machines and allowed for trust funds to benefit nongaming tribes.

The Indians could now have full blown Las Vegas style gambling within California's borders.

Another victory was handed out too when the charges of money laundering against Mark Nichols and Greg Cervantes were dismissed by a federal judge. On December 16, 1998, U.S. District Judge Audrey B. Collins handed out a 16-page opinion which declared that Nichols and Cervantes were "versed in the minutiae" of election law regulations as proof that they were knowledgeable of whether or not they were committing a crime. But, she went on to say that the law was ambiguous as to what a contributor was and that doubts in the law were to be "resolved in favor of the defendants."

Nichols and Cervantes were delighted with the ruling even though it still left them culpable for one felony conspiracy count each and two misdemeanor counts of making contributions in another person's name.

The U.S. Attorney's vowed to appeal and on February 9, 1999 Mark Nichols high hopes of complete dismissal of the charges were dashed against the rocky shore of mainland legal views when another federal judge refused to dismiss the last remaining charges. This cleared the path for prosecutors in the remaining charges against Nichols and Cervantes in their attempts to defraud the Federal Elections Commission. U.S. Attorneys said they may still seek a reversal of the earlier dismissal and Nichols and Cervantes attorneys claimed they might seek an appeal against the recent court ruling.

In September, 1999, Mark Nichols gave California Governor Gray Davis the highest honor known to any Indian tribe and an honor that is rarely given to anyone except a real Indian. Nichols gave Davis an Eagle feather in a ceremony befitting orchestrated to celebrate the conclusion of negotiations on the compact detailing the states involvement with tribal casinos. This was in addition to the $113,000 donation made by Nichols and the Cabazons to Davis' election campaign.

Unfortunately, there was one hiccup in the event. The California Department of Fish and Game determined that it was illegal for a person to own the feather of an Eagle, which is an endangered species. The fine for the possession of a single Eagle feather is a fine of $1000 and is punishable by up to 6 months in jail.

To mollify the issue, the Cabazon's stated that they did not "give" the feather to Davis. Rather, it was entrusted to him. For his part, Davis found an exception to the law saying he would safe keep the feather utilizing a California law that allows for the state to own endangered species in much the same manner as the state owns zoos. The feather remained on display in the Governor's office as a symbol of his treaty with the Indians.

For all his political wrangling, Mark Nichols now had a target on his back and was to be hung out to dry. On Thursday, October 14, 1999, Nichols and Greg Cervantes found no alternative except to plead guilty to the money laundering charges federal prosecutors were pursuing against them. Specifically, they admitted to funneling $41,000 to the Bill Clinton-Al Gore presidential campaign fund. Federal law limited the contributions to $2,000 per person, at the time. Under the plea agreement reached with prosecutors, Nichols would pay a fine of $200,000 to the court and $56,000 to the Federal Elections Commission and serve three years' probation. Cervantes would pay a fine of $13,000 and be on probation for a year. Their sentence would be officially served after the New Year.

When Nichols and Cervantes finally appeared before U.S. District Judge Audrey B. Collins for sentencing on February 28, 2000, the judge ordered Mark Nichols to quit associating with campaign fundraisers for 5 years. Prosecutors tried to sway the judge into imposing a 3 month prison sentence on Nichols. But, the judge denied the request. Instead, she ordered Nichols to 30 days of home arrest and increased his probation to 5 years, adding that he must not "associate directly or indirectly or indirectly with political fundraisers," including, but not limited to, benefits, fundraising dinners, or other events to collect money for political purposes. In essence, Nichols political career was over. However, his CEO career for the Cabazon Indians was not yet finished. The tribe gave Nichols an interest free loan to pay off his fines. He would continue on as the chief administrator of the tribe – for a while.

In March of 2000, Proposition 1A, also known as the Gambling on Tribal Lands Amendment, was passed by 64.5% of California voters. The statewide ballot initiative, funded largely by contributions of Indian tribes and their casinos modified section 19, Article IV, of the California constitution further reinforcing Tribal Rights to conduct all types of casino gambling on Indian reservations while simultaneously limiting state rights to regulate them.

Much of the success from the effort to get this initiative passed can be laid at the feet of Mark Nichols and the Cabazon Band of Mission Indians. Nichols may have been under investigation for falsely filing campaign contributions; he and the tribe may have pushed the envelope on Indian casino operations – some may say they broke the laws to get the machines running. Certainly they orchestrated many other nefarious schemes and plots that we don't even know about, because we only know what was written about and presented in court and anyone who knows anything knows that you never catch the criminals for every one of their backhanded deeds. You only catch them at the one they did a little too openly. For all their underhanded and law breaking ways, the Nichols family, from their father through every one of his sons, created the empire John Philip Nichols had begun some 20 years earlier. The day Proposition 1A passed; there was a lot less need to operate from the shadows.

But Nichols was still obligated to fulfill the terms of his plea bargained conviction and during his probation, on July 30, 2002, Mark Nichols and the Cabazon tribe members met with the New York Gubernatorial Candidate Andrew Cuomo at the Fantasy Springs Casino to donate $25,000 to Cuomo's campaign as payback for

Cuomo's helping the tribe when Cuomo was Bill Clinton's Secretary of Housing and Urban Development. During his tenure as Secretary, Cuomo had been instrumental in assisting the tribe to obtain a designation as an "empowerment zone." This granted them access to federal financial benefits – grants and tax breaks – for the improvement of impoverished tribal lands. At the time, the tribe was making millions and millions of dollars annually from their casino. Though Cuomo's opponent and countless commentators asked him to return the tainted money, I found no record that he did.

In 2003, the Cabazon Band of Mission Indians gave $75,000 to Governor Gray Davis's re-election campaign against Arnold Schwarzenegger. Davis lost the election.

Embezzlement

Apparently, not all government officials can be bought and in 2001 the Nichols family had a bad year.

On March 17, 2001 the family patriarch, John Phil Nichols, had a seizure resulting in a heart attack. He died the same day. His obituary in the Los Angeles Times both praised and scandalized him, saying, he had launched the Cabazon Band of Mission Indian into business ventures of card rooms and bingo parlors, the sale of tax-free cigarettes and discount liquor and that under his leadership the tribe had benefitted from improved health care and educational opportunities. The Times highlighted Nichols as the leader of the legal fight when the Cabazon's and the Morongo Tribes teamed up to win a victory for Indian tribes throughout the nation in the Supreme Court. The resulting landmark decision guaranteed Indian sovereignty and created the opportunity for Indian gaming. The Times also vilified Nichols for his conviction in the 1984 murder-for-hire plot and noted his two years in prison. John Philip Nichols was 76 at the time of his death.

Meanwhile, back at the reservation, the youngest of the Nichols brothers, 46 year old Robert Moses Nichols had a good job.

He'd been promoted from working as the card room manager in 1996 at the Fantasy Resort and Casino to his new position as Director of Gaming Operations in 1999. Less than a month after climbing to a new rung on the ladder of corporate success he was fired after being caught with his hand in the cookie jar. Someone in the tribe must have had concerns about the Nichols's and their money managing ability. Two generations of Nichols had built the tribe from poverty to some of the wealthiest Native American people in the country. But, the Nichols family had left a trail behind them and someone must've had enough; because on November 30, 2001, Robert got a Thanksgiving surprise when he was indicted by a Federal Grand Jury out of Los Angeles on charges of embezzlement.

Assistant U.S. Attorney Elliot Krieger said Robert may have stolen more than $500,000 from the tribe's casino from 1996 to 1999 though they could only prove $17,200 was gone. Robert was indicted on nine counts of embezzlement and one count of theft. Authorities felt they had proof Robert was going to the card room cashier windows at the casino and cashing false "paid-out slips." Robert claimed he needed the money as reimbursement for tournaments and other promotions that either never really happened or had already been paid. A Federal Court would soon issue a summons for Robert, then living in Yucca Valley, to surrender himself to authorities.

On December 20, 2001, Robert pleaded innocent to the charges. In the interim, he also was under investigation for bilking $23,500 from Las Vegas casinos.

In April of 2002, Robert Moses Nichols changed his plea to guilty on five counts of embezzlement and theft in a plea bargain with the U.S. Attorney's office. His crimes carried with them the possibility of up to 25 years in prison and a $1.25million fine which would be determined at a July 22nd sentencing hearing. He would also be prohibited from working in or for a California or Nevada casino ever again.

According to the Wall Street Journal, Robert Nichols was

sentenced to one year in prison and forced to repay the money he stole from the tribe. Like his father John Philip Nichols, Robert could never work in a casino again.

Mark Nichols Ousted

When it rains, it pours, even in the arid landscape of desert casinos.

In May of 2005, the Cabazon Band of Mission Indians voted unanimously to fire Mark Nichols as CEO, Duff Wrenz as Chief Operating Officer and Greg Cervantes as Public Affairs Director, for mismanaging of tribal funds. Nichols was not fired over the IRS audit of a $145million tax-exempt building bond, which was to be utilized for essential public services and instead was questionably purposed to finance the construction of the current 250 room Fantasy Springs Hotel and its adjoining 97,000 square foot Convention Center. That tolerant attitude changed when the tribe found itself in a financial quandary and had to disband their police force and fire departments, including possibly having to auction off their squad cars, fire trucks and other public safety gear to maintain fiscally responsible. The tribe had had enough. Too many irregularities were found in the budget review and the blame was laid plainly at Nichols feet. Even the tribe's Treasurer, his now ex-wife, Virginia Welmas-Nichols, voted to oust him.

Nichols executive leadership position was his downfall, as he was opposed to reorganizing in the face of declining casino profits when the country slipped into the early stages of the looming national economic depression. The ramifications of the impending IRS audit and the competition from other tribes expanding casino operations in the desert were becoming serious issues. To top this off, Nichols formerly friendly Cabazon Tribal Council friends (now totaling 35 members of the tribe) didn't see eye-to-eye with him on his opposition to reorganizing.

Mark Nichols and the other two executives supporting his policies were escorted out of the casino and shown the way off reser-

vation immediately by tribal and casino security, ending nearly 30
years of the Nichols family leadership over the Cabazon Band of
Mission Indians.

Cutting the public safety departments saved the tribe $5.5mil-
lion annually. The damage done by Nichols relentless desire to expand his lucrative empire at the expense of the Indians was
detrimental to the tribe's budget, but not significant enough to warrant bankruptcy. Tribal second vice-chairman Marc Benitez said it
would take about a year to restore full stability and budget security.
Some large scale projects would be put on hold temporarily as the
tribe restructured but, he felt assured that the profits from the casino
would eventually restore the tribe to its pre-existing budgetary levels
and beyond.

A Google search about Mark Nichols life after his being
ousted from the Cabazon tribe revealed he had 13 followers and
132,028 views on his Google Plus page. It also showed he wrote the
following quote in a January 26, 2013 blog posting, his only blog
posting:

"The only suggestion that I offer is watch for any angst developed by forcing the process. Remain relaxed and settle into it.
You're not going anywhere as part of you is already there. Let
thoughts pass as you feel for that completely relaxed feeling, relax
into it further and just let thoughts float by and keep relaxing deeper.
As you integrate all of our masks fall away as the stream of thoughts
dissipate and evaporate leaving you integrated in your pre-adulter-
ated center. Remember you are already there; it's not a matter of
going somewhere. Effort can become an obstacle. May you and all
that is, know they are one. Namaste."

On his Google Plus page, Mark Nichols showed his place of
residence to be Pau Pau, Moorea, Tahiti. On his Facebook page,
Mark Nichols showed his residence to be Mount Shasta, California,
and he claims to be living the life of a painter and poet. His page also
showed a lot of photographs of himself in his glory days as CEO for

the Cabazon tribe when he ran their casino and other operations, standing alongside such notables as Al Gore, State Assemblyman Cruz Bustamante and California Senator Barbara Boxer, among others.

Robert Booth Nichols

There is one character in the Nichols saga whose tale is best told on its own. His tale is such a mystery that I felt it best to give him his own chapter.

Born, March 6, 1943, Robert Booth Nichols led a life of normalcy. He dropped out of high school and worked as a salesman for a security alarm company. The location of his childhood is unknown. Much about him is unknown. What is known is that he became involved with what he thought was the CIA; recruited when he was 22 or 23 years old and thereafter lived mainly in the shadows of the real world; popping up into verifiable existence from time to time. On a few of those occasions when he did surface, Robert Booth Nichols claimed to be involved in, or to have knowledge of, nearly every national and international conspiracy of the day; from the Bay of Pigs to the Iran-Contra Scandal and beyond. As the 1980s slipped into the 1990s, Nichols' life seemed to take on an even nastier turn in the darker shades of his nether-world and continued up until his death, or disappearance – another uncertainty. The full truth may never be known about this man.

To tell his tale, I have to ask the readers forgiveness for digressing into this sub-chapter. Much of Nichols life has nothing to do with Palm Springs or the Cabazon Band of Mission Indians. The part of his life that was spent out here in the desert is so significant that I cannot feel I have done the story of Indian Casinos and sovereignty justice without completing this one biography.

In Cheri Seymour's book The Last Circle: Danny Casolaro's Investigation into the Octopus and the PROMIS Software Scandal, Seymour says plainly that Robert Booth Nichols was not related to

John Philip Nichols. Yet, in another document (which I have now laid aside and cannot easily reference because the foot-high mounds of research I have accumulated) I know I came across a paragraph which stated that a Jim Nichols, who was attending law school in the 1970s, told another reporter that he had a brother who had gone down a very dark path and had been disowned by the family. Either way, I can no longer verify Robert Booth Nichols family tree. Perhaps that is what he intended when he gave up a traditional hard-working life and became a spook long long ago.

He described his first three jobs in a deposition taken in 2008: "The first one was when I first met them, was to speak to a woman who stayed at the Surfrider Hotel and find out why she was in Honolulu and who she was seeing and have cocktails with her. If possible…"

"A Chinese woman that was in Honolulu that stayed at the Princess Kalani Hotel and to see who she was seeing and what she was doing…"

"A trip to Australia to see who was speaking, to the best of my recollection, and negative – when I say negative, to see who they felt were being anti-American interest in an area that was formally an R and R location, Sydney, for U.S. forces."

One very specific rule that his handlers told Robert he had to obey was that he was never ever to pay taxes again in his life. Something most Americans wish they could get away with doing. He was also promised complete immunity from federal law for anything he might do in the future. This worried Nichols in the beginning. He was receiving a paycheck from what appeared to be a regular U.S. company at the time. Throughout his life, the company that paid him might change but, it was always a front for what he was really doing. He questioned his handlers on this. They told him again and again that he was supposed to never file a tax return again in his lifetime. He was also told never ever to publicly reveal the projects he worked on. They would all be covert operations in the United States national security interests.

Over his life, he was involved in many secret operations. Here's a list of a few I have found reference to:

Nichols claimed that Sam Giancana was his business partner and that Nichols mentor was the head of the Yakuza in Hawaii.

He ran drugs to and from a Singapore drug lord in exchange for weapons.

He helped create the drugs for weapons pipeline that started as the October Surprise, aimed at keeping the U.S. embassy hostages in Tehran, Iran, thereby depriving Jimmy carter the chance of appearing a capable President and allowing Ronal Reagan to win the Presidential election in 1980. After Reagan's victory, these same channels flowed into a new conspiracy which became the Iran-Contra Scandal.

He helped facilitate a covert business venture called The Company whereby a group of agents, local police officials and judges, grew marijuana and made methamphetamine on Federal land and on an Indian reservation. This occurred in and around Marin County for the purposes of distribution and sale in Los Angeles, and eventually other major cities in the United States as a way to generate cash to fund other covert operations.

He was involved in the Lockerbie Pan Am Flight 103 plane bombing over Scotland in 1988.

He created a drugs-for-weapons exchange with warlords in Lebanon, under the guise of rebuilding the country, as part of a CIA covert operation in the 1980s.

He claimed involvement with the Mai Hua and Tong crime families of China.

He sold the PROMIS Software to Iran and other Middle Eastern countries to help the U.S. spy agencies keep an eye on these countries.

He was supposedly a long time co-criminal aligned with the Gambino crime family and a personal friend of John Gotti.

He was involved in the Music Corporation of America's mob connections and was investigated by the FBI for corrupt ties to Hollywood.

He believed that his actions over his lifetime were entirely legal and that his orders were given from the highest authorities within the government: the office of the President, especially during the Ronald Reagan and George W. Bush administrations.

As early as 1978, the FBI kept a file and ongoing investigation on Robert Booth Nichols for his involvement in narcotics trafficking, money laundering and other criminal activities...

This is just the tip of the iceberg.

It seems that the concept of drugs for guns was a cash business which became a staple in much of Nichols life. He was a good looking man by most people's accounts, standing over six feet tall with a resemblance to Clark Gable and he had an athletic build, although he started to gain weight around the middle as he matured.

Robert Booth Nichols legal business activities included:

He is credited with the invention of an automatic machine-gun pistol that packed more power than the commonly popular MAC-10.

He owned a company called Meridian International Logistics, which also owned Meridian Arms. He was an advisor to Wackenhut Corporation during his time at the Cabazon reservation in Indio and simultaneously sat on the board of FIDCO, First Intercontinental Development Corporation, which, among other things, made and sold the Bradley personnel transports to the U.S. military. It was while serving in these capacities that he sought to facilitate weapons manufacturing for John Philip Nichols and the Cabazon Band of Mission Indians.

In 1992, he started a company in Hawaii called Pacific Rim Services; and that same year, he was an official advisor to the movie *Under Siege* starring Steven Segal and Tommy Lee Jones and played a role as a ranking officer aboard the ship.

From 1989 to the early 1990s, Robert Booth Nichols became embroiled in two lawsuits. One whereby he sued an FBI agent named Thomas Gates for slander in the amount of $11million for causing him a loss in business in Australia. The other lawsuit was against the City of Las Angeles whereby he claimed financial loss stemming from the revocation of his concealed weapons permit affecting his ability to procure military weapons contracts. He lost both lawsuits and thereafter began expanding his fraudulent financial schemes.

In 2004, he orchestrated a scheme to defraud which would be his eventual downfall.

On December 16, 2008, while trying to resolve accusations against him for high financial crimes, Robert Booth Nichols gave a deposition of his lifetime activities to U.S. Attorney Jeff Alberts in New York, in front of three witnessing FBI agents. Two months later he would be dead.

The scam began, as it usually does, by finding a mark. In this case, the fall would be attributed to Sam Israel, a Wall Street trader who mismanaged a hedge fund called Bayou Group, LLC that was more than $100million out of balance. Israel was desperately searching for an investment that would right his books and return his fund to profitability and respectability. Besides being incredibly in debt to his own investors, Israel had been kicked out of his house, his wife had left him, and he had a cocaine and alcohol habit.

It was spring 2004 and Israel heard of a man who knew of a top secret computer program that kept track of where and when the Federal Government injected money into the market and a man who knew of secret investments only meant for the mega-wealthy. Robert Booth Nichols told Israel he traded in Treasury Notes secured by tons of gold at the U.S. prime bank in Atlanta. The T-Note was worth $250billion and leveraged by liens against it. Only the most influential of banks traded in these. It was a secret and secure market which was generally only invested in by the wealthiest of families: The Rothschilds, the Vanderbilts, and the Rockefellers, and who knows

261

who else. Nichols said, if they used some select bankers he knew in Europe they could get in and out of the T-Note, making millions, maybe hundreds of millions of dollars, in a very short time and none of the principal parties would know about it. The interest alone on the T-Note would be worth millions of dollars even if you only owned it for a day. All Israel had to do was trust him.

So, trust him Israel did.

The two began jet setting around Europe at an alarming pace, meeting bankers at odd hours and having clandestine meeting with unique individuals who had English and Arabian accents. By the third stop, Nichols told Israel the time was ripe and Israel should deposit $150,000,000 into Barclay's Bank of London. Israel did what Nichols asked. Then, Nichols told Israel they'd missed their opportunity by mere minutes and they began jet setting again. At one point, during the wee hours of the darkened morning, Israel was so frustrated with Nichols that he stormed out the back door of their hotel and saw a man wearing a turban staring at him. The man spoke to him in English, saying something about the investment. When Israel questioned him, the man claimed to not speak English. In his frustration, Israel fought with the man, and then pulled out a gun, which Nichols had given him to carry, and shot the Arab. The turban exploded in a spray of blood and brains. Nichols came outside and told Israel they had to get away before the police showed up. When they were safe in another hotel less than an hour later, Nichols made a call and said he'd taken care of the body. No news of the murder ever made it to the media. During the later trial and lawsuits that would emerge from the fraud, Israel would say he finally determined the murder to be an elaborately staged ruse. Nichols would deny it even happened.

Israel took his money out of Barclay's and put it into another bank in Germany. Nichols was depressed. He borrowed $10million off Israel and promised to pay it back when the investment worked out. As collateral, Nichols offered Israel a bond worth $100 million from a safe deposit box he had in Mayfair, England. Israel and Nichols went to the bank together to get the bond. At the bank, Nichols passed a retinal scan and they were led to the vault where Nichols pulled a very old looking money box from his safety deposit box. He told Israel that if the box wasn't opened at exactly the right angle, it would explode. Nichols carefully opened the box and then set it down. From inside it, he tossed Israel a tape and told him it was the Zapruder film, the real one, which showed who really killed John F. Kennedy.

It never did.

Nichols and Israel jet-setted around Europe some more, always chasing the elusive clandestine meeting with a banker who could get them access to the secret market. After spending more than a million dollars on hotel, air and train travel, Israel realized he would never get the investment and his $10 million loan to Nichols was lost too. His money had been frozen in the German bank after it mysteriously disappeared from his account for a few hours and then returned.

Israel went home dejected. The Securities and Exchange Commission audited the books on Bayou Group, LLC, and Israel found himself under investigation and then a defendant in a criminal lawsuit for embezzlement from his investors. He filed his own lawsuit against Robert Booth Nichols ho claimed that the entire investment was legal and he had no idea that Israel was a fraud. The case dragged on for a few years with Nichols plying all sorts of legal wrangling to stall and negotiate a settlement or a plea bargain.

On December 16, 2008, as part of a settlement Nichols gave his deposition to U.S. Attorney Jeff Alberts. In it Robert Booth Nichols detailed his life story, many of the covert operations he'd performed under the handling of men whom he presumed were CIA agents (although now he wasn't so sure they'd ever really worked for the country he loved) and the Prime Bank fraud he pulled on Israel. He'd negotiated a financial settlement with Israel which he would, of course, never pay.

On Valentine's Day, February 14, 2009, Robert Booth Nichols was in Geneva, Switzerland, with a New York stockbroker friend, Mark Stolz, who found Nichols dead after he missed a meeting. Nichols appeared to have had a heart attack, although the coroner also noted a substantial blow to the head was more likely the cause of death. Stolz cremated the body the same day and then notified the U.S. Embassy in Bern, who in turn notified Nichols next of kin.

Many believe Robert Booth Nichols is still alive today, leading a new life, with a new identity. Some think that perhaps his handlers killed him for publicly stating too much about his past and the operations they secretly worked.

Sam Israel was found guilty of securities fraud and then tried to fake his own death in a bridge jumping suicide. When his girlfriend was about to be thrown in jail for aiding and abetting the escape of a felon, Israel turned himself in to face a 22 year prison sentence.

Alvarez Murders Revisited

In August of 2009, Riverside County Investigators decide to reopen the investigation into the murder of Fred Alvarez, Patricia Castro and Ralph Boger. Later, sources would confirm that the investigation was opened up at the urging of Boger's daughter Rachel Begley. Only, this time, the state's Attorney General would head the investigation since then Riverside County District Attorney, at that time, Rod Pacheco was a distant cousin, to the man who would be charged for the murders of Alvarez and friends: former informant Jimmy Hughes.

According to the Indian media source, NativeTimes.com, Rachel Begley had secretly captured Jimmy Hughes on videotape in 2008 saying that the murder of her father was a "mafia (style) hit job" that was "a lot bigger than the murder of this guy or that guy." This new evidence and more would reopen the case.

As the new theory went, Hughes, (now 52) was no longer

considered the $25,000 bag man for the 1981 killings. Instead he was being charged with committing the act of murder himself; and conspiring with John Philip Nichols, Nichols' son John Paul Nichols, and others. He was being charged with three counts of murder and one count of conspiracy to commit a crime

A Special Governor's warrant was issued for Hughes arrest. He was now the leader of the Jimmy Hughes Ministry which, according to its website, claimed that since 1995 the church provided services to battered women, drug addicts and others, in Central America. The ministries headquarters was in Miami, Florida. Hughes was arrested at the Miami-Dade International airport on September 26 as he was about to depart on a plane headed for Honduras. He would be extradited to face charges in about a month and would be held in Miami until his extradition.

Hughes hired legal counsel and fought the extradition. He was eventually escorted back to Indio to face investigators, who though they tried and tried, were not able to gather enough evidence to prosecute. The only evidence which did come forward exonerated Hughes. But, prosecutors refused to reveal that evidence. California Deputy Attorney General Michael Murphy suddenly and immediately dropped the case and on July 1, 2010, Jimmy Hughes walked free from jail, never to be seen again. Authorities believe he returned to Central or South America to work for a drug cartel.

John Philip Nichols had died eight years earlier in 2001. His son John Paul Nichols was not to be found. Authorities tried to contact him at a New York City address and at an Indio Golf Course home. Their attempts were unanswered. Another man, Glen Heggstad, was mentioned in the warrant, though not charged. He was interviewed by Riverside County Sheriff's detectives who would not reveal the specifics of their conversations with the informant. Heggstad had been friends with Alvarez, who had told Heggstad that he feared for his life when he uncovered information regarding Nichols illegal activities. This information included mismanagement of tribal money during the early beginnings of the tribe's casino ventures when Nichols was trying to work with the Wackenhut Corporation to build weapons for the Nicaraguan Contra rebels. Linda Streeter, the now grown daughter of Fred Alvarez who had been only 12 at the time of her Dad's murder, told the Associated Press that Alvarez's fears grew from the fact that his mailbox had been shot up and that his motorcycle began having many unexplained breakdowns due to mysteriously missing parts, during the time leading up to his death.

In her book on Danny Casolaro and The Octopus, author Cheri Seymour postulates that the reason Jimmy Hughes was never prosecuted stems from his religious involvement in the Full Gospel Businessmen's Fellowship International. The Fellowship membership greatly overlaps the Reagan administration, high level Secret military organizations and Central and South American Politico-Military organizations. Seymour basically states that he had people in higher places watching out for him when he was about to take the fall.

In July, 2011, The Desert Sun ran an article where former Hells Angel sergeant-at-arms Glen Heggstad spoke to a reporter about his involvement with the 30-year-old murders and the recently closed investigation by the state Attorney General's office. Shortly before the article, the police had arrested Heggstad on the grounds that he knew Jimmy Hughes and knew that the murders were about to happen and did nothing to stop them. He was accused but let go due to lack of evidence.

Heggstad said state Attorney General Murphy had lied in the felony complaint which prompted the Governor to issue the warrant and that the statements were made to shut Heggstad up about the crime so the truth couldn't easily come out. It was done as a way to keep the truth out of court.

According to Heggstad, the reason the authorities didn't want him on the stand was he'd make a terrible witness for the state. He had a long record of fighting and disturbing the peace. He'd even served a year in jail when he attempted to bribe a witness to miss a judicial hearing. Furthermore, he claims that in the 1970s and 80s; he conspired with police to retrieve stolen merchandise for people when the police couldn't legally do anything about it. He claimed that at the time, he knew most of the thieves in town and often would get a tip via a phone call from the police and then he'd go and forcibly get the "goods" back. He would receive a commission based on 50 percent value of the merchandise and then would give the police officers a referral fee, though not all officers accepted the fee. Through his work, he became nicknamed "Crazy Glen" Heggstad and other people, non-police related, began to hire him to handle divorce cases and private investigator work. It was for this kind of work that Jimmy Hughes and Fred Alvarez approached him, Heggstad said.

Heggstad said Fred Alvarez and himself had become friends who shared a mutual love of riding their Harley-Davidson motorcycles. The two would occasionally go riding across the vast desert back road landscapes in the days when it was legal to ride without helmets, sporting only sun glasses as head gear with the wind whipping through their long hair.

It was Alvarez, who broached the subject with Heggstad one day, while Alvarez was sitting on his sofa smoking one joint (marijuana) after another, sharing his fears about non-Indian Nichols getting the Cabazon Band more and more involved in the arms manufacturing business. He was very concerned that a government hit man was going to take him out. Heggstad said it was hard to take Alvarez serious. He was ranting. However, Alvarez had three pieces of damning evidence that he was being followed: his mailbox had been shot up, as a warning he thought; his house had been ransacked; and his motorcycle engine unexplainably fell out onto the road while he was riding it. The engine incident simply could not have happened without someone tampering with it because Alvarez maintained his motorcycle himself and kept it secure in the living room of his Rancho Mirage home.

Heggstad claimed that while Jimmy Hughes was working as Security Chief at the Bingo Parlor and Poker room for the Cabazon's, Hughes approached "Crazy Glen" looking for work. He remembers it plainly because Hughes still had the crew-cut military hairstyle and wore goofy shoes. Hughes said he was willing to do just about anything necessary: bodyguard, hit man, collector, he didn't care. But Heggstad didn't need any help. Also, Heggstad simply didn't believe that Hughes was willing or able to do everything he claimed and as far as Heggstad was concerned, Hughes was full of crap.

After the Alvarez murders, Heggstad ran into Hughes again and Hughes immediately asked Heggstad if he believed him now? Hughes never actually admitted to the murder but, "Crazy Glen" thought the implication was clear.

Heggstad said that the detectives assigned to the cold-case informed him that multiple informants sad Hughes had made similar statement a half dozen times to other people. But, the Desert Sun could not get authorities to repeat that claim officially. Furthermore, Heggstad said he still has his doubts about Hughes committing the murders – because what kind of professional goes around whispering tales about his dirty deeds to others?

In his Desert Sun interview, Glen Heggstad shared the same information he told police detective John Powers two years earlier. Heggstad said that when detective Powers called him, he was in Mexico and they arranged to have dinner together to discuss the case. Heggstad was willing to repeat his conversations with both Hughes and Alvarez. Powers told Heggstad that he had someone claiming that Heggstad had been told or hired to "lean" on Fred Alvarez, but that he'd also been told that Glen had not taken the job. Heggstad told Powers that it was the cop who was crazy. Heggstad told the Desert Sun that even over 30 years his memory wasn't that bad. There was no way that he'd gone from beating up drug-crazed thieves to murdering someone. Powers tried diligently to get Heggstad to offer up new evidence, even saying the conversation was "off the record,' though in reality, Heggstad could be called as a witness later.

In another conversation, Heggstad says he told Powers not to call him as a sworn witness out of concern for his reputation being damaged. He didn't like the thought of headlines that might read "Former Hells Angel Turns State's Witness." So, instead, the police named Heggstad as a co-conspirator in the case against Hughes. Heggstad hired his own lawyer and waited for the detectives to come calling with an arrest warrant. Friends and family suggested he take it on the lamb, hop on his motorcycle and run away but, Heggstad didn't want to run. He stayed and the police never came. For nine months he chewed his nails, worrying about a knock on door as prosecutors and investigators tried to develop a case against Jimmy Hughes during 2009 and 2010. Eventually the police gave up and Hughes was released.

When questioned by the Desert Sun, detective Powers couldn't recall the conversation with Glen Heggstad and the cold-case division supervisor, Sergeant Scott Brown wouldn't comment because the case was still open. It is still open today, 34 years after the killings occurred.

Afterword

If this story intrigues you, as it did me, please take the time to Google some of the subjects involved, the people, the conspiracy names, and definitely Danny Casolaro, The Octopus and Robert Booth Nichols. In these nearly fifty pages of writing I barely scratched the surface of this tale. If I had written it in its entirety, it would've become a book in its own right. Other authors who have done so either did an incredible job or were found dead of an apparent suicide. The best book on this subject that I have found is The Last Circle: Danny Casolaro's Investigation into The Octopus and the PRMOIS Software Scandal by Cheri Seymour. Buy it online and read it. Cheri Seymour should have received a Pulitzer for all she uncovered. Nathan Baca, a local reporter from KESQ TV made a series of news reports about the Cabazon Band and the Octopus murders and won an Emmy Award. Despite these efforts, the story is often buried by the main-stream national media. I can only guess that the reasons for the media staying away from the story is that it is well connected to high level government officials and the facts are difficult to verify as they are mired behind veils of secrecy under the guise of national security whether it was legal or not.

Sources:

ABC NEWS, 20/20, 1985

Associated Press, CABAZON TRIBE FIRES THREE TOP EXECUTIVES FIRED IN SHAKEUP, http://legacy.ut-sandiego.com/news/state/20050506-1121-ca-tribalshakeup.html, (May 6, 2005)

Associated Press, CABAZON TRIBE FIRES THREE TOP EXECUTIVES IN SHAKE-UP, SignOnSanDiego.com, (May 6, 2005).

Associated Press, UNSOLVED 1981 TRIPLE MURDER IN CALIFORNIA WAS HIT JOB, AUTHORITIES SAY, Fox News, (October 2, 2009).

Rachel Begley, PRESS RELEASE- "OCTOPUS-COLD-CASE FILE STALLED AT DOJ, http://12160.info/profiles/blogs/press-release-octopus-cold-case, (December 27, 2010 at 2:12am).

John Connolly, BADLANDS: HOW DID A FORMER CIA MAN TAKE OVER A TRIBE OF IMPOVERSHED INDIAN NEAR PALM SPRINGS? Spy Magazine, (April 1992).

Paul Feldman, BID TO OUST TRIBAL LEADER ENDS IN DEFEAT: CABAZON INDIAN: THE TWO DISSIDENTS ARE FINED $50,000 EACH AND FURTHER PENALIZED AFTER A MISCONDUCT HEARING STEMMING FROM THEIR CHALLENGE, Los Angeles Times (.com), (June 22, 1991).

Gillian Flaccus, COMPLAINT: KILLING OF TRIIBAL LEADER WAS HIT JOB, www.nativetimes.com, (October 2, 2009).

John M. Gonzales, 3,000 RALLY FOR INDIAN CASINOS, Los Angeles Times (.com), (March 25, 1997).

Tom Gorman, DISPUTE STALLS LAND DEAL FOR IMPOVERISHED TRIBE, Los Angeles Times (.com), (September 26, 1997).

Bill Hammond, TIME FOR CUOMO TO RETURN PILE OF DIRTY MONEY, NY Daily News (.com), (August 1, 2006). William Hammond, Jr., CUOMO TOOK CAMPAIGN CASH FROM INDIANS HE HELPED, http://www.freerepublic.com/focus/news/733878/posts, (August 15, 2002).

Paul Jacobs and Daniel M. Weintraub, CALIFORNIA ELECTIONS: INDIANS GIVE LARGE SUMS TO DEMOCRATS: TRIBES SEEKING TO EXPAND THEIR CASINO BUSINESS SUPPORT BROWN AND UMBERG BECAUSE THEY HAVE FOUND REPUBLICANS UNRECEPTIVE TO THEIR INTERESTS, Los Angeles Times (.com), (October 26, 1994).

John Kendall, ADVISOR TO INDIANS JAILED IN MURDER-FOR-HIRE PLOT, Los Angeles Times (.com), (January 19, 1985).

Guy Lawson, THE DISGRACED WALL STREET TRADER WHO FAKED HIS OWN DEATH BY PRETENDING TO UMP INTO THE RIVER AFTER CIA AGENT TRICKED HIM INTO HANDING OVER MILLIONS IN WORLD'S WILDEST CON, The Daily Mail (.com), (August 11, 2012).
Jonathan Littman, TINY TRIBE SHOWERED WITH FUNDS, San Francisco Chronicle, reprinted in the Pittsburgh Post-Gazette, (September 9, 1991).

James May, FISCAL TROUBLES LEAD TO CABAZON SHAKE-UP, Indian Country (.com), (May 16, 2005).

Dan Morain, AN EAGLE FEATHER-AND CONTROVERSY-FOR GOVERNOR: RITUALS: IT IS A MISDEMEANOR TO POSSESS THE ITEM WITHOUOT A PERMIT. TRIBAL OFFICIAL'S GIFT TROUBLES SOME INDIANS, Los Angeles Times (.com), (September 9, 1999).

News Brief, TRIBAL OFFICIAL'S BROTHER EMEZZLED CASINO FUNDS, Casino City Times (.com), Gaming

News, (May 17, 2002).

News Brief, THE REGION, Los Angeles Times (.com), (May 31, 1985).

News Brief, TRIBAL OFFICAL'S BROTHER EMBEZ-ZLED CASINO FUNDS, CasinoCityTimes.com, (May 17, 2002).

Obituaries, JOHN PHILIP NICHOLS, LEADER OF CABAZON TRIBE, Los Angeles Times (.com), (March 26, 2001).

David Rosenzweig, 2 CASINO EXECUTIVES AC-CUSED OF LAUNDERING, Los Angeles Times (.com), (Jun 19, 1998).

David Rosenzweig, JUDGE DISMISSES COUNTS AGAINST TRIBE EXECUTIVES, Los Angeles Times (.com), (December 16, 1998).

Peter Sanders and John R. Emshwiller, AT INDIAN CASINOS, ODDS GROW LONGER FOR SOME TRIBES, The Wall Street Journal (.com), (September 27, 2005).

David G. Savage, SUPREME COURT RULES STATES CAN'T REGULATE INDIAN GAMES, Los Angeles Times (.com), (February 16, 1987).

Cheri Seymour, THE LAST CIRCLE, DANNY CASO-LARO'S INVESTIGATION INTO THE OCTOPUS AND THE PROMIS SOFTWARE SCANDAL, Trine Day LLC, (2010).

Staff Reports, CABAZON BAND OF MISSION INDI-ANS, CALIFORNIA, Indian Country Today Media Network (.com), (December 12, 2001).

Staff Reports, EX-CASINO WORKER FACES EMBEZ-ZLEMENT CHARGES, Los Angeles Times (.com), (December 1, 2001).

Staff Reports, INDIANS FIRE THREE CASINO EXEC-UTIVES, Los Angeles Times (.com), (May 7, 2005).

Staff Reports, 2 TRIBAL LEADERS GUILTY IN CAM-

PAIGN DONATION CASE, Los Angeles Times (.com), (October 15, 1999).

Staff Reports, TRIBAL LEADERS LOSE ROUND IN CAMPAIGN GIFTS CASSE, Los Angeles Times (.com), (February 9, 1999).

Staff Reports, RESERVATION LANDS, Los Angeles Times (.com), (September 27, 1996).

Amy Taxin and Gillian Flaccus, ARREST IN 1981 TRIBAL MURDERS REVICES OLD MYSTERY, www.native-times.com, (November 20, 2009).

Monica Torline, GLEN HEGGSTAD NEVER CHARGED, BUT LOOKING FOR VINDICATION FOR 1981 'OCTOPUS MURDERS', The Desert Sun (.com),(July 3, 2011).

United States Bankruptcy Court, Southern District of New York, DEPOSITIONS OF ROBERT BOOTH NICHOLS, United States of America vs. Samuel Israel III, Case No. 05 Cr.1039 (CM), and Bayou Management, LLC vs. Robert B. Nichols, Ellen M. Nichols, Samuel Israel II, and John Does 1-5, Case No. 08 Civ.6036 (CM), Fink and Carney Reporting and Video Services, New York, New York.

Philip Valenti, CABAZON: HOW 'INDIAN GAMING' BEGAN, Executive Intelligence Review, published by Lyndon Larouche, (January 15, 1993).

Various contributors and references, ROBERT BOOTH NICHOLS, Prison Planet Intelligence Wiki (.com), http://ppia.wikia.com/wiki/Robert_Booth_Nichols.

Various writers, ROCCO ZANGARI, Mafia.wikia.com/wiki/Rocco_Zangari.

Various writers, CALIFORNIA VS. CABAZON BAND OF MISSION INDIANS, Wikipedia.

The Trials and Tribulations
of
Ginny Foat

She was born Virginia Galluzzo, in Brooklyn, New York, on June 2, 1941; the war baby of Gus and Virginia Galluzzo, who would fight her own battles all through life, again and again succumbing to the demons of dark choices; running from and hiding from the ghosts of her past. Yet, she was also a fighter and an adventurer, always looking for her next victory, her next mountain to climb.

In 1954, her family moved to upstate New York, to the rural town of New Paltz, when Ginny was only in middle school. One friend claimed that even then, Ginny had a sort of "Wild Blood" in her. She was pretty and electrifying, very much alive. Her figure developed at an early age, when most of her friends still had coltish knees and gangly arms. Decades later, she would tell a Rolling Stone magazine reporter that she had an uncanny desire to climb the tallest peak in the nearby Shawanguk Mountains looming over their small town. Problem was this mountain was private property. Determined as she was, young Ginny made friends with the daughter of the owner of this local Everest and in a trade of dinner at Ginny's for an escort up the mountain a deal was struck to allow Ginny permission to climb. Ginny's determination won out.

As she matured, her figure blossomed in the visage of Marilyn Monroe, Jane Russell, or Sophia Loren. Full figures were in and Ginny had curves in spades. She was beautiful and attracted men.

The first significant man, in a list of many, to come her way was Fred Schindler, a high school sweetheart who lasted till the year after school ended. In 1960, school was a year out of her life and she didn't miss it a bit. That same year, so was Fred. They could be friends; but, not lovers.

Ginny was a hard worker. She wanted things in life and she didn't mind earning them. She'd to work as a waitress back in high school; after she became an airline stewardess for Alleghany Airlines, , and then landed a job at a car rental agency. None of these jobs gave Ginny what she wanted in life. They were all jobs that women were supposed to have. But, she wanted more. She wanted a unique life that one day she could look back on and say she'd done it her way.

In August of 1960, she married her first man, a New Paltz local: Danny Angelillo. The wedding was an extravagant affair: 200 guests and all the flowers and frills. It didn't last. Before the first year ended the marriage was annulled.

Shortly thereafter Ginny found herself a counselor at a Wiltwyck boy's home for troubled teens.

John Sidote

Her next man would be a life changer. He would take her from the small town girl with big dreams to see the world – or at least the southern and western United States – and they would have love and romance and adventure. They would see strange and unique places, meet interesting people and then kill them. Her soon to be husband was named John Sidote. She met him in 1964 and he was 26, she now 23, when they met at the Villa Lipani bar in New Paltz. John was an ex-marine, married at the time he and Ginny met, to Eileen, since 1959. They had a baby. He'd worked at the bar for three years and had made his family a home in a house they were paying a mortgage on, with two new cars, presumably on payments. As a bartender, Sidote was known to play the field a little. But, it was the love free 1960s and regardless of his happenstance indiscretions, he considered himself faithful to Eileen.

Then Ginny Foat and a group of female friends came into his bar one night and John Sidote forgot all his other commitments in life. Maybe he was never as faithful as he claimed and was only married because it was the thing to do for a hometown boy whose parents lived within the same city limits and wanted to do the right thing. Or maybe he'd only made his commitments while he was biding his time and waiting for the future to come rushing in. Regardless of what else was going on in his head, when Ginny came within sight of John there was an attraction between the two from the word GO. He loved her bombshell curves and she was instantly attracted to his tough guy looks. Some say he resembled a cross between a thinner Charles Bronson and a hunkier Sonny Bono. Though, Ginny and her friends jokingly referred to John as the white Sammy Davis, Jr. After that first night, Ginny came again. Then one more time and she and John finally hooked up after an evening of him serving her Cutty Sark and plying her with smiles, laughter and songs. John was known to occasionally take the microphone and lead the band in a rendition of 'That Old Black Magic.' Later, in prison interviews, John would admit Ginny was three sheets to the wind that first night when they slipped away, after his shift, to the motel across the parking lot. Then, she hesitated, wanting it to be more special, her to be more special in his eyes; something more than a quick fuck. So instead, they went to the local all night diner and had coffee till she sobered up and could drive herself home.

The night ended; but, the reckless affair continued.

John's marriage lost any semblance of substance under Ginny's musk. It reeked of a crumbling foundation and the morality of his decisions would haunt John forevermore. He had a family he'd started, the sort of thing that God and humanity coveted and called special. Yet, the sexual attraction between him and Ginny was like a volcano, ready to explode at any moment and unstoppable. He'd never had a woman create the sort of feelings Ginny inspired in him and he didn't want them to end.

In the summer of 1965, John was supposed to take his wife, Eileen, on a vacation to Atlantic City, yet instead, somehow ended up taking Ginny to Montreal. They had so much sex, John claimed; they both came home with rug-burned knees.

John sought answers for his crumbling marriage and moral choices in one bottle after the next. One night, while Eileen was visiting her family in the Bronx, John brought Ginny home to his house, his bedroom and told her that he wanted to leave Eileen and to leave New Paltz. John would be the first in his family to get a divorce.

He and Ginny invited an eighteen-year-old co-worker from John's bar, Wasyl Bozydaj, to come along and the three of them loaded up John's new white convertible Pontiac Bonneville and drove to Cocoa Beach, Florida, where John had a friend. They felt they could find jobs there as well as anywhere and it was a long way from upstate New York. Bozydaj did most of the driving. John and Ginny drank and fondled in the back seat. They had $1500 between the three of them.

Florida didn't last. Neither did their money, and the three went on to Baton Rouge, Louisiana, then New Orleans, to find work at a place called the Ponderosa Grill and Lounge on Canal Street, near the French Quarter. It was a low-brow place, known by the NOPD, as a place corrupt with vice, gambling, cheap drinks and lewd dancing. The Ponderosa owner was a local connected mob guy named Murphy "Happy" Ditcharo. Some would say Happy was a Don. He put Ginny's curves into a barmaid's outfit and let her go-go dance for tips. While the skinny tough guy, John, would work the door as a bouncer.

The Ponderosa gave them jobs, a little food, but not much cash. Most nights they'd only earn about $10 each a day and half of that would go to pay for rent at a cheap hotel nearby. Bozydaj worked at a hamburger joint a little further away. He would use the car while John and Ginny walked to work. At least John's drinking had come to an end. He couldn't afford the alcohol. Life was hard in New Orleans, not the panacea of freedom they all thought they were leaving upstate New York for and they hatched a plan to help supplement their income.

Moises Chayo

In the late summer of 1965, Moises Chayo had come to New Orleans to tend to his 24-year-old son, Raymond, from the Ochsner Clinic while he was treated for phlebitis (the inflammation of veins in the leg that generally lead to blood swelling and blood clots) for nearly three months. On November 22nd, Moises was to check out Raymond. He never arrived. Nor did he the next day, or the next. The police were called. No leads were forthcoming after more than a week and finally Raymond flew home alone to Argentina.

About a week before Christmas, Moises showed up. His body was found in a ditch alongside a road in Jefferson Parish, south of New Orleans, further out in the bayou. The body was seriously bruised and discolored and decomposition had further reduced its condition, making identification difficult. The skull showed a torn scalp with lacerations, five in all, down to the bone. Moises had been beaten to death. His attackers had taken his money and in their rush to rob him of the $1400 he had, they'd missed a solid gold wrist watch and gold writing pencil.

Western Bound

Whether it was hours or days after Moises Chayo death is unknown. What is known is that Ginny and John left New Orleans quickly after November 22, 1965, flying to Houston, Texas. They called Wasyl BozydaJ to drive out and pick them up. As a group, they decided to drive west to Carson City, Nevada, to find work in the casino's and restaurants of the Carson-Reno area. John spent some of his travelling money on drinking again. He and Ginny, she now 24, were no longer the starry-eyed love-struck couple they once were. They fought. She was not happy with their lot in life. John yelled at her

279

that he'd left a family and home behind. She put the blame squarely on John, saying he'd made his own choices. Ginny gave up drinking. John continued.

In Carson City, jobs were not easy to find. John dubbed the Reno area "Dogpatch" and blew their last $400 gambling. They wanted to go even further west and visit California, a land of opportunity in their eyes if ever there was one. But, they needed funds to do it.

Donald Fitting

In court testimony 11 years later, John Sidote would swear to the following happening in 1965: Ginny was the lure. She was to attract a man that they would rob. They were at Harrah's Casino in Lake Tahoe. John spent the same evening getting smashed – not part of the plan. A vacationing San Francisco hotel clerk would be their victim. His name was Donald Fitting. John lost interest in gambling and went to the car to pass out in a fit of drunkenness. He awoke to darkness in the lower hills near Carson. The sounds of gunfire startled him to consciousness. Ginny had put three holes into Donald's head. The car was a bloody mess, literally. Ginny cleaned it while John slipped back into a drunken stupor.

The take was only $20 this time and a diamond ring that Ginny would later hock in Hermosa Beach, California, for $200. She would testify that the ring had belonged to John.

No Regrets

Ginny got another waitressing job in Huntington Beach, California. Together, she and John also ran a telemarketing service for a family photographer. Bozydaj went back to New York. John remained at Ginny's side and was perplexed at how she had done what she had to Donald Fitting and then had no emotional scars, no remorse. He continued drinking. She was a social butterfly. Their relationship was deteriorating fast. They seldom talked. Instead they played board games when alone at night. Finally, John had had enough and after a particularly vicious game of Scrabble, where the tiles spelled out accusatory words back and forth between the two, John lost his control, flew the pieces aside and hit Ginny over the head with the board.

Despite their frustrations, on New Year's Day, 1967, John Sidote and Virginia Galluzzo married and with $1000 borrowed from Sidote's parents, went into a partnership with another couple on a bar of their own in an underdeveloped area near Torrance, California. They appropriately called it the No Regret's Bar. But, despite their efforts, the bar didn't succeed. One night, John and a few of his friends had a showdown with a Samoan group of ruffians who felt insulted. A fight ensued and John retrieved a pistol from a friend's car. He fired warning shots into the air to break up the ruckus. One of the bullets did not go straight up. It went through the windshield of the Samoans station wagon and straight through the head of one of the Samoans, killing Okeni Moe, 18. John would be found guilty of manslaughter and sentenced to six month to fifteen years in Chino Prison.

At first, Ginny was the considerate housewife; attending visits, giving money, showing concern for her husband behind bars. In 1969, she even wrote letters to the Parole Board in John's defense, saying he was needed at home because life was so hard. But, as time went by, she became distant, aloof, distracted. She missed visits. Claimed a car wreck made visiting impossible and then started showing up with bruises and a black eye. Through a friend, John found out Ginny had fallen in with a petty hoodlum named Richard "Blackie" Busconi. At least until that spring. Busconi was murdered in the parking lot of a San Pedro bar. Ginny became a suspect in Busconi's death. She was accused of being the getaway driver in a failed robbery. The detectives questioned John too and he was mentally tortured with details of Ginny's affections for Busconi. But, no one talked. John even claims to have passed a lie detector's test. Eventually the case was dropped. Not enough evidence. It still remains unsolved.

While in prison, John received a letter from a Mrs. Foat, saying Ginny had seduced her husband, Raymond, sexually. Mrs. Foat begged John to get his vivacious wife away from her husband. A provocative photograph of Ginny and Raymond was enclosed. During one of her infrequent visits, Ginny confessed experimenting sexually with a lesbian. As an inmate, John Sidote was a model prisoner. He would be semi-released in the summer of 1970, having served less than three years of his sentence.

John bit back his rage and left prison each morning on a work-parole program. In a borrowed car, he would drive early each day first to Ginny's house and seek some husband-wife companionship. He could squeeze in about one hour before he was due at his job in Torrance at the Grand Prix Auto Repair shop. Ginny wasn't interested. He would crawl into her bed and then have to crawl back out. There would be no sex. She didn't even want to talk to him. She would feign sleep or just out and reject him.

John's frustrations exploded one morning and he started choking Ginny. He couldn't believe after all they'd been through that she would treat him thus. He wanted to kill her. But, he wanted to return to prison even less. He checked himself and threw Ginny aside, then stormed out. A week later he filed for a divorce and never saw her again.

Becoming Ginny Foat

Raymond Foat liked Ginny from the start. She was beautiful, as he called her, "…a looker." He was a 43 year old British gentleman and he hired Ginny as a waitress at the Princess Louise restaurant in 1969, after she had lost the No Regrets. The Princess Louise II was located on a luxury liner moored of the Southern California coast, a sort of precedent to the Queen Mary in Long Beach. She was a good worker and gained a promotion to become Raymond's administrative assistant where she was known to get the most out of the other workers.

They simply wanted to work for her.

The problem was Raymond Foat was married, though separated, and his wife soon became jealous of Ginny, accusing Raymond of having an affair with her; something Raymond denied. Mrs. Foat even mailed a letter to John Sidote's prison address seeking help. The only help that came was Raymond Foat moved to Vancouver, BC, Canada in 1969 and Ginny moved back home to her parent's house in upstate New York to get further away from John Sidote. Her New York escape was short lived however and she called Raymond Foat in Vancouver and asked if he would hire again for his new restaurant, the Princess Louise II. Of course, he said. Together again, this time there was no doubt that Ginny and Raymond were to be a couple, they quickly fell deeply in love.

In May, 1971, Raymond and Ginny married in a posh ceremony on a friends yacht and, in 1972, moved back to California; this time to Anaheim. Raymond became the general manager of the Quality Inn Greenhorn restaurant, near Disneyland. Ginny was the catering manager. They moved to nearby Canoga Park where they purchased a home together and made the idyllic California life together. They had three dogs, a boat and a Cadillac. They vacationed regularly to places like Palm Springs England, New York and Las Vegas. Though they tried, children were not forthcoming. About a year later, Raymond left The Greenhorn and took a position at the Disneyland hotel. Ginny and a partner, Dan Marcheano, started her own catering business, Affairs Unlimited. To help establish the venture she tried to get a small business loan and instead got a slap in the face: The banks would only lend her the money if her husband put the loan in his name.

In response to her first brush with sexual discrimination, Ginny became involved in the Orange County chapter of the National Organization for Women and often Raymond would come home to a living room full of ladies talking of politics and protest planning. She and Raymond had gotten the loan together and Ginny's business was getting stronger fast, growing into a fine venture; but, Ginny was also finding pleasure in helping others. Other women needed help getting reestablished too. Many of them were divorced or from abused homes. Some had children. They needed assistance getting child support, welfare, food stamps. Sometimes the authorities needed a little pushing to do their jobs. Because of Ginny's past, she could honestly connect with the ladies in the group. She claimed a fear of men, leaning on her marriage to John Sidote often as an emotional link to embrace others. The San Fernando Valley Chapter was just starting up and Ginny easily became a leader within its unorganized ranks. She was charismatic and organized and became a leader. As Ginny became more and more involved with NOW she cared less and less for men and instead interacted more and more with women. She told her friends in NOW that she never really wanted to have children with Raymond.

Ginny on the other hand, continued to grow in the NOW ranks, climbing from a local organizer to a state co-chair on a task force on self-employed women. She was 35 and had matured well into the role of a respectable woman. She was still beautiful. She was now more. She was charismatic and had also become a very capable organizer, a person to be looked up to. Unfortunately, the evidence from an old crime came back to haunt her.

The Donald Fitting Trial

Ginny's ex-husband John Sidote had ran into a bad spell and after a seriously long bout with alcoholism had walked into an Albany, New York, police station and started talking while going through serious withdrawals. He was delirious and seeking help and rambling on and on about how his life had gone downhill since leaving his first wife and getting involved with Ginny and their eventual break-up. He was a broken man. A couple officers heard fragments of incidents that they thought worth investigated and gave John a bottle of vodka to settle his nerves. John talked more and before the police were done with them he'd confessed to his and Ginny's involvement in the murders of both Donald Fitting and Moises Chayo. According to John: he and Ginny had conspired together to rob Moises Chayo. John had hid in the trunk and Ginny had been the beautiful bait that lured the Argentinean man with the prospect of sex out to the bayou south of New Orleans. Once there, Ginny popped the trunk of the Pontiac and John came out. When Moises refused to submit to robbery, John and Ginny bludgeoned him to death with a tire iron. In Carson City, John confessed, that he and Ginny had needed money again bad enough that Ginny committed the crime against Donald Fitting herself while John was drunk in the back of the car. New York police contacted Nevada and Louisiana officials. John was arrested immediately.

Nevada authorities issued a warrant for Ginny's arrest on the Donald Fitting Murder. They had found a woman's shoe print at the scene of the crime. California police delivered the warrant and arrested Ginny at her Canoga Park home in 1977 and Governor Jerry Brown did not fight extradition to Nevada. After five months in jail, Ginny was transferred to from Sybil Brand Prison for Women in Los Angeles to Carson City, Nevada, to face charges. A warrant was issued for Ginny by Louisiana authorities too, who wanted her back in New Orleans on the Moises Chayo murder. Louisiana decided to wait for Nevada to try and convict her first. John Sidote's Louisiana warrant was also deferred, and he was extradited to Carson City, Nevada, to face charges on the Donald Fitting Murder. Ginny claimed she had nothing do with the Donald Fitting murder. That it had been all John's doing and, after plea bargaining with the District Attorney, John pleaded guilty to robbery and voluntary manslaughter in exchange for his testimony against Ginny.

The judge was harsh on John Sidote and handed out a 25 year sentence for the murder of Donald Fitting. John was furious. He expected a much lighter sentence and thereafter refused to cooperate with authorities to convict Ginny. Ginny's case would be dismissed for lack of evidence. John's would not. Ginny would go free.

PALM SPRINGS TRUE CRIME

By 1976, Raymond Foat was done with the anti-man group, the bra burning and everything else the feminists were known for. To raise funds for Ginny's defense he had torn asunder everything they had built together. He'd mortgaged the house to the hilt and Ginny's ownership in the catering business had been sold. He wanted to move to Hawaii. But, Ginny wanted to become more involved with NOW. They filed for an amicable divorce. While she'd been in jail, the organization had also raised funds for her defense. They'd helped her find the attorney, Orange County lawyer, Robert Tuller, who provided solid representation; and they'd published an article making the first public claims that Ginny was a bettered woman at the hands of John Sidote, laying the foundation for her story of how a young woman with ambitions could temporarily go down the wrong road with a forceful man.

Political Ambitions

She returned to California a victorious hero who survived trumped up charges that were alleged to derail her valiant political career. Her time in jail, the accusations, and the legal triumph bolstered Ginny's standing in NOW and catapulted her status to that of a war veteran within the burgeoning political action committee. Other strong members began to congregate around her: Jan Holden, Kay Tsenin, and Los Angeles NOW chapter president Shelly Mandell. Ginny transitioned her catering business into a fundraising company, called Anodos, and soon was mixing and mingling with celebrities and powerhouse activists: Lily Tomlin, Jane Fonda, and more; hooking her star to theirs created a meteoric rise for Ginny's own political currency.

Still, all was not golden in Ginny's new life. The Nevada trial had had at least one somewhat negative effect. It brought to life the fact that Ginny had never actually completed her divorce to John Sidote. Papers had been filled out, yet the divorce was never completed. When Raymond Foat found out this detail he halted his own divorce proceeding in 1979 and instead got an annulment. Also, in 1979, Ginny made a good impression on Jean conger, a veteran of NOW operations, when Ginny was a coordinator of the 1979 national conference. Jean was impressed at the womanliness of Ginny. Here was no combat boot wearing, butch haircut dyke; but a sweet, gentle manicured, hair-dooed, nicely dressed lady who could speak her mind and inspired others. One of Ginny's inspired admirers was John O'Leary, a former leader of the National Gay Task Force. He knew Ginny both before and after her legal problems and he liked the newly transformed Ginny who'd become such a political achiever. In 1980, she became the Kennedy delegate to the Democratic convention and was hired by the Amalgamated Clothing and Textile Workers to help organize its California boycott of the J.P. Stevens Company.

In 1981, at 40, Ginny remarried for the fourth time, to Jack Meyer; a video business owner who had been friends with Ginny for a couple of years via her catering and fundraising businesses. According to Ginny's friends, Jack was classy. He had money and he was nice, presentable. Stylish. Unfortunately, Jack wanted Ginny to sign a difficult pre-nuptial agreement and the marriage lasted only a month. It ended in yet another annulment.

That same year, Ginny's star within NOW had risen to the heights of state level recognition. She had a talent for uniting other organizations to NOW's cause. Labor Unions and California's Democratic Council allied with Ginny and she with them. In San Diego, she had successfully spoken in front of a large crowd of United Steel Workers representatives from ten western states, gaining their support for the new Equal Right Amendment going through congress. This sort of leadership was respected by many within NOW and frowned on by others. Ginny packaged an Equal Rights Amendment organizing kit and travelled throughout California and other states to other NOW chapters, empowering other women to take active roles within their communities, their spheres of influence, affecting their political leaders and those around them. There were those who were both jealous and/or considered Ginny to be too ambitious within the group. Many NOW members claim that California membership in the organization doubled due to Ginny's efforts. One former state president, Jean Bendorf, considered Ginny's packing a state level meeting with women sympathetic to a bylaw change to be an affront to the old guard within NOW. Other's loved Ginny and reached out to her to affect change or to get things done. Ginny was known for being a straightforward thinker who could get things done. She showed little emotion and a sort of reliable toughness within the women's movement. She paid attention to detail and by the end of 1981 she had successfully ran for and been elected to the California State Presidency of the National Organization of Women. In this position, there were sixty chapters of the organization under her control. Twenty percent of all NOW members nationwide lived in California. Ginny was encouraged by her friends and allies to consider running for the national presidency.

Politics and business continued to mix for Ginny. She and Shelly Mandell and two other women wanted to purchase a restaurant together and call it Ladies' Entrance. To ensure no obstructions to obtaining a liquor license, Mandell claims, at Ginny's request, she asked an associate to run a government background check on Ginny for this reason. The check came back with a mark on it. Though Shelly Mandell would not say what, Ginny was told to not apply for a liquor license. The restaurant fell through. But, Mandell decided to back Ginny in her pursuit of a national candidacy and was able to unite about a dozen state leaders to support Ginny in her bid.

Then, in the summer of 1982, during a strategy meeting, a hammer dropped on Ginny. She was pulled aside to take a phone call from former NOW Secretary, Jean Conger, who informed Ginny she could not lend her support. Ginny's inexperience, the intense spotlight the president had to live in, could cause problems for the organization in light of Ginny's shadowy past. Conger also said she knew that there had never been a trial in Louisiana and felt this left Ginny exposed. Ginny denied there was still a loose thread in New Orleans. Conger was not so sure. Ginny hung and returned to the meeting shaken and white. She felt Conger might have designs of her own on the presidency. In checking around, Ginny found out Conger had been urged to call Ginny by her old friend and former president of the Hollywood chapter, Jan Holden. Shelly Mandell urged Ginny to call a lawyer and make sure there was no issue with Louisiana left unresolved. Instead, within a week, Ginny withdrew her candidacy for the national presidency.

By October, 1982, Ginny had regained her composure and threw her hat in the ring for vice-President. But, some of her friends did not back her, claiming that they were already committed to other candidates by then. There was also a whisper campaign to be floated against Ginny, breathing life into the rumors of her unresolved murder cases. Ginny accused Shelly Mandell of starting the rumors. Mandell denied the claim and asked Ginny of there was any truth to the stories. Ginny denied the accusations yet again and lost the election. Her rivals threatened to reignite the allegations again and again if Ginny continued to seek higher offices.

The Moises Chayo Trial

Then a very funny – not haha funny, but funny strange – thing happened. In December 1982, unbeknownst to Ginny, Shelly Mandell, using her position as an assistant to then Los Angeles City Councilman Marvin Braude, ran a more thorough background check on Ginny; claiming she did so to verify once and for all that there was no sordid past in Ginny's life, so Mandell could suggest Ginny's appointment to a Human Rights committee. Mandell claimed she did not want any embarrassing backlash to come forth if there was a skeleton in Ginny's closet. Ginny knew nothing of Mandell's efforts or intentions and Mandell stated that if Ginny was clean she could then suggest her name for the committee. If Ginny was not, she would likely bury her intentions and cause Ginny no harm. The truth of the situation would remain forever unknown. But, what is definite is that Shelly Mandell wrote a letter, on City Council stationary, to the Jefferson Parish Police Department in Louisiana seeking information in regards to one Virginia Galluzzo, also known as Ginny Foat.

The letter would move slow through the mail during the holidays and not end up on any one's desk until January 3, 1983 where it was finally acted upon. A sheriff ran Ginny's information through the National Crime Information Center database and the computer spat out the details for a warrant from 1977 relating to the 1965 murder of Moises Chayo that was never enforced. The Jefferson Parish authorities reached out to Los Angeles authorities and asked for Ginny to be arrested and extradited to Louisiana.

January 4, 1983: another horrific happenstance coincided with John's Louisiana misfortune. John Sidote, who had been paroled on his 1979 conviction several months earlier, had gotten horrendously drunk and been arrested in Carson City, Nevada. Apparently, he'd been struggling to keep his job while his new girlfriend was sick during the holidays and the pressure didn't mix well with vodka. He'd fallen asleep at the wheel, crashed into a stop sign and ended up in jail, violating his parole and inspiring the police to run a fresh warrant on him. They also found the open Louisiana warrant that had been put on hold back in 1977 when he'd been prosecuted in Nevada. His New York drunken confessions were still on tape, and though John remarked that the Louisiana charges had been dropped during his plea bargains in Nevada, Louisiana officials called him a fugitive. John was booked and earmarked for extradition to Jefferson Parish where a pending trial would achieve greater incarceration than a parole violation for drinking.

January 11, 1983: Ginny and Kay Tsenin are headed for the Burbank airport in her 1977 blue Chevy Caprice to do what was called "airport duty" for NOW. Behind them pulls an unmarked police vehicle which follows the two ladies to the passenger unloading area of the airport. Six cop cars await her. Officers have weapons drawn. A helicopter buzzes overhead. Ginny is arrested on the old warrant and shepherded off to another stay at the Sybil Brand Women's Facility. This time she's placed in maximum security and while her lawyer's vigorously oppose extradition, Ginny shortly thereafter finds her transported, booked, processed, indicted and on trial in Jefferson Parish for the murder of Moises Chayo.

Back in California, the National Organization for Women was quick to disassociate Ginny's legal problems from themselves. NOW issued a statement that basically said that Ginny's problems were her own and that NOW would press on with or without her. Ginny's friends couldn't be sure of her guilt or innocence. Some still admired, prayed for her release and loved her. Others took political advantage of the vacuum in the wake of her confinement.

In Louisiana, the prosecution readied its case. The trial was assigned to Judge Robert Burns in Gretna, Louisiana who gave the defense a break by deciding that evidence from the Carson City case was inadmissible and the prosecution could not use it against Ginny in Louisiana. Still, the District Attorney's had John Sidote as their primary witness against her and he seemed very willing to cooperate this time. Plus, Louisiana law would not favor Ginny. It was an anti-ERA state, so there would be no political rallying of NOW to try and support her in the public eye. And, the bar for proving murder was a low one. In Louisiana, the court had only to determine that Ginny had aided or abetted in the fatality of Moises Chayo. They did not have to be convinced she had swung the tire iron. The mere fact she had lured the man, enticed him to the murder scene would be enough to land her in jail for the rest of her life.

In April, three months after her arrest, Ginny was finally able to post a bond of $125,000 and allowed to leave jail so long as she stayed in the vicinity of New Orleans. She found herself a residence and her and her attorneys doubled their efforts in preparing her de-

291

fense. She also began to work on her life after the trial. She claimed to be innocent, intended to win the trial and she wanted to be able to reclaim her life. A defense fund was created by some of her NOW colleagues and more than $100,000 was raised.

In October, Judge Burns granted a postponement that moved the trials start date back a month. Both prosecuting and defense attorney's felt that recent headlines in The Time Picayune/The States newspapers had caused an unfair bias that would make seating a jury difficult. In the meantime, the judge ordered all parties involved in the case to keep their mouth shut and not leak anything to the press so the case could be tried on the merit of law and the court of public opinion. Newspaper around the country were writing about Ginny Foat, the feminist movement, and the possibility of her being either a woman wrongly accused or a woman hiding the double life of politics and crime.

On November 7, 1983, the trial began with a jury of six men and six women. In most states, the prosecution goes first, giving the defense the chance to rebut witnesses and hear the entire case against them first, thereby allowing those accused to face their accusers. But, in Louisiana proceedings are reversed, they still practiced Napoleonic law and the defense has to go first and the prosecution is allowed to rebut the defense. The first four days of trial were all Ginny's. She wasted no time in telling her tale of a woman being beaten by a man she mistakenly fell in love with, one who quickly went from falling in love with to be living in a cage with a husband who drank too much and was violent in his temper. Ginny's attorney, John Reed, claimed he beat her whenever things didn't go his way and she was just a young fearful Catholic girl, ashamed of her relationship and of her earliest path. He said Ginny had already had one divorce at the time and didn't want a second. Furthermore, he said she had already had one child out of wedlock and instead of having an abortion she had given the child up for adoption. Because of these things, she tried and tried to make the relationship work to no avail. Her only escape was to run away when John was first arrested after the bar fight and subsequent death of the No Regret's patron and even while John was behind bars he still threatened her with the likelihood of putting her behind bars too if she didn't continue to do his budding – a threat he eventually carried out in 1977 when Ginny was first placed in jail awaiting trial for the murder of Donald Fitting. Now, John Sidote was doing it again. He was doing it because he was a hateful, revengeful man who wanted to lessen his own criminal sentences. In short, John Sidote was lying about Ginny. He had made a deal with prosecutors to testify against her to save his own skin and receive immunity from prosecution. Ginny's attorney put forward the defense that Ginny not only never murdered Moises Chayo; but that she never even met the man. The night of the murder, she had fallen asleep over a book.

The prosecution put forward their chief witness, John Sidote, who testified that despite her beauty and youth, Ginny was a bulldog of a woman who once she set her sights on something did not back down. She was not only capable of the murderous act. But, she had struck the decisive blow, killing Moises Chayo with a tire iron from behind while John held his attention with the threat of robbery. Ginny was no misunderstood and frightened angel. She was a conniving conspiring woman who planned, participated and partook in the crime every step of the way and then shared in the loot. Prosecuting attorney's told the court and jury that regardless of the 18 years that had passed since the crime was committed they had evidence proving that Mrs. Foat had participated in the slaying of Moises Chayo. If the trial had been only one year after his murder they would have more witnesses. But, there was no doubt that Moises had been killed, his body tossed in a roadside ditch, and that Ginny had done it. They went to say that Mr. Sidote's testimony stemmed from a voluntary confession, when he went into the New York police station to clear his soul of guilt and the prosecutors made sarcastic references to the defenses assertions that Mr. Sidote had threatened Ginny with jail or violence if she were to leave him. As proof of John Sidote's humility, they offered as evidence the fact that he had not talked to Ginny for seven years before he confessed the crime to the police in 1977.

On November 16, 1983, only a little more than a week after the trial began, both the defense and the prosecution rested. The jury was allowed to go deliberate. They returned only two hours later and declared Ginny Foat an innocent woman. One juror said after, they had covered the decision from all angles and had only needed one vote as jurors. They were all in agreement that Ginny was not guilty. The judge told reporters that he thought she got a fair trial and a few hours after the verdict was returned Ginny and her attorney held a press conference. Ginny was smiling from ear to ear. She had tears of joy and an uplifting new look on life again. She claimed her victory a victory for all women and that all she wanted now was to put her life back together and pay of her legal debts.

After the Trial

Two years later, Ginny had not fully regained her former life. She was a free woman. But, rejoining NOW with any semblance of her former position was not to be. Instead she moved to Marin County, north of San Francisco, founded Legal Advocates for Women and along with a group of investors purchased The Langtry, a Victorian bed and breakfast manor house intended as a safe haven for women travellers. The press still occasionally followed up with her and in a December 29th, 1985, Los Angeles Times article she told a reporter that at times she still woke up in the middle of the night, drenched in sweat, and afraid that the police would be waiting to escort her away to jail again.

Ginny had made some headway against her legal debts which amounted to $270,000. To help her in this endeavor, royalties from her biography: Never Guilty, Never Free, by herself and Laura Foreman, Random House, paid off a big chunk of her debt and actress Marlo Thomas bought the movie rights. But also in 1985, the California lawyer who had fought her extradition to Louisiana and then helped prepare her defense, Robert K. Tuller, sued her over $9,800 that he felt he was still owed due to travel costs in going back and forth to the Gretna, Louisiana court and that due to the high publicity of Mrs. Foat being the president of California's NOW at the time, in addition to fees she was accumulating from a speaking tour now that she was a free woman, he had every anticipation of being paid back in full and only filed because the statutory curfew for suing was approaching. He did add on 18% for interest, attorney's fees and other costs.

Such would be the story of the rest of her life it seemed. Ginny would be forever dogged by the haunting remains of her undignified past. In November, 1987, she was again interviewed by the LA Times and stated that there were still people who thought she had gotten away with murder, despite being acquitted. She kept mostly to the background in political events. Though she did protest the Pope visiting San Francisco, helped Representative Pat Schroeder raise $15,000 in a bid for the U.S. Presidency and was co-chair on the San Francisco Mayoral campaign of John Molinari. Her biggest return to the spotlight was when she went on the Oprah Winfrey show speaking on behalf of battered women. Still, from time to time, she would be painfully reminded of others doubts as to her innocence. Marlo Thomas never did produce the movie of Ginny's life, letting her partner, Kathie Berlin, state that they just couldn't make it work and that the complexities of Ginny's life were too daunting.

Happiness would find a way into her life. On August 22nd, 1988, Ginny met the woman who would become the love of her life: Pamela Genevrino. Together they would navigate the waters of young lesbian love in a time when such a thing was not socially or politically acceptable. But, from the time the two met till forever more, the two would be inseparable. Almost thirty years later, in 2006, Ginny and Pamela decided to get married. It was a time of controversy to do such a thing. Proposition 8 had yet to be approved by

California voters. But, Ginny felt it the right thing to do. As she wrote on her Facebook page August 22, 2015, on the 27th anniversary of her meeting Pamela, Ginny writes, "In 2008 we 'legally' married thinking we would do it for political reasons – let people know how important it was before they voted on Proposition 8. But, when we actually said the words and repeated the vows we both were crying like babies. This year we are celebrating the victory in freedom to marry, but in no way is equal to freedom to love."

Palm Springs

The years moved on and so did Ginny. She participated in politics when it suited her and helped others as she could. In 1989, she purchased a vacation home in Palm Springs and went from being an infrequent visitor to a second homeowner in the desert. Somewhere over the years she came out declaring she was a lesbian. In 1999, after finishing up a non-profit job in New York City, Ginny and her partner decided against their first instinct of moving there and instead sold their Los Angeles home and moved into their vacation home in Palm Springs, becoming full-time desert residents. Ginny purchased a building and opened a store on North Palm Canyon.

As an uptown Palm Springs merchant, she became involved with the districts business association. The area was struggling. It was not the trendy showcase it is today. Business owners were hard working and yet still having difficulty attracting a steady stream of clients. Ginny became president of the Uptown Business District. Under her leadership, the stores initiated what was called First Friday, where on the first Friday of every month they put out light food and drinks and invited customers to their stores for special deals. Still, they wanted more and sought the city's help. Ginny and other merchants didn't think the city was supporting them enough and one day she got very mad at the city's business liaison. She thought she and her business cohorts were only getting lip service. They weren't really being heard and it was then that she decided to really make a difference and do something about it.

In 2003, Ginny ran for the City Council seat in Palm Springs. In doing so, she'd decided to no longer hide from her past, but rather to embrace it honestly and openly. After all, she's an open book; two in fact. Her own biography: Never Guilty, Never Free had been released eighteen years earlier and another: Feminism on Trial-The Ginny Foat Case and the Future of the Women's Movement was released just a year later. She told a Los Angeles Times reporter that if she had to talk about her past, she would. But, she preferred to talk about how to make Palm Springs, a city of 44,000 people and one of the most openly gay cities in America a better place. Her platform would include the issues close to the hearts and minds of Palm Springs citizenry: empty store fronts needed to be filled, the city budget needed to be spent more wisely, a new animal shelter and public safety.

She'd be one of thirteen candidates vying for two open council seats and whether or not she was elected it seemed Palm Springs was at a turning point. The mayoral job was being contested in a hot race by an openly gay black man against a staunch white family establishment man. There were enough gay candidates running for the City Council seats that that it was possible the Council would end the elections with a gay majority. In the past ten years or so, the City had become more and more gay friendly as events like the White Party and the Dinah Shore golf tournament became more embedded in the city's destiny, introducing homosexuals to a city that at the very least was neutral towards their lifestyle, and the real estate markets of San Francisco and West Hollywood were so extravagantly high that a same sex couple could sell their inner-city properties for a hefty sum and relocate to the desert in a trendy mid-century home with a surplus of savings.

Ginny got a boost in her campaign. She was the only candidate who received the backing of the Democratic Party Central Committee and the AFL-CIO union. Their support would help tremendously in getting out the votes she needed to get elected. When the votes were finally cast, Ginny came in third for the two seats. But, since one of the existing won the Mayor's seat, she was selected to fill his now vacant term. She was officially a City Council member. She won again in 2008 and again in 2012.

In 2015, Ginny ran for Mayor of Palm Springs. She came in second. She very well might have won if the sitting Mayor, Steve Pougnet, had not been caught in a scandal. It seemed that since 2013, Pougnet had been receiving a $200,000 a year consultants' fee from a developer to assist in reading environmental reports, understanding government assistance funds, acquiring a very lucrative City land purchase, and helping navigate the permitting of this developers projects. The FBI and Riverside County District Attorney's office raided Palm Springs City Hall and the scandal blew up into national headlines, bringing negative publicity to the city. The electorate responded by voting out any incumbents.

If Ginny Foat had not run for Mayor during the mid-term of her existing council seat, which is up in 2016, she might very well have been booted from the City Council. As it was, she remains on the Council for another year and her future beyond that is still unwritten.

Sources:

Julie Amparano, CLEARED OF MURDER BUT HER NIGHTMARE HANGS ON: GINNY FOAT-THE WHISPERS CONTINUE, Los Angeles Times (.com), December 29, 1985.
Kate Buckley's Palm Springs Blog, AN INTERVIEW WITH GINNY FOAT, PalmSprings.com, April 26, 2012.
Kate Coleman , MYSTERY WOMAN: THE SECRET LIFE OF GINNY FOAT, FEMINIST LEADER AND MURDER SUSPECT, California Magazine, May 1983.
Ginny Foat, NEVER GUILTY, NEVER FREE, Random

House, September 1985.

Fay S. Joyce, EX-NOW FIGURE FACES LOUISIANA MURDER TRIAL, New York Times (.com), October 8, 1983.

Fay S. Joyce, HUSBAND BEAT FEMINIST, MURDER TRIAL JURORS TOLD, New York Times (.com), November 11, 1983.

Ellen Hawkes, FEMINISM ON TRIAL: THE GINNY FOAT CASSE AND THE FUTURE OF THE WOMEN' MOVEMENT, William Morrow & Co, May 1986.

Grace Lichtenstein, GINNY FOAT'S FEMALE TROUBLES, Rolling Stone magazine, May 12, 1983.

Barbara J. Love and Nancy F. Cott, edited by, FEMINISTS WHO CHANGED AMERICA, 1963-1975, University of Illinois Press, September 2006.

Frances Frank Marcus, GINNY FOAT, THE EX-NOW LEADER ACQUITTED OF MURDER IN LOUISIANA, New York Times, (.com), November 17, 1983.

Pat Morrison, and Alan Citron, AND JUST WHO IS THE REAL GINNY FOAT? The Milwaukee Journal, January 21, 1983.

Louis Sahagun, EX-FEMINIST ICON SEEKS OFFICE, Los Angeles Times (.com), October 9, 2003.

Staff reports, FEMINIST'S MURDER TRIAL POSTPONED, News Brief, New York Times (.com), October 12, 1983.

Various contributors, GINNY FOAT, https://en.wikipedia.org/wiki/Ginny_Foat, Wikipedia.org.

Sonny Bono Congressional campaign photo.

Was Sonny Bono Murdered?

There is a conspiracy story on the internet that claims Sonny Bono was murdered for his knowledge of a certain group of high level United States military and espionage secret agents involved in the sale of guns and drugs for profit. I cannot claim to know whether or not it is true. The details it provides are so closely connected with another story in this book: Tribal Casinos, The Octopus and Indian Head Nichols – that I felt it justifiable to insert Sonny's murder conspiracy into this book.

While I found this same story located in several places online, they all seemed to originate from a reporter named Bob Burns for the tabloid magazine The Globe on April 14. The exact year was never disclosed, however, it had to some year shortly after 1998. My source of choice became a website operated by a gentleman named Dave Martin, a privately possessed American patriot and government whistleblower who investigates and writes his own website articles, going by the online moniker DC Dave.

Dave's findings led him to support the following beliefs:

Sonny Bono was a very experienced skier who somehow crashed into a tree in Heavenly Valley Ski Resort, located in South Lake Tahoe, CA, on January 5, 1998. There were no witnesses and the autopsy report was not released to the public. At this time in Sonny's life, his popularity was growing and his capabilities in Washington were also on the upswing. His clout in political circles was increasing. He had been a proponent of Newt Gingrich's Contract with America and it seemed his voter base was very secure within his district of the Coachella Valley, thereby guaranteeing him a future in the Republican Party and American politics. Sonny was a driven man who, as he said at least once himself, "…had a knack for being good at things most people didn't think he could do."

Unfortunately, shortly before his death, Sonny had details of extensive covert government actions come across his desk that he didn't think appropriate and, if the story of DC Dave is true, Sonny was determined to uncover the truth. It may have been this very information which led to the death of Sonny Bono.

The information which reached Sonny's desk was a 10-year study presented by a citizen-investigator named Bob Fletcher and his findings detailed a certain group of high level military and top level U.S. government officials who were making millions of dollars selling drugs and guns in Central America and Southeast Asia. Sound familiar? Remember The Octopus in an earlier story within this book about the origins of Indian Casinos? Sonny may have stepped into a rattlesnakes nest when he decided to make the allegations of covert operations being funded without the approval of Congress. In December of 1997, Sonny received horrible findings of corruption, including videotaped evidence that just such a group of rogue agents were acting without government oversight and he was determined to make it his #1 priority upon returning to Congressional session in January.

Before he could act on this information he was dead.

It was determined that Congressional offices, where the phone calls between the information's suppliers and Sonny staff had occurred, were most likely bugged.

The best evidence that Sonny was ambushed and killed on the ski slopes by assassins lies within the newly obtained autopsy report that up until now was hidden from the public. According to Bob Burn's article, Fletcher stated this report was made public due to the efforts of retired FBI agent Ted Gunderson, who was also a confidant of reporter Danny Casolaro's prior to his death for investigating the espionage industry's drugs for arms transactions that were the basis for the shadowy Wackenhut Corporation and their tentacles known as The Octopus. Yet, half a decade later, according to Dave Martins website DCDave.com, Fletcher denied his own news article in The Globe, when on May 13, 2008, he stated "Gunderson has had absolutely nothing to do with this investigation." Could The Globe's reporter, Bob Burns, have been misled by a supposedly retired FBI agent whose only intent was to confuse the real story?

In the five-page report, prepared by Dr. David E. Palosaari, official Pathologist for Washoe County at the time, determined Sonny's death was caused by "craniocerebral injuries due to blunt force trauma" consistent with a skiing accident.

Others who have read the autopsy report note inconsistencies with this conclusion. Namely that upon inspection of Sonny's body he had a black eye, swollen lips, a bloody nose, a bruised jaw, and two of his upper teeth were knocked out. Arguably, these injuries may have been caused by a traumatic accident such as running into a tree at high speed, although they are severely extensive even for just such an event.

However, there was also a small series of fractures in a "central depressed region" on the side of Sonny's head which indicated a curved object may have been used to dent in his skull. Generally speaking, skiing accident victims do not get up after running into a tree to do it a second time from a new angle. Moreover, the non-governmental experts who reviewed the autopsy determined the indented fractured bone pieces on the side of Sonny's head were more likely caused from blows emanating from a round-edged weapon wielded by someone taller than Sonny's 5 foot 9 inch frame and the killer was most likely left-handed, attacking from behind, since the blow was done to the back right side of Sonny's skull. Furthermore, Sonny's injuries were limited to his head. He had no smashed ribs, no broken knees, no neck trauma – and that is extremely rare – and no hand injuries that would have been consistent with someone trying to ward off running into a tree at speeds high enough to cause a severe head injury. Also, there was no mentioning of tree bark, plant debris, or rough bark-like impressions on Sonny's face within the autopsy report.

Another factor contributing to the suspicion of Sonny being stalked and beaten up alone on the mountain is the fact his ski goggles were not damaged. If he had been skiing at the time he'd suffered all these injuries his goggles should have been battered just as bad. They were not. Therefore, it is considerably likely someone, or even likelier two someone's stopped Sonny on the slopes, using his good nature against him, feigning interest in his celebrity or seeking an answer to some simple question, and then they attacked him.

The possibility of two assailant's surfaces when looking at how much blood was on Sonny's back after his death. His clothes were supposedly soaked with blood, yet he had no back injuries. This could suggest he was held by someone and the attackers close vicinity kept the blood from spraying away from Sonny's body. There was also a small L-shaped tear in the back of Sonny's jacket, suggesting a struggle had ensued before his death.

There are several possible direct-link motives for someone wanting Sonny Bono dead. Apparently, his mother, Jean, thought it likely her son was murdered. She died in 2005 and had tried unsuccessfully to get a more thorough investigation into Sonny's death.

Definitely, when looking at the repellant voracity in which rogue FBI, CIA and other covert agencies were willing to go to defend the secrecy of their drug running and arms dealing in Central America and Asia, it is easy to believe that just such an accusation from a popular Congressman might invoke a fatal assault as a means of silencing him.

There were also other tentacles upon which Sonny was treading which might have inspired his critics to take deathly actions upon his person.

Sonny Bono was a ranking member of the full House Crime

Committee investigating the FBI and ATF's April 19, 1993, attack on the Davidian Branch compound in Waco, Texas, utilizing CS gas, a type of tear gas used for riot control. The FBI did this as a means to extricate the holed up members from their armed bunkers. In Sonny's questioning of U.S. Attorney General Janet Reno, under the Bill Clinton Presidency, the congressman was severely harsh in his criticisms of Reno not doing a more exhaustive study of the CS gas before it was used on the Davidians to end the 51 day siege. The hazards of just such a use, within the confined spaces of their hideout, had caused the chemically induced strangulation-like-deaths of four ATF agents and six followers of David Koresh within the compound called the Mount Carmel Center. After the initial raid, the onsite church building caught fire under controversially disputed circumstances and 80 followers of David Koresh were burned to death. The fire victims included 22 children under the age of 17. Fire conveniently covers up chemical death mistakes. Don't you think?

During the government's invasion, David Koresh's death is attributed to his right hand man, Steve Schneider, who FBI agent's claim shot Koresh in the head with a .22 caliber pistol, after determining the cult leader was a fraud, and then used the gun on himself to commit suicide.

During Sonny's questioning of Janet Reno on August 2, 1995, he was relentless as he accused the Attorney General of not knowing the full and damaging potential of the CS gas. He pointed out how with just two aids and himself in a single day had found out that toxicology studies proved high levels of the gas would cause the membranes of a child's lungs to secret a mucous in heavy enough amounts to fill the bronchial tubes, thus causing the children to choke, drown, and die on their own saliva. He found it impossible to believe the entire Department of Justice could be unaware of the likely effect of using this compound on the Davidian group.

In considering Sonny's determination to turn over the rocky foundations of the FBI, ATF, and other United States spook agencies, it is justifiable to consider he might have been killed by revenge assassins of the Waco fiasco who didn't want him to further investigate their activities. His investigations might ultimately have lead to embarrassing convictions which may have upset the Republicans apple cart destined to take back the White House as the Clinton Presidency entered its final years.

Or, Sonny Bono may have been murdered by the deeply embedded rogue agents who were implicated in the secret files which were to be Bono's next act of uncovering secret government operations in the drug running and arms dealing enterprises of those high level military and espionage officials who had also already murdered so many others who had tried to drag what has become known as The Octopus. Is it difficult to imagine these shadowy people would not want to have their activities drug into the bright light of the day or the even brighter lights of a Congressional hearing?

We may never know the truth.

Sources:

RamenRider, SONNY BONO GRILLS JANET RENO OVER WACO, https://www.reddit.com/r/conspiracy/comments/3lnuw3/sonny_bono_grills_janet_reno_over_waco/, Video Submitted September 20, 2015.

Dave Martin, THE COVER-UP OF SONNY BONO'S MURDER, http://www.dcdave.com/article5/080406.htm, April 6, 2008.

Unknown author, THERE IS NO STATUTE OF LIMITATIONS ON MURDER, http://www.theforbiddenknowledge.com/hardtruth/statute_of_li mitations.htm, Waco Tapes: 7:48:55 a.m., Central Times (4/19/93).

Various contributors, DAVID KORESH, https://en.wikipedia.org/wiki/David_Koresh#Raid_and_siege_ by_federal_authorities, Wikipedia.com.

STATISTICS

Palm Springs Crime Rates by Year										2010 Pop. 44,552		
Type	2001	2002	2003	2004	2005	2006	2007	2008	2009	2010	2011	2012	2013
Murders	4	3	5	4	4	3	5	2	1	1	1	3	0
Rapes	21	22	29	17	23	21	15	16	16	22	16	18	19
Robberies	112	112	90	107	112	128	121	134	117	69	88	104	99
Assaults	312	260	266	259	208	153	166	212	163	190	151	177	137
Burglaries	771	993	924	852	872	858	1,128	795	750	607	742	883	712
Thefts	1,701	2,061	2,039	1,984	1,659	1,888	1,975	1,591	1,382	1,188	1,266	1,112	1,342
Auto Thefts	445	457	393	599	571	446	416	286	229	178	296	237	296
Arson	35	20	25	28	39	29	n/a	27	26	18	16	18	9
City-data.com crime index (higher means more crime, U.S. average = 292.4)	542.1	569.5	549.2	542.6	498.9	470.1	494.5	422.3	364.9	318.3	372.3	391.7	365.9

According to City-data.com research, Palm Springs has 58 registered sex offenders as of Nov. 18, 2015.

Palm Desert Crime Rates by Year										2010 pop. 48,445		
Type	2001	2002	2003	2004	2005	2006	2007	2008	2009	2010	2011	2012	2013
Murders	1	0	unknown	1	2	3	2	3	1	0	2	0	2
Rapes	6	9	unknown	11	6	18	16	9	5	6	2	6	7
Robberies	47	37	unknown	41	38	66	48	42	30	30	40	49	30
Assaults	122	105	unknown	112	99	82	26	10	8	12	32	49	30
Burglaries	538	536	unknown	861	714	730	847	778	705	638	593	727	572
Thefts	1,399	1,325	unknown	1,871	1,691	1,792	1,837	1,695	1,114	1,150	1,439	1,477	1,511
Auto Thefts	206	181	unknown	240	257	233	230	149	108	123	115	118	132
Arson	1	5	unknown	4	4	4	11	5	5	3	3	5	4
City-data.com crime index (higher means more crime, U.S. average = 292.4)	333.9	304.6	unknown	390	342	375.6	352.7	283	207.9	199.7	243.1	267.8	256.8

According to City-data.com research, Palm Desert has 29 registered sex offenders as of Nov. 18, 2015.

309

PALM SPRINGS TRUE CRIME

| Rancho Mirage Crime Rates by Year | | | | | | | | | | | | 2010 pop. 17,218 |
Type	2001	2002	2003	2004	2005	2006	2007	2008	2009	2010	2011	2012	2013
Murders	0	0	unknown	0	1	0	0	1	0	0	0	0	0
Rapes	5	2	unknown	0	0	3	3	3	1	3	1	7	1
Robberies	3	1	unknown	11	4	7	13	9	13	7	6	4	8
Assaults	42	18	unknown	35	37	17	11	1	3	7	12	12	17
Burglaries	159	180	unknown	274	253	288	290	245	204	197	243	282	156
Thefts	358	375	unknown	598	688	633	703	605	361	332	444	411	443
Auto Thefts	46	61	unknown	89	110	67	74	48	39	26	36	33	37
Arson	1	1	unknown	0	2	5	0	2	0	1	0	2	0
City-data.com crime index (higher means more rime, U.S. average = 292.4	307.7	270.6	unknown	382.8	387.1	345	355.6	298.3	212.1	199.7	239.6	264.3	209.8

According to City-data.com research, Rancho Mirage has 0 registered sex offenders as of Nov. 18, 2015.

| Cathedral City Crime Rates by Year | | | | | | | | | | | | 2010 pop. 51,200 |
Type	2001	2002	2003	2004	2005	2006	2007	2008	2009	2010	2011	2012	2013
Murders	7	7	2	1	3	4	4	2	3	3	4	2	4
Rapes	31	7	16	16	10	15	18	22	15	17	15	10	9
Robberies	86	53	48	53	44	62	49	54	62	49	53	68	44
Assaults	148	152	158	169	195	152	133	163	123	180	154	124	92
Burglaries	463	495	556	676	559	501	501	554	430	556	790	626	399
Thefts	798	807	849	960	1,023	871	906	825	596	660	713	653	417
Auto Thefts	477	411	380	602	497	337	380	254	195	289	280	297	302
Arson	0	0	0	1	0	0	1	5	6	9	7	10	1
City-data.com crime index (higher means more rime, U.S. average = 292.4	417.9	346	327.7	373	336	293.4	283	279.8	226.7	274.1	308.1	263.5	201

According to City-data.com research, Cathedral city has 40 registered sex offenders as of Nov. 18, 2015

310

Type	2001	2002	2003	2004	2005	2006	2007	2008	2009	2010	2011	2012	2013
Indian Wells Crime Rates by Year											2010 pop. 4,958		
Murders	0	0	0	0	0	0	0	0	0	0	0	0	0
Rapes	0	1	1	0	2	1	1	0	0	1	0	0	n/a
Robberies	1	2	2	0	2	1	2	1	2	1	0	1	2
Assaults	9	1	5	8	3	3	0	0	1	2	0	1	5
Burglaries	41	61	63	79	53	81	109	66	58	67	47	58	48
Thefts	116	98	130	176	183	165	151	139	105	105	102	141	116
Auto Thefts	15	9	16	9	13	13	12	7	7	5	2	4	8
Arson	1	0	0	0	0	1	1	0	0	0	0	0	0
City-data.com crime index (higher means more crime, U.S. average = 292.4)	268.9	256.9	288.7	317.6	302	291.6	299.5	202.6	174.8	195.7	145.2	198.7	191.4

According to City-data.com research, Indian Wells has 1 registered sex offender as of Nov. 18, 2015.